PATRICIA K. OURADA, attended the College of St. Catherine in St. Paul, Minnesota, and the University of Colorado at Boulder, and received the Ph.D. degree from the University of Oklahoma. She is currently Professor of History in Boise State University, Boise, Idaho.

The Civilization of the American Indian Series

The Menominee Indians

The Menominee Indians

A HISTORY

By Patricia K. Ourada

with a Foreword by Donald J. Berthrong

UNIVERSITY OF OKLAHOMA PRESS : NORMAN

Library of Congress Cataloging in Publication Data

Ourada, Patricia K   1926–
    The Menominee Indians.
    (The Civilization of the American Indian series; 146)
    Bibliography: p.253
    Includes index.
    1. Menominee Indians—History.   I.   Title.   II. Series.
E99.M44087   970'.004'97   78–7942
ISBN 0–8061–1486–X

To
My Parents

MARTIN AND LUCILLE OURADA

Foreword

In the forests of northern Wisconsin live an Indian people, the
Menominees, who have survived the vicissitudes of Anglo-Euro-
pean encroachments upon their lands. Speaking the Algonquian
language, their hunters ranged along the shores of Lake Michigan from the Escanaba River to Milwaukee and westward to
the Mississippi River. When first visited by French explorers
and missionaries, the Menominees maintained their principal
village at the mouth of the Menominee River where they fell
under the influence of French fur traders and missionaries.
Today, 80 per cent of the Menominees profess the Roman
Catholic faith, although a minority cling to traditional Indian
beliefs and rituals. Rapidly, they came to depend upon traders
for guns, metal products, and other artifacts while continuing
to utilize wild rice, fish, the animals of the forests, and maple
sugar for their food supplies.

While the Menominees warred against their traditional enemies—the Chippewa and Sioux—they remained loyal to the

ix

nation claiming their allegiance. Their warriors fought under French leadership at Braddock's defeat in 1755 and were with their French friends in 1759 on the Plains of Abraham when Quebec fell to English troops. Throughout the American Revolution, Menominee warriors served the British on the western frontier and during the War of 1812. Although Tecumseh failed to elicit a response from the Menominees, they later followed Tomah as he fought beside Robert Dickson in his western Great Lakes campaigns. Contingents of Menominees fought at the Battle of the Thames and against United States troops in 1814 on Mackinac Island as the war was ending in the Old Northwest. After the Treaty of Ghent, the Menominees pledged their allegiance to the United States. When the drums of war sounded thereafter, Menominee men volunteered for duty during the Civil War, the Spanish-American War, World War I, and World War II.

For their loyalty, the government of the United States callously forced the Menominees to cede their forests, lakes, and streams. First, one-half million acres of their domain became the home of tribes of the Six Nations, while in 1837, by the Treaty of the Cedars, four million acres containing prime, virgin white pine forests were ceded to satisfy the avariciousness of Wisconsin lumbermen. When the land cessions were concluded, the Menominees retained ten townships as their reservation, but even that land had to be defended from illegal timber cutting. Still, after 1908, with the assistance of the Bureau of Indian Affairs (BIA) and the United States Forest Service, their lumbering enterprises flourished. Led by educated and mixed blood leaders the Menominees were able to maintain some independence and a satisfying life in their forests.

Tribal success and wealth marked the Menominees as "ready for release" from federal supervision. In 1948, Republicans in Congress designated the Menominees and nine other tribes as no longer requiring assistance and supervision of the BIA. "Termination" became the new policy for Native Americans

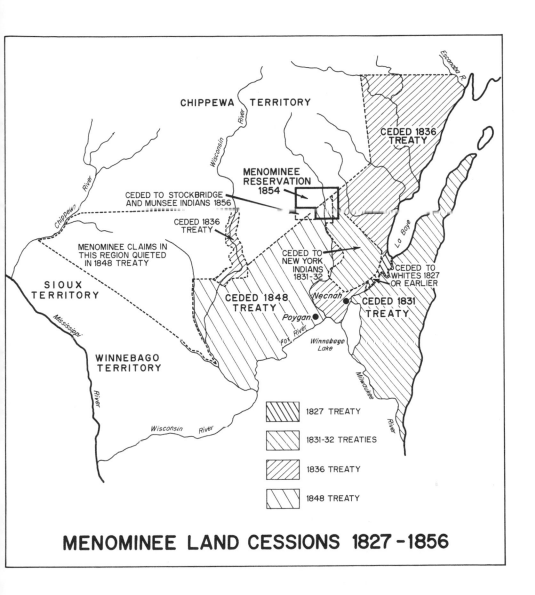

MENOMINEE LAND CESSIONS 1827-1856

during the administrations of President Dwight D. Eisenhower. With the tribe possessing a ten million dollar trust fund in the United States Treasury, Congressmen decided to distribute $4,700,000 of the trust funds to all enrolled tribal members and simultaneously terminate all relationships and treaty guarantees between the Menominees and the United States government. In 1953, attracted by the large proposed per capita distribution of their trust funds, the Menominees voted 169 to 0 to accept the money and termination. Public Law 399 passed Congress one year later which provided that the Menominees submit a termination plan no later than the end of 1957, but final implementation was delayed for four years.

Termination was a disaster for the Menominees. The Menominee Enterprises, Incorporated (MEI), which managed tribal business operations lost money; health care programs and education languished; unemployment reached nearly 25 per cent; and Menominee County, the former reservation area, suffered from the lowest per capita income in Wisconsin. Realizing that the Menominees could survive only by selling their lands, now private property, to real estate developers and lumbermen, dissenters to MEI leadership began to meet. In hard economic fact, the Menominees were costing the governments of the United States and the State of Wisconsin far more money than the BIA programs required before termination, but the Menominee plight was rapidly worsening. Organizing as Determination of Rights and Unity for Menominee Shareholders (DRUMS), dissident leaders drove toward repudiation of MEI leadership and restoration of federal tribal status and their reservation.

The cost of the victory of DRUMS was high. On December 22, 1973, Public Law 93–197 restored tribal status to the Menominees. Five DRUMS members controlled the nine-member Menominee Restoration Committee which was charged with writing a new constitution under which the tribesmen could manage their own affairs under the protective shield of federal power. Deep, galling bitterness is the residue of the factional

The Menominee Indian Reservation in the
Middle Western United States

leadership struggle between the MEI and DRUMS. But, at least, the Menominees have saved their forests and rivers for tribal purposes. The DRUMS leaders sincerely believed that without achieving that goal the Menominees would disperse and dissolve in the engulfing sea of white America.

In this volume Patricia K. Ourada presents a concise yet comprehensive history of the Menominees. She corrects Chief Reginald Oshkosh's complaint that: "The quiet, industrious tribe of Indians goes unchronicled, but the ones who made trouble are always talked about." With great skill and steady judgment, Dr. Ourada narrates for the first time the known history of the Menominees. No one interested in the history of Native Americans should fail to profit from this study which spans time from prehistory to the present day.

DONALD J. BERTHRONG

Lafayette, Indiana

Acknowledgments

For the completion of this history of the Menominee Indians
I am indebted to my parents, friends, and teachers for their
belief in the project. Dr. Donald J. Berthrong, head of the
Department of History, Purdue University, formerly at the University of Oklahoma, and Dr. Savoie Lottinville, director emeri-
tus of the University of Oklahoma Press, gave inspiration, expert counsel, and encouragement throughout the preparation
of this manuscript.

Many librarians and archivists generously gave of their time
and materials during the research phase of the study. I wish
to thank the library staff at the University of Oklahoma, particularly Mrs. Alice M. Timmons, library assistant, Phillips Collection, Mr. Jack D. Haley, assistant archivist, Western History
Collections, and Mrs. June Witt, clerical supervisor, Western
History Collections. The staff at the Federal Records Centers
and the National Archives were considerate and helpful, especially Mr. R. Reed Whitaker at the Federal Records Center in

Kansas City and Mr. Bruce C. Harding in Chicago. The materials and facilities at the Great Lakes–Ohio Valley Ethnohistory Archives at Indiana University and at the Wisconsin State Historical Society were excellent. The late Mr. Atlee Dodge of Keshena, Wisconsin, read the manuscript and shared it with members of the Menominee tribe.

Mrs. Josephine A. Gil, assistant to the chairman, Department of History at the University of Oklahoma, kindly agreed to type the final draft of the manuscript. The excellence of the work attests to her patience and skill.

I am also indebted to Alice H. Hatton who assisted with compilation and proofreading of the index.

The many people associated with me at Boise State University, Boise, Idaho, in Norman, Oklahoma, and in Menominee, Michigan, are too numerous to mention, but their help and encouragement will always be remembered with appreciation.

PATRICIA K. OURADA

Boise, Idaho

Contents

Illustrations

The
Menominee
Indians

I

Wild Rice People

I am born to create animals for my uncles.
I can create my fire that the sparks may reach
*   the sky.*
My arrow I am going to take out, so that while
*   the earth stands there will be enough to*
*   eat.*

Mä'näbus

White Indians? The idea stirs the imagination and conjures up ghosts of proud Viking sons and descendants of the lost Welsh prince, Modoc. "Beaux hommes!" said the French when they first encountered the Menominees in 1634. Modern Menominees scoff at the notion of a European background. Old Menominees explain their relatively light copper complexion in their ancient myth of tribal origin. This myth serves the Menominees not only to trace their ancestry, but as the base for social organization, family precedence, and civil government.

The Great Mystery, who made the earth, permitted the Great Underground White Bear with a copper tail to emerge from the earth at Mini'Kani near the mouth of the Menominee River and to assume human form. The White Bear's need for a brother prompted the Great Mystery to permit one of the spirits, known as Thunderers from above the earth, to join the bear man. Eagle descended and became a man. Other Thunderers joined the pair, and Nama'kukiu, the Beaver Woman, also became a gener-

3

ic brother to the group, as did the Wolf. The entire family lived together along the waters of the Menominee, where wild rice grew and sturgeon abounded. Menominee totems or gentes derive from this original grouping and include the Bear phratry, Big Thunder phratry, and Wolf phratry. Within each phratry are various subphratries and totems, each having an animal name. The Bear clan remains the principal phratry, and from it come the great first chiefs of the tribe, while war chiefs descend through the Thunderer phratry.[1]

No date can be ascribed to the presence of the Menominees along the Menominee River, but recent archaeological research at the Menominee Riverside Site reveals that men have inhabited the shores of the river for the last three thousand years.[2] Indians of the Old Copper Culture and early Wisconsin mound builders once occupied the vicinity.[3] The early Menominees, believed to be indigenous to the area, belong to the Woodland culture pattern. Most aspects of their culture reflect adaptations to the environment.

The Menominees were Algonquian-speaking Indians who maintained a central village at Mini'Kani near the mouth of the Menominee River. They roamed over an area extending from the Escanaba River in the north to the Milwaukee River in the south, and as far west as the Mississippi River. After white contact and the beginning of the fur trade, tribal bands moved from the parent settlement. The Oká′to Wini′niwûk, Pike Place people, dwelt at the mouth of the Oconto River; the Pä'sä′tiko Wini′niwûk at the mouth of the Peshtigo River; the Mätc Sua′mäko Tusi′nini˘, Great Sand Bar people, lived on the sand dunes at Big Suamico on the shore of Green Bay; and the Kaka′-pa'kato' Wini′niwûk, Barricade Falls people, lived at Keshena Falls on Wolf River, the present home of the Menominee people. Other groups of Menominees dwelt at Little Suamico, Sturgeon Bay, Lake Poygan, Portage, Winneconne, Manitowoc, and at the distant points of Prairie du Chien, Michilimackinac, and Milwaukee.[4]

The Menominees, like other central Algonquian tribes, Chip-

pewas, Ottawas, Potawatomis, Crees, Sacs, Foxes, and Kickapoos, built low, dome-shaped wigwams as their winter homes.
Arched saplings formed the frame of a wigwam and overlapping
mats served as the outside wall covering. The Menominees
made mats of birch bark. Cattail-reed and cedar-bark mats
were also used. The cattail-reed mats provided an indoor wall
covering, twelve to fifteen of which walled the average bark-
covered wigwam, assuring watertightness and providing insula-
tion. Slender lake shore reeds, bleached, dried, and dyed, were
woven into rugs for the interior of the dwelling. The Indian
women achieved beautiful colors for the reeds from common
woodland dyestuffs that included blueberries, blackberries,
bloodroot, wild plum, lambs-quarters, and the inner bark of
sumac, butternut root, and chokecherry.[5]

Rectangularly shaped houses of peeled logs covered by bark,
with high sloped roofs, provided spacious and cool accommoda-
tions in the summer months. Each lodge had a central fireplace
and a smoke hole with a ventilator flap of bark in the roof. At
one time the Menominees used a type of Eastern Woodland
long house as a multifamily dwelling. Since historic times, the
long house served only as a ceremonial structure.

In the long house the Mitä'win, or Medicine Lodge, oldest of
the Menominee ceremonial societies, assembled to pay honor
to the Algonquian demigod and folk hero, Mä'näbus.[6] According to the myths, Mä'näbus came among the Menominees to
help them to improve their lives. He did so by giving them the
Mitä'win Society endowed with power to cure diseases. He
gave them fine medicine bags made of animal skins. Each bag
contained samples of powerful medicines. Mä'näbus taught the
Menominees the use of the medicines and gave each a special
song. The number of songs in a bag indicated its powers. To
accompany the medicine rituals Mä'näbus offered a medicine
dance which had been given to him by the gods below in repara-
tion for the death of Wolf, the brother of Mä'näbus. The
Mitä'win, using the procedures prescribed by Mä'näbus, conduct membership rites, private memorial services for deceased

5

members, and ceremonies to cure the sick. Walter J. Hoffman in *The Menomini Indians* and Alanson Skinner in the *Material Culture of the Menomini* record their attendance at meetings of the Menominee Medicine Lodge, and each describes the rituals in his study.

Besides the Mitä'win, Mä'näbus gave the Menominees drums and flutes with which to accompany their songs, fire for warmth, power to be successful hunters and great warriors, and special power to kill O'wasso, the bear. A hunter killed a bear only to appease hunger, or to provide a winter covering. The hunter first offered apologies to the Great O'wasso before making the kill. Members of the Bear phratry avoided eating certain parts of the bear such as the head and paws. Mä'näbus also taught the Menominees to play lacrosse as a means of honoring him. He gave them tobacco to be used as an offering, maple sap to provide work, and the fish net with which to secure food. Like other folk heroes, Mä'näbus traveled widely and had many adventures both mirthful and harrowing. Included in his escapades are stories of how he gave the kingfisher its white breast, the buzzard its bare, ugly head, and the hell-diver its red-rimmed eyes.

After he had given the Menominees the powers needed for achieving earthly success, Mä'näbus moved away to live in solitude. Many Menominees in later generations set out on the quest to find Mä'näbus in order to ask special favors, and Menominee braves have communicated with him in their spirit dreams. Legend says his abode is at Mackinac Island. Father Claude Allouez, an early visitor to the Island, observed that

> the legends about the Island are pleasing. They say it is the native Country of one of their Gods, named Michabous—that is to say "the Great Hare," Ouisaketchak, who is the one that created the Earth; and that it was in these Islands that he invented nets for catching fish, after he had attentively considered the spider while she was working at her web in order to catch flies in it.[7]

Other societies functioned among the Menominees at an early date. They include the Wa'bano Cult of prophets, who derived skills from the Morning Star, the Je'sako, or divines, who could return a departed soul back to its body, and who could remove a sorcerer's arrows from a patient by means of a sucking tube. The Menominees also possessed a Buffalo Dance, Rain Dance, War Dance, Scalp Dance, Harvest Dance, All Animals' Dance to honor the totemic ancestors, and a Beggar's Dance at maple sugar time. Witchcraft has always been deeply rooted among the Menominees. Since the witches' power was gained through patronage of the evil spirits, they were greatly feared and the cause of much suffering. The Thunderers were also feared, and a Thunder cult developed to pay tribute to these spirits and to seek their help. Small carved wooden puppets were used as magic charms to protect health, to serve as family gods of good will, or as tribal spirits to bring harm to the enemy. The Menominees developed prayers, songs, and feast days to honor these spirits.[8]

Besides housing, the environment provided the Menominees with clothing, food, and material for transportation, the modes of which best suited the prevailing conditions. Deerskin, tanned soft and supple, and sometimes bleached snowy white, made leggings, breechclouts, skirts, and single-piece moccasins, seamed up the toe. These items of apparel were trimmed with dyed porcupine quills and shell beads. The art of quilling was a very old Menominee craft. The quills were softened in water and flattened and smoothed with a tool of antler or bone. The quills were dyed and sewn on the garment, medicine bag, or bark box in accordance with the pattern drawn on the object. Carefully designed floral patterns distinguish early Woodland work from that of other culture groups. In the severe winter months deerskin, bearskin, and rabbitskin robes provided needed warmth. Evidence exists that the Menominees' scanty summer attire distressed the Jesuit missionaries as much as their obvious indifference to winter's cold impressed them.

For centuries wild rice served as the basic food of the Menominees. The Menominees were so dependent upon the wild grain, *zizania aquatica,* that other Indians called them Mano'min

7

ini'niwûk, or Wild Rice men, and the French called them Folles Avoines, Wild Oats people.[9] Tradition makes wild rice a gift of the spirits from beneath the earth that the Thunderers carried to the lakes and river shores of the Menominees. The Jesuit missionaries provided the first written accounts of wild rice among the Menominee Indians. Father Marquette in 1673 observed:

> The wild oats, whose name they bear because it is found in their country, is a sort of grass, which grows naturally in the small Rivers with muddy bottoms and in Swampy Places. It greatly resembles the wild oats that Grow amid our wheat. The ears grow upon hollow stems, joined at Intervals; they emerge from the Water about the month of June, and continue growing until they rise about two feet above it. The grain is not larger than That of our oats, but it is twice as long, and the meal therefrom is much more abundant. The Savages Gather and prepare it for food as Follows. In the month of September . . . they go in Canoes through These fields of wild oats; they shake its ears into the Canoe; on both sides as they pass through. The grain falls out easily, if it be ripe, and they obtain their supply In a short time. But, in order to clean it from the straw, and to remove it from a husk in which it is Enclosed, they dry it in the smoke, upon a wooden grating, under which they maintain a slow fire for some Days. When the oats are thoroughly dry, they put them in a skin made into a bag, thrust it into a hole dug in the ground for This purpose and tread it with their feet—so long and vigorously that The grain separates from the straw, and is very easily winnowed. After this they pound it to reduce it to flour—or even, without pounding it, they Boil it in water and season it with fat. Cooked in this fashion, the wild oats have almost as delicate a taste as rice has when no better seasoning is added.[10]

A much tastier one-dish meal was made of blueberries, wild rice, boiled duck, and maple syrup.

Just as the river banks provided wild rice, the rivers yielded fish. The Menominees have always enjoyed spearfishing, and were adept at spearing the sturgeon as the huge fish swam up the river to spawn. Spearfishing was often engaged in at night in the shallow water, with the water illuminated by means of tightly rolled birch-bark torches smeared with pitch. For off-shore fishing the torch was affixed to the prow of a canoe. Nets, strung across the mouths of the rivers emptying into Green Bay, were also an effective means of catching fish.[11] Ducks and geese, attracted to the shoreline by ripening wild rice, were easily snared or caught in nets. Besides wild rice, other plants utilized by the Menominees included tree lichens, arum-leaved arrowhead, swamp milkweed buds, wild onions, spikenard root, May apple, high-bush cranberry, hazelnut, beechnut, and the inner bark of the bittersweet vine. A variety of berries added refreshing flavor to Menominee cooking and included wild strawberries, sand cherries, chokecherries, blackberries, blueberries, and raspberries. The wild gooseberry and frost grape were also highly prized foods.

The bark of the paper birch tree was perhaps the most useful of nature's gifts to the Menominees.[12] With it the Menominees crafted ceremonial masks, wigwam mats, storage boxes of all sizes, baskets, dishes, buckets for collecting maple sap, and canoes. The birch-bark canoe of the northern Woodland peoples was eagerly accepted by the first white comers to the area, since it proved to be best suited to light, fast travel. The canoe, a craft about twenty feet long and two feet wide with small ribs and rails of cedar, could carry four men or eight hundred pounds of baggage. Yet, it was so light that a man could easily portage it around impeding rapids. The Abbot of Gallinée in 1669 observed, while on a voyage from Montreal, that canoes "are so fragile that to bear against a stone a little, or to step on to them a little heavily, is sufficient to make a hole, which can, however, be mended with pitch." He further found "that to be in one of these vessels is to be always, not within an inch of death, but within the thickness of five or six sheets of paper."[13] The Abbot commented on the temporary shelters built for the night's lodging when it rained. He said:

> you have to go and peel the bark off trees, and the bark is arranged on four small branches with which you make a hut to protect you from the rain. The Algonquins carry birch bark with them, small pieces sewn together, so that they are four fathoms long and three

9

feet wide. They roll up into a very small compass; and under three of these strips, hung on poles, eight or nine men can easily be well sheltered.[14]

In winter when the forest trails were filled with untracked, drifted snow and the lakes and rivers were frozen hard, the northern Woodland Indians donned snowshoes. The Menominees used four kinds of snowshoes. Named for their shape, there were catfish, bear's paw, pointed, and keen-shaped snowshoes. The rounded front end of the shoe was made of a bent strip of green ash. The strip was tied together at the heel. Two rib crossbars were added for strength, and leather thongs were woven in every other section of the shoe. The wearer bound the snowshoes to his feet by means of a rawhide thong.

The severe winter weather kept the Indians closer to home than in the summer months, but the central Menominee village teemed with activity throughout the year. There is evidence that the Menominees engaged in a limited exchange of goods with nearby tribes. From the Ojibwa in the north they secured copper for making points and ornaments, and they had catlinite from the Siouan controlled pipestone quarries of Minnesota. Father Jerome Lalemont on a trip into regions of Lake Superior in the year 1666 wrote:

> This lake which is more than eighty leagues long by forty wide in certain places, is studded with Islands picturesquely distributed along its shores. The whole length of its coast is lined with Algonkin Nations, fear of the Iroquois having forced them to seek asylum there. It is also enriched in its entire circumference with mines of lead in a nearly pure state; with copper of such excellence that pieces as large as one's fist are found, all refined; and with great rocks, having whole veins of turquoise amethyst.[15]

It has been suggested that Lake Superior copper in its pure form was so easily procurable that the discovery of the art of smelting and casting metal was thereby greatly inhibited in the northern Woodland area.[16] Menominee tradition says copper was heated to make it malleable. Many copper artifacts of the Late Archaic

10

culture, including points, celts, awls, fishhooks, and toggle-head harpoons, have been recovered at archaeological sites within the confines of old Menominee territory.[17] Stone pipes remain as a last remnant of the stonecutting art. Heavy catlinite pipes were used in religious ceremonies, war and peace councils, and for recreational smoking. The stems of the catlinite pipes were usually carved from wood. The catlinite bowls of the pipes were sometimes carved in the form of animals or fish, and regular pipes frequently had floral or animal designs incised on the sides. The Menominees made pottery vessels from clay mixed with pulverized clam shells and molded over a ball of basswood-bark twine. An opening was left at the top, and after the clay mixture had dried, the twine was pulled from the opening, leaving an earthen shell. The bowl was finished by covering the rough interior with a thin coating of new clay. Tortoise shells, native copper, and birch-bark bowls and dishes were also used. The Menominee crafts of ribbon embroidery and basket making date only from historic times and were introduced into the tribe by other Indians.[18]

The Iroquois Wars brought hundreds of displaced central Algonquian Indians, representing many tribes, into the Menominee culture area, even though the wars never directly involved the Menominees or their Winnebago neighbors. Within the shadow of recorded history the Menominees engaged in a war that resulted in a great loss of life among them. The Sturgeon War lacks a historic date. Writers have surmised that since the Jesuit Father, Claude Allouez, who visited the Menominees in 1669-70, found them hungry and "almost exterminated by war," that the war must have occurred about that time. Just as there is no proof of the time, there exists some conjecture and legendary interpretation of the events. The war developed when the Menominees built a log wall across the Menominee River to prevent the sturgeon from ascending the river. This action deprived the bands of Chippewas living upstream of fish. Prior to this occurrence, the two tribes had lived harmoniously, and the sister of the Menominee chief had married the Chippewa chief. When the Chippewa chief learned that the river had been barred, he sent his son to the uncle with a request that the river be opened. In answer to the request the Menominee chief stuck a sharpened animal bone through the forehead of the youth. This indignity brought swift retaliation as the Chippewas descended the river to the Menominee village. Many village dwellers were killed in the raid. This skirmish marked the beginning of the Sturgeon War which pitted the central Algonquian tribes, who came to the defense of the Menominees, against the powerful Chippewa bands. Na'banois and Nipigon are listed as Chippewa leaders in the war. This war brought privation, suffering, and death to the Menominees and created a situation that belied the naturally rich Woodland resources that surrounded the Menominee people.

The Menominees survived the ordeal of war, however, and to this day live in their native habitat as guardians of Spirit Rock, one of the last surviving links with their ancient past. This rock is situated just north of Keshena Falls and can be visited by anyone passing through the Menominee reservation. Legend says that a Menominee brave, summoned by Mä'näbus in a dream, set off with seven companions to visit the god. Mä'näbus answered the requests of those braves who sought to become great hunters, warriors, or lovers. One of the group, however, angered the god by asking for eternal life. Mä'näbus seized the warrior and cast him to the ground. "You shall be a stone, thus you will be everlasting."[19] The legend concludes by admonishing the Menominees that when the stone finally crumbles away their tribe will be extinct. Thus it is, that in the night kindly spirits come to the rock to lay offerings of tobacco at its base to appease the wrath of the great Mä'näbus, and thereby hopefully preserve the existence of the Menominees.

II

French Relations

Very soon now you will see someone coming over the water.

A Dream Spirit to a Menominee Warrior*

The French quest for a general Indian peace which would promote the fur trade and enable the continued search for a short-
cut to the Orient brought Jean Nicolet into Green Bay in the fall
of 1634. He had been commissioned by the Company of One
Hundred Associates to journey to the Men of the Sea, the
Siouan-speaking Winnebagoes, to conclude a peace with them.
As the Frenchman and his Huron Indian guides paddled their
canoes along the shoreline of LaBaye, they came upon the Menominee Indian village, two days distant from the Winnebagoes.
Nicolet tarried there, while a runner carried news of his coming
to the Winnebagoes. Conversant in the Algonquian language,
having lived eight years among the Nipissings in Canada, Nicolet could talk with the Menominees, although their dialect dif-
fered distinctly from the northern Algonquian tribes.

The Menominees, like the other tribes encountered by Nico-

*Bloomfield, *Menomini Texts,* 77.

let, must have shown terror at the sound of his pistols. Nicolet, too, must have expressed surprise at the sight of the *beaux hommes,* men of a lighter complexion than any Indians he had ever seen.[1] It is not known if the Menominees followed Nicolet to the foot of Green Bay, but the news of his arrival attracted four or five thousand Indians to the meeting at which a peace was concluded. The pelts accepted by Nicolet as gifts and the news of a Great Sea just three days journey away were of greater significance to the Frenchman than the pledge of peace secured that fall of 1634. For the Menominees, the arrival of the first white man from over the water presaged changes in their lifestyle and native freedom.

The Iroquois Wars which erupted in 1642 delayed the return of the French to Lake Michigan. Although penetration south of Lake Superior was postponed, the French profited from trade in the regions of Lake Superior. Pierre d'Esprit, the Sieur Radisson, and his brother-in-law, Médart Chouart, Sieur de Groseilliers, made three voyages along the south shore of Lake Superior in the late 1650's. Their fourth voyage, undertaken in 1661, brought them southward to Green Bay. Radisson's *Journal* of this voyage describes the abundance of fish and game and the aborigines' fear of guns and desire for hatchets and kettles. The descent of the lake was so successfully achieved that Radisson triumphantly proclaimed, "we weare Cesars, being nobody to contradict us."

Radisson and his companions visited the Menominees. This encounter was recorded in the *Journal.* It states:

> We came to a cottage of an ancient witty man, that had a great familie and many children, his wife old, nevertheless, handsome. They weare of a nation called Malhommines; that is, nation of Oats, graine yt is much in yt country. Of this afterwards more att large. I tooke this man for my ffather and ye woman for my mother, so the children consequently brothers and sisters. They adopted me. I gave everyone a gift, as they to mee.[2]

This is the only time that Radisson speaks of having been adopted by the Indians. Radisson and Groseilliers and a group of sixty

14

wandered in the wilderness, half-starved and attempting to cope with the cold and deep snow. That winter the Frenchmen and their Huron and Ottawa guides reached the country of the Dakota Indians west of Lake Superior. Radisson did not return to his adopted family among the Menominees, nor is it known how many of the French *coureurs de bois* remained in the Green Bay area in 1661.

Nicolas Perrot, noted Canadian *coureur de bois* and French commandant in the Northwest, and Toussaint Baudry embarked in 1667 on a fur trading expedition that brought them into Green Bay.[3] While there, a crisis arose between the Menominees and a band of Potawatomis residing at the foot of Green Bay. The Menominees, while hunting, had killed a Potawatomi warrior en route to a nearby Outagami village. In retaliation the Potawatomis tomahawked a Menominee brave found among the Winnebagoes. Fearful of an attack on their defenseless women and children, since most of their young men were away on their first visit to Montreal, the Potawatomis implored Perrot to help them secure peace.

Perrot went to the Menominee village, having sent word in advance of his coming. News of his impending visit "caused universal joy" among the Menominees, and their youths came to meet him "bearing their weapons, and their warlike adornments, all marching in file, with frightful contortions and yells." After smoking the calumet, they escorted Perrot to the village "with assiduous attentions." At the village Perrot addressed an assembly of the people, expressing God's anger at them for being at war with the Potawatomis. He offered a gun and porcelain collar to bind the Menominees to himself as he had done the Potawatomis. He asked, "What will you have to fear if you unite yourselves to us, who make guns and hatchets, and who knead iron as you do pitch?" He warned them that in the past they had been evenly matched with their enemies, but the French had now promised the Potawatomis "articles suited for war." He threatened, "Would you abandon your families to the mercy of their [fire] arms, and be at war with them against the will of the French?" The father of the murdered Menominee accepted Perrot's gifts and pledged support to the French and to the living Spirit, "who had domination over all other men."[4]

This encounter marked the beginning of a long association between Nicolas Perrot and the Indians along the shores of Green Bay. In the spring of 1670, Perrot joined a flotilla of canoes, manned by nine hundred men en route from Green Bay to Montreal. A year later he served as interpreter to Simon François Daumont, Sieur de St. Lusson, when on June 14, 1671, in the presence of representatives of fourteen Indian nations, including the Menominees, he took formal possession of Sault Ste. Marie and adjacent territory.[5] Perrot became commandant for the French post at Green Bay in 1685.

During this same period of widespread French fur trading activity in the Green Bay area, LaBaye became a center for Jesuit mission work. Although of short duration, 1669–84, the Jesuit contact had a profound and enduring effect upon the Menominees. Today, 80 per cent of the Menominee people profess the Catholic faith. As early as 1641 two Jesuit missionaries, Isaac Jogues and Charles Raymbault, established a mission at Sault Ste. Marie. When in the next year the Iroquois Wars broke out, the missionaries had to abandon hope of extending their field of labor. "By 1650, all upper Canada was a desert, and not a mission, not a single Indian was to be found. . . . six missionary fathers had fallen by the hands of the Iroquois, another had been fearfully mutilated in their hands."[6]

Father Claude Allouez, accompanied by two French voyageurs, arrived at the Menominee village on November 27, 1669.[7] Of his first encounter, he wrote:

> while we were trying to paddle with the utmost vigor possible, we were perceived by four cabins of savages, named Oumalouminek [Menominees], who forced us to land; but as they were pressed with hunger, and we were at the end of our provisions, we could not remain long together.[8]

Allouez proceeded onward to the Oconto River, which he reached on November 29, 1669. There he found French *coureurs*

16

de bois who had preceded him, and on December 2, he established St. François Xavier Mission at which he spent the ensuing months preaching to the Indians wintering in the vicinity. In the spring of 1670, Father Allouez delighted in the return of warm weather. "Bustards [cranes], ducks, swans and geese are in great number on all these lakes and rivers," and, "we saw two Turkeys perched on a tree, male and female, resembling perfectly those of France." On March 17, 1670, while preaching at a newly settled Outagami village on the Little Wolf River, four Menominee Indians "arrived from a place two days journey hence, bringing three Iroquois scalps and a half-smoked arm, to console the relatives of those whom the Iroquois had killed a short time before."[9] The Outagamis, refugees from the Iroquois attacks, did not have canoes and relied upon other tribes to avenge their losses in the Iroquois raids. That very month the Outagamis had been attacked, their men killed, and thirty women taken captive in a surprise raid.

On May 6, 1670, Father Allouez returned to the village of the Menominees on their river, where he discovered their language to be Algonquian and "in harmony with their disposition: they are gentle, affable, sedate; they also speak slowly."[10] Father Allouez reported that he was well received. "Take heart, they said to me, instruct us often, and teach us to speak to him who made all things." Father Allouez named the Menominee mission and the river St. Michael's.

Father Louis André came to minister among the Menominees and the Indians along the shores of Green Bay in 1671. From that date until his recall in 1684, Father André attended to the spiritual and material needs of his extensive parish.[11] Some Menominees resented the influence of the missionaries on their children. Louis André attempted to appeal to the children. He taught them to sing songs set to French music. He composed songs against the superstitions and vices most opposed to Christianity, "and after teaching the children to sing them to the accompaniemen of a sweet-toned flute, he went everywhere with these little Savage musicians, to declare war on Jugglers,

17

Dreamers, and those who had several wives."[12] Father André's descriptions of his life and successes among the Folles Avoines present an interesting commentary upon life among the Menominee Indians three hundred years ago. "None of them have been angry with me because I decried the false divinity of the sun, of thunder, of the bear, of mississippi (the underground panther), of michabous, and of their dreams, nor because I spoke against superstitious feasts and against Jugglers."[13]

Father André recounts the "unexpected blessing" that God granted the Menominees in April of 1673. The sturgeon had bypassed their river that spring, but had already appeared in the nearby Peshtigo and Oconto rivers. Desperate in their desire for sturgeon, the Menominees erected an altar to the sun surmounted by a picture of the sun painted on a board. André persuaded the Indians to replace the sun board with a crucifix. "On the following morning sturgeon entered the river in such abundance that these poor people were delighted . . . after that, it made them so docile and so attentive to me that I was astonished . . . even the warriors obeyed me . . . and only a few of them blackened themselves and fasted in order to dream of the Nadouessi [Sioux], their enemy."[14]

That same spring in May, the Menominee village received a distinguished visitor, Father Jacques Marquette. It was on this visit that Father Marquette described wild rice. When he told the Menominees of his plans to visit the remote nations along the Great River,

> they were greatly surprised to hear it, and did their best to dissuade me. They represented to me that I would meet Nations who never show mercy to strangers. They also said that the Great River was very dangerous . . . that it was full of horrible monsters, which devour Men and Canoes together.[15]

Thanking them for their advice, Marquette assured them that he had no fear, and leaving the Menominee village, he proceeded along the bay.

Father André endured hostile actions and hardships, as well as rewarding moments, while ministering to the needs of the six villages of Indians which were his parish. In 1676 a non-Christian Menominee burned André's "little house." The missionary believed this was done to allay the grief of the warrior, whose small children had recently been murdered, even though one of them had been baptized. Untiringly, Father André journeyed from village to village, traveling by canoe in summer and on foot over the bay ice in winter. Father André's simple observations tell the story of the haunting cold: "the cold has been extraordinary in this country; on one occasion the Chalice stuck to my lips," and "opposite the fole avoine, the ice was three feet thick—that is, where the bay begins."[10]

The recall of Father André to Quebec in 1684 deprived the Menominees of their missionary, but St. Michael's mission continued to be served sporadically by the missionaries, Charles Albanel, Antoine Silvy, Henry Nouval, Jean Enjalran, and Jean Chardon, all of whom spent some time at the central Jesuit mission of St. François Xavier at De Pere. That mission was burned and abandoned in 1728. The Jesuit missions in North America fell victim to the conflict within the Jesuit Order over papal policy, to the growing commercial expansion of the French fur venture, to the renewal of war by the Iroquois as they sought to capture the Illinois-Great Lakes trade, and to the intense French-English rivalry that led to international warfare in the eighteenth century.

Throughout the mission period French exploration continued. In September, 1679, the Sieur de La Salle's sailing ship, *Griffin,* the first sailing vessel on the Great Lakes,* put in at Green Bay to collect the furs cached there. Because of the approach of fall storms on the lake, La Salle ordered the *Griffin* to return to Niagara by way of Michilimackinac. The ship never completed her voyage. She was lost in a storm somewhere between Green Bay and the Straits of Mackinac. To this day no evidence of the

---

*On the voyage from Niagara to Lake St. Clair the *Griffin* carried thirty Frenchmen, three Recollect missionaries, weapons, provisions, and seven iron cannons.

vessel has been found. La Salle, then en route to the Mississippi River, left the *Griffin* at Green Bay and continued his journey by canoe. He did not learn of the fate of his ship until the following year.

An Iroquois attack on the Illinois valley in 1680 disrupted both the fur trade and exploration throughout the Northwest. An Algonquian confederacy was quickly organized in the Illinois area and French forts were erected at Chicago and on the Illinois River near Utica. These measures thwarted the Iroquois raids of 1682 and gave new courage to the Indians, who reacted with increasing suspicion towards the activities of the French among them. Depredations were made against the Jesuit missions, and the Indians turned from trade with Montreal to intertribal trade. In 1682 Louis XIV of France expressed opposition to continued exploration, which tended, he said, only "to corrupt the settlers by hopes of profit and to reduce the income from beaver-skins."[17]

Undaunted by the king's attitude, Daniel Greysolon, Sieur Duluth, who had returned with the Recollect Father Hennepin from the Mississippi by way of the Fox River and Green Bay, planned to control the fur trade by uniting all of the northern tribes into a French alliance. While at Michilimackinac in 1684, preparatory to visiting the western tribes, Duluth undertook to punish Indians guilty of an attack on a French fur trading party in the vicinity of the Keweenaw Peninsula in the fall of 1683. Duluth wrote Governor La Barre, in April, 1684, of his apprehension of a Menominee Indian charged, along with two sons of the Ottawa chief, Achiganaga, with the murder of two Frenchmen, Jacques Le Maire and Colin Berthot, and their party of ten Indians. Father Albanel informed Duluth that the Menominee was living among relatives at Sault Ste. Marie. Duluth with Jean Peré and Messieurs the Chevalier de Fourcille and La Chardonnière went to the Sault and arrested the Menominee. Jean Peré also brought Achiganaga and his sons from Keweenaw to Michilimackinac. There several meetings were held with the Indians who assembled on behalf of the accused. On March 29, 1684, Duluth presented the evidence to a convened panel of Frenchmen, who decided that two of the accused should pay the death penalty for the deaths of the two Frenchmen. The Menominee accused of being the instigator of the crime and the elder son of Achiganaga were sentenced to death. As a favor and with the hope that the Indians would not retaliate, Achiganaga's younger son's life was spared. Duluth wrote:

> After this I left the council, and informed the Reverend Fathers, so that they might baptise those two wretched men which they did. An hour afterward, I put myself at the head of 42 Frenchmen, and, in sight of more than 400 men, and 200 steps from their fort, I had their heads broken in.[18]

This unexpected action, the first execution for crime in the area of the Great Lakes, set a precedent for future French action. No longer could the Indians expect to expiate their crimes with an offering of beaver skins. A new respect for French authority developed among the tribes and the Great Lakes became a safer highway for the white man to travel.

La Barre, meanwhile, prepared to move against the Iroquois, and Duluth was summoned to join an expedition for that purpose. Olivier Morel, the Sieur de La Durantaye, and Nicolas Perrot reestablished the French allegiance of the Green Bay tribes, and a group of one hundred LaBaye Indians, Winnebagoes, Sacs, Foxes, and Menominees, joined their French-Ottawa allies at Lake Erie. This action marked the first time that the Menominee Indians responded to the appeal of the white man for aid. The failure of the La Barre expedition of 1684 at Lake Ontario saved the western Indians from further participation against the Iroquois at that time. La Barre lost the governorship, and he was replaced by the Marquis Denonville. From that time forward the prestige of France declined in the western territories. The English began to trade at Mackinac and other Great Lakes points, and the French worked the interior, much to the distress of the Green Bay Indians, traditional enemies of the

Sioux. In 1687 the Menominees again joined a Perrot expedition of one hundred warriors for Denonville's war against the Iroquois.

Perrot's troop traveled by way of Michilimackinac and Lake Huron to Detroit. En route down Lake Huron the force captured the English trader Johannes Roseboom and his canoes with twenty-nine white men and five Mohawks.[19] The prisoners were returned to Michilimackinac where their trade goods, enough to buy eight thousand beaver pelts, were distributed among the Indians in the war party. At Detroit the western troops joined forces and proceeded into Lake Erie, where they captured a second British trade flotilla, commanded by Major Patrick McGregory. The force now consisted of Menominees, Potawatomis, Winnebagoes, Foxes, Kickapoos, Miamis, and Mascoutens. It was directed by Nicolas Perrot, Olivier La Durantaye, Daniel Duluth, and Henri de Tonte. This army joined with Governor Denonville's Canadian force on July 4, 1687, at Irondequoit Bay, from which place they laid waste the Seneca fields and four villages already partially burned by the fleeing Senecas.[20] Denonville later wrote that "the war was an absolute necessity, for without it all was lost." He explained that "it is certain that had the two English detachments not been stopped and pillaged, . . . all our Frenchmen would have had their throats cut by a revolt of all the Hurons and Ottawas, whose example would have been followed by all the other Farthest Nations, in consequence of the presents which secretly had been sent." Denonville's letter stated that if the attack had not been made, the Great Lakes Indians would have "pulled off the mask, submitted to the Iroquois, and placed themselves under the protection of the English." Denonville's expedition, as well as the building of a permanent fort at Niagara, prompted the Iroquois Confederacy to swear vengeance against the French. This time they did so under the aegis of the British Crown.

Protective of French interests, Governor Denonville sent Nicolas Perrot into the interior in the autumn of 1688. On May 8, 1689, he reasserted the French claim to the land, specifying the lands extending from Green Bay to the Mississippi and St. Croix rivers.[21] Great unrest pervaded the area of the Great Lakes in the ensuing years, and Sioux Indians regularly attacked the lake settlements. The Menominees, like their neighbors, were confused by reports of the Hurons making a separate peace with the Iroquois. In the hope of preventing a Sioux war and retaining the peace and loyalty of LaBaye Indians, Perrot in 1695 accompanied ten or twelve canoes of Indians, Potawatomis, Sacs, Foxes, Outagamis, and Menominees, to Quebec where they met with Count Frontenac, who in 1689 had been reappointed governor of New France. Onunguisse, the Potawatomi chief, was spokesman for the group. Chief Kioulous-Koio represented the Menominee Indians and voiced accord with the speech of the Potawatomi. Frontenac begged patience and submission from the tribes and congratulated the Menominee chief on attempting to keep the Fox Indians from defecting to the Iroquois. Frontenac warned those who seemed disposed to go to the enemy to note with what indifference the Miamis were devoured by the Iroquois. He said, "When he will have no more meat do you imagine that he will not eat you. He wishes to be alone." Frontenac then proclaimed Perrot's authority as commandant of Michilimackinac to be the official voice of the French for the tribes present.[22]

French policy changed drastically in 1696, following a decline in the European fur market and amid growing reports of a harmful liquor trade with the Indians and abuse of the Indian women by the French. In response to the opposition, royal orders were sent to close the posts, revoke the trading licenses, and prohibit all further trade except with Indians who voluntarily traveled to Montreal.[23] By 1698 the edict was in effect and the upper lakes returned to their original state. A few missionaries and *coureurs de bois,* in violation of the order and under penalty of being sentenced to the galleys, braved the wilderness alone. In that same year Count Frontenac died and Louis Hector de Callières became the governor-general. Callières subsequently made peace with the Iroquois, secured an exchange of prisoners and acceptance of the treaty among all of the tribes,[24] and then concentrated French attention on their new venture in Louisiana.

Although Queen Anne's War broke out in 1702, and the French and English and their Indian allies fought in Acadia, Newfoundland, and New England, the Menominees lived free of further French entanglement until 1712, when they and all of the tribes on the western frontier became embroiled in Fox affairs. The Fox Indians had recently confederated with the Iroquois and English, and a large band of them pledged the destruction of Fort Detroit and the murder of the Frenchmen there. En route to Detroit, where they planned to build a fortified village preparatory to their attack, the Foxes attacked a settlement of Illinois Indians, killing a large number. In the spring of 1712, a Potawatomi raid against the Mascoutens was successful, and the Foxes, Mascoutens, and Kickapoos were infuriated by the attack. Expecting a siege and having only twenty French soldiers at Fort Detroit, Commandant Sieur du Buisson hurriedly summoned the aid of the Ottawas, Illinois, and Green Bay Indians.

Once again the Menominees sent braves to the defense of the French. They arrived at the French garrison of Detroit on May 13, 1712, and laid a merciless siege to the village of Foxes and Mascoutens. From elevated ramparts gunfire and fire arrows rained down upon the pallisaded village. Pemoussa, the Fox chief, sued for peace, which the allied Indians rejected. The attack resumed. After a nineteen-day siege Pemoussa and Allamina of the Foxes again came forward under a flag of truce. Their proffered peace to return to their western Lake Michigan home was rejected. When in desperation the Foxes attempted to escape at night, they were pursued and slaughtered. This victory forced the British to abandon hope of establishing themselves at Detroit, and thus peace returned for a time to the Great Lakes. The Indians, however, instead of bringing their furs to Montreal, as was hoped, sought trade with the English, who liberally plied them with liquor and trade goods. The loss of the fur trade and the unrest among the northern Indians prompted France to reopen Fort Michilimackinac.

Incensed by their terrible losses at Detroit, the Foxes fortified Butte des Morts on the Fox River, and there, in 1716, the French Captain Louis de Louvigny, commandant of Michilimackinac, attacked the Fox stronghold. The bombardment of the fort by cannon and mortar fire brought capitulation. The Foxes promised peace and delivered up hostages, including Chief Pemoussa, who died of smallpox upon reaching Montreal. They refused, however, to attend the peace conference and soon renewed their incursions against neighboring tribes and allied themselves with the Sioux and the Chickasaws.[25]

In 1718 the Menominees were still together in their Menominee River village when they were visited by Sieur de la Mothe Cadillac, who was up from Mobile in search of silver mines. Cadillac, a former commandant at Michilimackinac, described the country from the Straits of Mackinac to the Mississippi as well as the Indians found on the land. He took time to record the physical qualities of the Indians whom he saw. This is something that the Jesuit Fathers did only in general terms, they being more interested in the Indian's sorcery, heathenism, and general living conditions. Of the Menominees, Cadillac observed:

> The Malhomine or Folles Avoines are so called from the river on which their village is situated, where the land produces an enormous quantity of wild oats, which they reap and gather in as we do our corn. They boil it with game or fat. It is a wholesome food. There is no tribe in which the men are so handsome or have such good figures. They are not so swarthy as the others, and if they did not grease themselves they would surpass the French in whiteness. Their women are also very pretty, and more gentle than their neighbours.[26]

Disappointed over the loss of the fur trade at Montreal, the French Crown on April 28, 1716, authorized the reestablishment of twenty-five licensed traders in New France.[27] Once again, trappers, traders, and missionaries traveled the Great

Lakes. Father Charlevoix visited the Menominees in 1721. Of
his visit he wrote:

> we found ourselves abreast of a small island . . . which concealed
> from us the entrance to a River on which is the village of the
> Malhomines—whom the French have named Folles Avoines, ap-
> parently because they use that vegetable as their ordinary food.
> The entire Tribe is composed of this village, which is not very
> populous. That is a pity, for they are fine looking Men, and among
> the most shapely in Canada. They are even taller than the Pou-
> teouatamis.[28]

Stinging from defeat, the Fox Indians sought new allies and
found them among the Sac and Winnebago Indians. The Menominees were also approached but refused to join with the treach-
erous Foxes. By 1724 Lake Michigan's western shores were
again embroiled in a war waged between the Fox and Sauteur
(Ojibway) and Illinois Indians. On August 23, 1724, Sieur de
Lignery, commandant of Michilimackinac, held a council of
Sacs, Foxes, and Winnebagoes at Green Bay. These Indians refused to lay down their war clubs raised against the Illinois.
Following the meeting, warfare against the Illinois Indians and
their allies was earnestly renewed. Claude du Tisné, the French
commander among the Illinois, complained to the governor-
general that the "Renards dance around our scalps with their
allies."[29] On June 7, 1726, de Lignery again met with the war-
ring tribes at Green Bay where the Indians agreed to make
peace. Good to their word, the Foxes were still professing loyalty to the French king when Faber du Plessis arrived in the
spring of 1727 to relieve Monsieur d'Ararton as commander of
the Green Bay post. By fall, however, British intrigue had dis-
suaded the Foxes from their French alliance, and the Indians
were once more on the warpath. Governor Charles de la Boische,
Marquis de Beauharnois, on October 25, 1727, informed the
French government that he would commence warfare against
them in the spring. In May, 1728, Louis XIV ordered the destruction of the Fox Nation.[30]

The Marchand de Lignery commanded the first French expedition of the Second Fox War. His force consisted of four hundred French and eight hundred Indians. The expedition left Michilimackinac on August 10, 1728. Father Emanuel Crespel, chaplain to the group, described the expedition. On August 15, 1728, the French landed at the Menominee village, "with a view to prove them to oppose our descent; they fell into the snare and were entirely defeated."[31] Father Crespel offered no explanation for this attack on the loyal Menominees. The de Lignery expedition failed to engage the Fox Indians and managed only to capture and cruelly torture some old men and women of the tribe. De Lignery also ordered the destruction of the French fort at Green Bay to prevent the Foxes from taking it. These actions by de Lignery were harshly condemned by Governor Beauharnois, who added in explanation that, "they say M. de Lignery was ill, and that he did not wish that any other should reap any glory from the undertaking."[32]

Pierre Paul, Sieur de Marin, headed a second expedition to aid the Winnebagoes against the Foxes in the spring of 1730. He and nine soldiers arrived among the Menominees at their village. There, he repaired and fortified a trading post that had been abandoned. Winnebago Indians arrived with three Fox slaves for Marin. The Winnebagoes, accompanied by four Menominee braves, returned to their village on an island in Little Lake Butte des Morts. This village was quickly attacked by Fox Indians, and after a forty-eight-hour battle, the Winnebagoes negotiated for a settlement. As retribution for the slaves that they had given away, the Winnebagoes surrendered the Menominees. Two of them were delivered bound, while the other two were decapitated and their heads given to the attackers. Unsatisfied, the Foxes demanded four Winnebago warriors. These were refused, and the battle resumed.[33]

The Menominees, uneasy when their young men did not return, sent scouts toward the Winnebago village. When they reported the state of war, the Menominee chief, Aus-kin-naw-waw-witsh, sought Marin's aid. Marin with five French soldiers and thirty-four Menominee braves set out by canoe to relieve the Winnebago village. On March 19, 1730, they portaged around the Kakalin Falls of the Fox River at Kaukauna and proceeded to the island. They landed at a point close to the entrenched Foxes, where they began to fortify their position. Contrary to Marin's order, a member of the expedition began chopping trees, and the noise brought the Foxes down upon the little group. Marin's men met the attack so successfully that the Foxes retreated to their fortifications. The latter shouted insults at the Menominees, informing them that their young men had been put in their kettles. Incensed, Aus-kin-naw-waw-witsh desired to war on both groups of Indians, but Marin prevailed upon them to concentrate on the Foxes.

The Fox warriors returned a second time seeking to establish a position from which to overrun the Menominee position in the approaching darkness. Ten Winnebagoes joined Marin's party, and during the night they assisted the group in reaching the Winnebago fort. An elderly Menominee couple residing among the Winnebagoes begged Marin to attack and punish the Winnebagoes for their recent treachery toward the Menominees. The immediate problem of the Foxes, however, took precedence. A battle raged for three days before the Foxes asked to talk. Marin refused to leave the fort as requested, and the fight continued. On the morning of the fourth day the Foxes demanded to know Marin's losses, a matter he refused to discuss. Actually, one Frenchman was dead and two others wounded, while three Menominees were killed and seven wounded. Sometime during the night the Foxes fled the island, and on the fifth morning ravens were seen alighting inside the Fox fortifications.[34] Marin and the Menominees escorted the Winnebago Indians to Green Bay and then proceeded to the French post at the Menominee village. The Menominees confessed to Marin their desire to destroy the Winnebagoes. Marin diplomatically persuaded them to do nothing about the matter until he had discussed it with their father, Onontio.*

*Onontio, the Iroquois name for the governor-general of Canada.

Although the Fox Indians fled the Green Bay area, the war against them continued among the Illinois and in the territory as far west as the Mississippi, thereby further decimating the ranks of the Fox and allied Sac nations. The encounter with the Winnebagoes and Menominees marked the beginning of their end. On September 9, 1730, on a plain extending between the Wabash and Illinois rivers, four hundred Fox men, women, and children were killed and five hundred more taken prisoner by a combined French and Indian army under the command of Nicolas Coulon, Sieur de Villiers. The prisoners were divided among the participating Illinois, Mascoutens, Kickapoos, and Potawatomis.[35]

In 1731 Sieur de Villiers was sent by Governor Beauharnois to restore the fort at Green Bay which de Lignery had burned. Indian revenge, once determined, is difficult to assuage, and attacks continued against the remnant Fox nation. In September, 1731, they were raided by Illinois Indians, and late that year a war party of one hundred and twenty-four Hurons, Iroquois, and Ottawas attacked them on the banks of the Wisconsin River, killing and capturing over three hundred.[36] Only fifty men of the Fox tribe remained free, and these their enemies had sworn to slay. The French Crown approved the total destruction of the Fox tribe and also urged the French allied Indians to war against the Chickasaws, allies of the British in the south. In the summer of 1733 the fifty remaining Fox Indians, forty men including Chief Kiala, and ten boys, ages twelve to thirteen, came to M. de Villiers at Green Bay to beg for mercy. Sieur de Villiers named four Fox Indians, including Chief Kiala and another chief, to accompany him to Montreal where the tribe's fate would be decided. The remaining Foxes moved into a nearby Sac village to await de Villiers' return. Governor Beauharnois decided that all of the Foxes should be brought to Montreal where they were to be dispersed among the "villages of settled savages."

De Villiers returned to Green Bay with this decision but was slain on September 16, 1733, by the Sac Indians, who refused to surrender the Fox refugees. The Sacs and Foxes fled the village, pursued by the French and two hundred Indian allies, among whom were the Menominees. Six Menominee Indians were killed in this final encounter of the Second Fox War. The Sacs fled to the Wapsipinicon River in Iowa, where they built a fort. They established the Foxes in another fort as their neighbors. Beauharnois ordered a new attack against them, and Nicolas Joseph de Noyelles was assigned the task. De Noyelles had to abandon his plan to destroy the tribes when most of his Indian allies refused to fight the Sacs and enfeebled Foxes. The Sacs agreed to separate from the Foxes and return to Green Bay. Meanwhile, one of the Fox chiefs at Montreal died. Chief Kiala was sent as a slave to Martinique, and his wife was given to the Hurons, who adopted her but from whom she later escaped.[37]

According to the census report of October 12, 1736, there were one hundred and sixty Menominee warriors. The report described armorial standards used by the Menominees that included the large-tailed bear, the stag, and "a kiliou, that is a species of Eagle (the most beautiful bird of this country)— perched on a cross." This latter standard is explained by the story that a former Menominee chief, failing to respond to ordinary remedies during an illness, called for the missionary, "who, Cross in hand, prayed to God for his recovery, and obtaining it from his mercy. In gratitude for this benefit, the chief desired that in his arms should be added a Cross on which the Kiliou has ever since been always perched."[38] The report also lists eighty Winnebago warriors, who since 1728 had left Green Bay and joined the Sioux, twenty Potawatomi warriors, and one hundred and fifty Sac warriors in the vicinity of Green Bay. In the area of the Fox River it cites one hundred migrant Fox men, eighty Kickapoos, and sixty Mascoutens.

In 1737 the Menominees and other tribes that had fought the Foxes sent delegates to Governor Beauharnois asking clemency for the remaining Fox Indians. Beauharnois honored their request and agreed to spare the lives of the remaining Fox and Sac Indians.[39] The Green Bay Indians, including representatives of the Fox and Sac Indians, were again in Montreal, accompanied by Pierre Paul Marin, in the summer of 1740. The meeting was one of good fellowship and mutual promises of peace. At this same time Sioux Indians began to raid the tribes along the western Lake Michigan frontier.

Tribes from this whole western frontier attended conferences in Montreal during the summer of 1742. The Menominees journeyed there along with Sioux, Foxes, Sacs, and Chippewas. This latter group met with Beauharnois on July 18, 24, and 25, 1742. The Foxes complained about offenses against them since moving "their fire" one day's journey from Green Bay. They reported that when they went to greet the Menominees, "we were surprised to see the heads of two of our men suspended in the air. We said: how can it be that we are killed by our true brothers?" In reply the Menominee spokesman said:

> It is true, My Father, that we did wrong in striking the Renards our brothers. The chiefs did not consent to it, and had nothing to do with it. A young Giddypate committed the deed that causes so much Trouble today. . . . the reason that you see so many of us, is that I have brought with me the more dangerous of the young Warriors, whom I have bound, so that, if the Renards wish to revenge themselves, they may do so more easily, as we have left women only in our village."[40]

Governor Beauharnois replied to each group. He told the Foxes of the Menominee people's sorrow over the wicked way of one of their members and reminded them that the Menominees had already sent them gifts to make amends, and that he too would add gifts to lessen their grief. Beauharnois praised the Menominees for their efforts to atone for the misdeed of one of their young men and also distributed gifts to their principal chiefs and "the Distinguished women" who had accompanied them.

In 1745 Jean Monier and Jean l'Eschelle, merchants of Montreal, entered into a business agreement to outfit the trading enterprises of Louis Matthieu Damours, Sieur de Clignancourt. The trading post at Green Bay was leased for three years to the three men in 1747. The lease provided for the exclusive control of trade throughout the post area. It restricted the quantity of brandy that could be brought to the post, not to exceed sixty-eight pots a year, and it forbade military men from engaging in the fur trade.[41] The lease was not renewed in 1750 apparently because of complaints from the tribes of exploitation by the Frenchmen sent out by the lease owners. Without competition at the French posts the traders charged excessive prices and openly cheated the Indians. Such actions led to widespread discontent and the Indians resorted to capturing trade canoes and jeopardizing the lives of the French among them. In 1746 Etienne Augé had been murdered by Menominee Indians because of his misconduct toward them in matters of trade.[42] The promise of better treatment came with the return of Pierre Marin to the Green Bay fort in 1750.

During this period France and England were once again at war. King George's War, the American phase of the War of the Austrian Succession, 1744-48, was fought in the East along the French and English colonial borders. In this war the French again relied heavily upon their Indian allies. The Menominees responded to the call for assistance, and Chief La Mothe headed a group of sixteen Menominees who went to war. In July, 1745, they were with Lieutenant Demuy's detachment which, besides sixty-nine Frenchmen and officers, contained four hundred Indians. This detachment was stationed for a time at Fort Frederic and, while there, they felled trees to prevent the use of the River au Chicot* by the enemy and went on raiding parties.[43] One such party of fourteen warriors was directed by Chief La Mothe and raided in the area of Albany. The foray resulted in securing the scalps of two Mohawks and a Dutchman. The Menominees left the battle area in August, 1747, and returned to Montreal with the scalps. La Mothe recounted the scenes of the ambuscade of their victims. The first Mohawk to be apprehended was tall and big, and La Mothe had ordered him to be taken alive, but Carron, a French-Ottawa trader adopted by the

*Wood Creek, Washington County, New York.

32

Menominees, had already killed him. At first it was believed that this Mohawk was the notorious Toyen-o-guen, but it was later discovered that the victim was Big Fish, an influential Mohawk chief.[44]

La Mothe also was among a delegation of Menominees that visited Montreal in the summer of 1751, when they assured the new governor, the Marquis de la Jonquière, that they would attempt to stop the bands of Winnebagoes from making further attacks against the Missouris. Some Menominees had also organized to raid the Missouris, but they were stopped by their own people before carrying out their plan.[45]

Despite their protestations of peace the previous summer, the Menominees on June 1, 1752, joined with the Winnebagoes, Foxes, Sacs, and Potawatomis in an attack against the Michigami and Cahokia Indians in the Illinois Valley. The attackers, who launched the raid in reprisal for the murder of seven Fox Indians, killed and captured seventy men, women, and children, burned ten or twelve cabins, and scattered the limbs of the dead. M. Adamville met the raiders following the attack and reported seeing sixty canoes and four hundred Indians. They showed Adamville thirty scalps and a number of prisoners. Adamville reported that the Indians appeared satisfied that by the attack they had avenged the deaths of their people.[46] Joseph Marin, son of the late Pierre Paul Marin, arrived as commandant at Green Bay, and in the summer of 1752, a general peace was made among the Lake Michigan Indians. This peace assured the French retention of their Illinois colonies of Cahokia and Kaskaskia.

France had a desperate need for manpower with which to fight the colonial wars with the more populous English outposts in America. Throughout the long colonial struggle France depended heavily upon her Indian allies to supply the needed manpower. The final war in the conflict for supremacy in North America was the French and Indian War, begun in America in 1754. The Menominees became involved in this long struggle as early as 1755, when some of their warriors responded to the call for troops at Green Bay by Charles de Langlade. Langlade, related to the Menominees by marriage, led a force of western Indians to Fort Duquesne. From there the Indians joined the French troops of M. Beaujou in attacking General Edward Braddock's army at the Monongahela River on July 9, 1755.[47] The surprise attack overwhelmed Braddock's forces and routed them. In their haste to escape the vicious attack many of Braddock's men drowned in the Monongahela. The Indians despoiled the bodies of the British and Colonial soldiers of their clothing and articles of value. They searched for the British supply of liquor, but Langlade had wisely disposed of it. Over twelve hundred of Braddock's two thousand soldiers perished in the battle. George Washington was one of the fortunate Colonials who survived the engagement. Both the French commander Beaujou and English General Braddock were mortally wounded in the encounter.

The next summer the Menominees served under Coulon de Villiers along the Oswego River in New York. There,

> with four hundred men he attacked a convoy of three or four hundred bateau [boats], each with two men, and three companies of soldiers . . . Villiers put them to flight and knocked off a great number, and would have knocked off a lot more were it not for the poor quality of the tomahawks furnished by the King's store, took twenty-four scalps and killed or wounded in their flight . . . about three hundred men.[48]

The Menominees proceeded to Presque Isle on Lake Erie where they joined Joseph Marin and the western Indians who had responded to the French call for help. Because of reports of smallpox at the French forts, all of the Indians, except the Menominees, refused to go to Montreal. The Menominees, pledged to the French cause and already exposed to the danger of war, risked death from the dread disease to accompany Marin to Montreal. They arrived there on July 11, 1756. Louis Antoine de Bougainville, aide-de-camp to General Montcalm, witnessed the Menominee arrival at Montreal.

They came in five great birchbark canoes with six scalps and several prisoners. Arrived opposite to Montreal, the canoes were placed in several lines, they lay to for some time, the Indians saluted with a discharge of guns and loud cries to which three cannon shot replied. Afterwards they came ashore and went up to the Chateau in double file, the prisoners in the middle carrying wands decorated with feathers. These prisoners were not maltreated, as is customary upon entering into cities and villages. Entered into M. de Vaudreuil's presence, the prisoners sat down on the ground in a circle, and the Indian chief, with action and force that surprised me, made a short enough speech, the gist of which was that the Menominees were different from the other tribes which held back part of their captures, and that they always brought back to their father all the meat they had taken. Then they danced around the captives to the sound of a sort of tambourine placed in the middle. Extraordinary spectacle. . . . These men were naked save for a piece of cloth in front and behind, the face and body painted, feathers on their heads, symbol and signal of war, tomahawk and spear in hand. In general these are brawny men, large and of good appearance. . . . One could not have better hearing than these people. The dance ended they were given meat and wine. The prisoners sent off to jail.[49]

On July 13 the Menominee chiefs with La Mothe as spokesman met with Governor de Vaudreuil. The Menominees professed a loyalty to the French that surpassed that of any other nation in the West and expressed their willingness to strike the English. Vaudreuil praised them for their participation in M. de Villiers' recent victory and presented them with two medals and eight gorgets for their warriors who had so recently distinguished themselves. He implored the Menominees to join his brother, Rigaud de Vaudreuil, on the forthcoming expedition.

Leaving their wounded and men to transport them home, thirty Menominees, led by Marin, left Montreal on July 18, 1756, bound for Fort Frontenac on Lake Ontario.* On July 30 Bougainville reported that a council was held to prevail upon the Menominees to remain. They received pork, wine, tobacco, vermillion, and eighteen strings of wampum. On August 1 the

*The Indian name for the French Fort Frontenac was Catarakaui.

Menominees along with the Guyenne and Bearn regiments mustered for an inspection by General Montcalm. Three days later the Menominees embarked for M. de Rigaud's camp at Oswego, twelve leagues distant, in company with the French commander Marquis de Montcalm, French voyageurs, and a group of engineers. The Menominees were used as escort and on details assigned to intercepting couriers on the trails and supply vessels on the streams and rivers. By August 13, 1756, Indian detachments were sent to harass the enemy at the British fort at Oswego. British Colonel Mercer, who commanded the fort, was killed on August 14, and one hour later the British surrendered. Montcalm's first victory in America yielded 1,700 British captives and all of their weapons and supplies. The prisoners were deported to Montreal. On August 17 the Menominees set out for Montreal no doubt with a consignment of prisoners.

The Indians had time to make it home for the rice harvest and fall hunt. The next summer found them again on the warpath for France. The loyalty, courage, and endurance displayed by the Menominee warriors was understandably admired by the French. The strength and skill of those men who traversed Lakes Michigan, Huron, and Ontario in fragile birch-bark canoes marked the Menominees as expert mariners. Although a peace-loving people, the Menominee warriors' valor in battle won them distinction in the ranks of the French army. Their faithful assistance made them an important allied power in French-Indian relations.

In 1757, Vaudreuil secured a renewal of the trading post contract at Green Bay for his brother, Rigaud de Vaudreuil, and his Montreal associates, Jacques Giasson and Ignace Hubert. The next year, eleven Canadians were murdered by Menominee Indians at Green Bay and the post warehouse raided. This drastic affair stemmed from the fact that for two years, because of the war, no ships had come from France with trade goods. As a result no presents could be distributed among the tribes now dependent upon the French for the much desired articles of trade.[50] Distressed by the murder of the Frenchmen, the Menominees sent seven of the offenders as prisoners to Montreal with their war party in July, 1757. There, the great Marquis de Montcalm witnessed the Menominee surrender of their prisoners.

> The Folles Avoines have sent as prisoners to Montreal the seven savages of their nation, who this winter have assassinated a French family at LaBaie. Three of them have been shot on the town square, and the other four must go to the war and expose themselves to danger in order to expiate their crime. This submission of an independent nation more than five hundred leagues distant, does great honor to the French name.[51]

The penalty extracted for the offense again indicates the desperate need of the French for fighting men.

The Menominees sat in war council with the Marquis de Vaudreuil and the Marquis de Montcalm. On July 12, 1757, an army of the West left Montreal with Montcalm at its head. Bougainville observed "the Indians of the Far West are the most superstitious of all. One must be very much on his guard not to do anything which they will regard as a bad omen. For example, if one touched the weapons of a warrior who was going on a war party, he would believe himself threatened with death and would take no part in the expedition." The Menominees with Marin left Fort Carillon (Ticonderoga) on July 16 to make a raid, and on July 18, Marin led three hundred Indians and eighty Frenchmen to the Chicot River. One hundred and twenty of Marin's men reported back to the French fort on July 22, having been dispersed by English war parties encountered en route. Marin with his best equipped men proceeded on reconnaissance toward the English forts of Lydius and William Henry. Marin's group returned to Fort Carillon on the morning of July 24 with thirty-two scalps and a prisoner. Meanwhile, a detachment of three hundred and fifty British troops from Fort William Henry was ambushed and annihilated by a French war party in which Le Chat and his command of Menominees participated.[52]

Plans were made by Montcalm for the destruction of the English forts, and he held war councils with his Indian allies.

LaMothe, chief spokesman for the Menominees, agreed with the general's plans. "As the Marquis de Montcalm profited by the chance fall of a great tree during the council to refer to it as a certain augury of the fall of Fort William Henry, La Mothe accepted the omen in the name of the Indians of the Far West."[53] The Menominees offered two detachments of men for Montcalm's army, sixty-two led by l'Original and sixty-seven by Le Chat. These one hundred and thirty-one Menominees were part of an Indian army of 1,799. Joseph Marin led the Indians of the western frontier. The total French army consisted of 8,019 men, commanded by General Montcalm.

The army departed Fort Carillon on August 1, 1757, some traveling overland and others going by water.[54] On August 3 Chevalier de Lévi led all of the Indians and his own nineteen hundred French troops as an advance guard in Montcalm's attack on Fort William Henry. By August 4 the French had positioned their troops and mounted their batteries, and light gunfire was exchanged with the fort. The Indians captured couriers, oxen, and supply vessels. Among the messages intercepted was a letter from British General Webb at Fort Lydius to Colonel Monro at Fort William Henry telling him that aid could not be sent. On August 9 Montcalm accepted the surrender of Colonel Monro and the British fortress. Before signing the capitulation, Montcalm received a promise from his Indian chiefs that their young men would not trespass against the British. The Indians, led by the Abnakis on August 10, violated the peace by plundering the fort and capturing five hundred British soldiers, some of whom they murdered before Montcalm could stop the carnage.

The Indians departed the next day for Montreal with two hundred English prisoners, arriving there on August 19, 1757. By August 29 the Indians agreed to surrender the Englishmen whom they had held and abused since their arrival at Montreal. One or more unfortunate Englishmen had even been boiled in the Indians' kettles, and their comrades forced to partake of the feast. Undismayed by the excesses of his Indian allies, Governor Vaudreuil gave presents of clothing, tobacco, brandy, lace, and vermillion to each tribe before sending them home. Meanwhile, the French salvaged the guns and supplies from Fort William Henry and then burned the fort. The field of battle in the French and Indian War shifted to Louisbourg, and later to the St. Lawrence Valley.

The Menominees returned to action in the summer of 1758. Again they served with Marin in an effort to intercept Robert Rogers and his rangers in the area of Wood Creek. Marin put his force of four hundred and fifty in ambush and intercepted the enemy. A two-hour battle raged between the French force and a British force of seven hundred select men consisting of the Connecticut regiment, a unit of light infantry under Captain James Dalyell, and Roberts' Rangers. Marin's unit was forced to withdraw, having lost one hundred and fifty men. That year French fortune faded rapidly in America. The loss of Fort Frontenac and the evacuation of Lake Ontario was a most serious blow to the French cause. Fort Niagara fell to the assault of Generals Prideaux and Johnson, and General Amherst seized the forts of Ticonderoga (Carillon) and Crown Point. By June, 1759, General James Wolfe arrived within sight of Quebec. The French reacted by camping their troops between the St. Charles River and the Falls of Montmorency in the hopes of obstructing the British passage. The French troops were divided into three corps, the left led by M. de Lévi, the right by M. de Vaudreuil, and the center by the Marquis de Montcalm. Included in Rigaud de Vaudreuil's command were the western Indians led by Charles de Langlade.

On July 9 the major part of Wolfe's troops disembarked below Montmorency Falls and camped across the river with their artillery. They regularly fired upon the French forces on the opposite shore. On July 25 a two-thousand-man British reconnaissance force might have been annihilated if Langlade had been able to spring his ambushed Indians against the enemy. The French officers did not issue the order to attack, and the opportunity to strike a major blow against Wolfe's force went unheeded except for a spontaneous Indian attack which killed sixty British troops. The Menominee Indians served in Langlade's command at Montmorency and in the Battle of the Plains of Abraham, September 13, 1759. Listed in the ranks of Langlade's troops are Chief Carron, his son, Glode, O-sau-wish-ke-no (Yellow Bird), and Kacha-ka-wa-sheka (The Notch Maker). Without doubt there was a large contingent of Menominees whose names have been lost to history. Langlade regarded the French capitulation at Quebec as premature and "effected through bribery," and in disgust he withdrew his Indian force from the battlefield.

By the fall of 1760 all French garrisons on the western frontier had been evacuated, and the British had already assigned officers to take charge of the posts. For the Menominees this meant that soon new officials would come to direct their future. The Menominees had acknowledged the French influences that first altered their life-style and their thinking. Through examples set by the French traders, missionaries, and soldiers, the Menominees learned the ways of the white man.

The traders craved beaver pelts, which for the Menominees meant trade goods. There is an Indian saying that the "beaver . . . makes kettles, hatchets, swords, knives, bread; and, in short, it makes everything."[55] The Menominees seemed to have adapted readily to the change from a subsistence to a partially trading economy. Part of each fall and spring hunt was devoted to trapping for furs and to gathering deer and bear skins.

The success of the French Jesuits is attested to by Father André's testimony and by the loyalty of the Menominee people to the Catholic religion. The religious influence brought comfort to the sick and dying, hope to the people in distress, and new symbols, music, and beliefs. For this new religion the Menominees abandoned their magic songs, their reliance on the Jugglers and thunder-spirits, and their native innocence in dress, morals, and social customs.

From the soldiers the Menominees learned of international warfare and governmental authority. No record exists to provide the number of young Menominee men who died in the French wars. One can only imagine the sadness in the Menominee village upon the return of each war party. The hand of French authority also rested heavily upon the Menominees at times, and white justice remained beyond the full acceptance of the Indians.

The French benefited from their contact with the Menominee Indians. They exploited them for their furs and their proudest warriors. They relied upon them as a peaceful force in a hostile country. Some Frenchmen found a new peace and joyous freedom in the land of the Menominees. These remained and married into the tribe. Although France lost her North American empire in 1763, echoes of her reign ring through every roll call of the Menominee Indians.

III

British Relations

The folls avoines behave with Spirit and Judgement, it is fortunate for us there are such Indians in such times.

Robert Dickson
February, 1814

A delegation of Menominee Indians met with Lieutenant James Gorrell, first English commandant at Green Bay, on May 23, 1762. An English occupation detachment from the 80th Regiment, commanded by Captain Henry Balfour and Lieutenant James Gorrell, had arrived at Green Bay on October 12, 1761. At that time the Bay Indians were away on the fall hunt. Lieutenant Gorrell found "the fort quite rotten, the stockade ready to fall, the houses without cover, and fire wood a distance from the fort."[1] Captain Balfour left the post in charge of James Gorrell and assigned him a sergeant, a corporal, fifteen privates, a French interpreter, and the English traders, Messrs. McKay and Goddard. The lieutenant's orders stressed the necessity of making friends with the Indians. Upon his arrival at Green Bay, Gorrell had no knowledge of the large number of Indians in the vicinity; moreover, he had arrived at the post without rum, wampum belts, or money with which to make friends. Wampum belts were purchased on credit from the Indians to be returned to them as tokens of British friendship. The Green

Bay fort, rebuilt by the soldiers, was named Fort Edward Augustus.

The first winter at Green Bay was a quiet time for the little English garrison. Each of the area's tribes sent young warriors to test the English reception. Lieutenant Gorrell reported they "were agreeably surprised to find that we were fond of seeing them." The Indian visitors received gifts of ammunition and flour and assurances of English goodwill. Three Menominee chiefs were in attendance at the first formal Menominee meeting with the British at Green Bay. During the conference the British officer stressed the victory of King George III over the French domain in America, and the king's desire to trade with the people in the newly acquired territory. The Menominees expressed their desire for presents, and they declared that they were poor and had recently lost three hundred warriors because of smallpox in addition to the many chiefs and braves lost in war. Little came from the conference, since Gorrell had little to give the Indians. He did promise to request supplies for them and a gunsmith for the English post.

Lieutenant Gorrell's position became precarious as orders were received to give the Indians only those presents necessary "to keep them in temper." Ensign Thomas Hutchins arrived in 1762 to inspect the post and to gain firsthand knowledge of the Indians.[2] He met with the Menominees, Sacs, and Foxes. The Indians requested flags and commissions in the English army inasmuch as they had received them from the French. Lieutenant Hutchins promised to act in this matter on behalf of the Indian chiefs. Once again the English officer had little but promises to offer the Menominees and their neighbors. The Menominee chiefs registered bitter complaints with Lieutenant Hutchins against the Chippewas who had murdered a Menominee warrior at Fort Michilimackinac. The Menominees said they were prepared to fight a war of revenge against the Chippewas.

At this same time an Indian voice was raised throughout the area of the Great Lakes and Ohio Valley calling for the Indians to unite in a common cause and drive the white man from their country. The Ottawa-Chippewa chief, Pontiac, was the master spirit behind the movement to destroy the western military posts. Pontiac met with the northern Indians at Milwaukee.[3] Except for Indians in the Milwaukee area, there was little response to Pontiac's appeal from the Green Bay Indians, especially the Menominees.

The outbreak of Pontiac's Rebellion at Forts Detroit, Miami, and St. Joseph inspired the Chippewa Indians to make a successful surprise attack on Fort Michilimackinac on June 4, 1763, while playing a game of lacrosse in front of the fort.[4] Charles Langlade was then an established trader at the fort. The French were unharmed in the attack, but Lieutenant Jemette and seventy English soldiers were murdered and Captain George Etherington, Lieutenant Lesslie, Henry Bostwick, and Alexander Henry with twenty soldiers were taken hostage. Ottawa Indians from L'Arbre Croche (Cross Village), hearing of the attack and angered at not being included in the plot, hastened to Fort Michilimackinac to claim the prisoners and hold them for ransom.

A summons for help reached Green Bay on June 11, 1763, when an Ottawa courier arrived with a letter from Captain Etherington. Lieutenant Gorrell sent word to the tribes in his command, and chiefs from all of the tribes assembled. They pledged support for an effort to rescue Captain Etherington and restore the English to Fort Michilimackinac. The Menominees promised protection over Fort Edward Augustus until the English soldiers returned. Gorrell's garrison, the English traders, and the Indian allies, Sacs, Foxes, and Winnebagoes, arrived at the main Menominee village on June 21, 1763, en route northward. There, Menominee chiefs and twenty warriors joined with the Menominees from Green Bay in Gorrell's party. Bad weather delayed the expedition until June 25, when the garrison soldiers, English traders, and ninety warriors crossed Green Bay.

The Green Bay expedition reached the village of L'Arbre

44

Croche where they were well received by the Ottawa Indians. The Ottawas, however, refused to release their English prisoners except for ransom at Montreal. Since the Chippewa Indians denied ships' passage beyond Fort Michilimackinac, the Menominee Indians with their Fox, Sac, and Ottawa allies in this venture went to Michilimackinac to negotiate a passage. After three days of talks with the Chippewas they agreed to release the hostages in their custody and to permit travel beyond the fort. Lieutanant Gorrell rewarded the Menominees with eight certificates of merit, and Captain Etherington permitted the traders, Bruce, Fisher, and Roseboom, to return with the Indians to Green Bay. Gorrell and his soldiers accompanied the Ottawa Indians to Montreal, where the prisoners were ransomed by General Thomas Gage.[5]

The Menominees with a considerable segment of western lake Indians took no part in Pontiac's war except to assist the English on the occasion of the Michilimackinac attack. In the summer of 1764 they did attend the large Indian congress at Niagara held by Sir William Johnson, British superintendent of the affairs of the northern Indians of North America. A total of 2,060 Indians attended the congress. Most of those attending had not participated in the fighting at the western forts. Sir William Johnson held private meetings with each tribe in attendance. The Menominees met with the British superintendent on July 17, 1764. Their spokesman stressed the loyalty of the tribe and presented two wampum belts from the Menominee council fires at Green Bay and on the Menominee River. Sir William Johnson expressed his appreciation for the help rendered by the tribe to the Green Bay garrison.[6] Chief O-ge-maw-nee accepted a certificate of award and friendship from William Johnson on behalf of the Menominee Indians. Supplies were also provided the group for their return home.

A final Menominee request before their departure from Niagara called for the regarrisoning of the post at Green Bay. In his "Review of the Trade and Affairs of the Indians," Sir William Johnson recommended to England that the British post be restored. Johnson's argument stressed the ease of water communication with Green Bay, which served all of the Indians west of Lake Michigan. The Menominees returned home for the winter, but early the following summer, 1765, they journeyed with the neighboring tribes to Michilimackinac for a peace conference. Captain William Howard expressed the British desire to keep the trade routes open with the western Indians, and the Indians pledged peace and promised to prevent the Chippewas from closing the routes. The Menominees requested Captain Howard to reestablish the military and trading post at Green Bay.[7] Before the Menominees left Michilimackinac word was received that two Menominee Indians had been murdered by the Chippewas. Captain Howard heard the renewed Menominee complaint against the Chippewas. He urged the Menominees to refrain from a war and to seek other concessions from their enemy for the recent losses.

Robert Rogers, newly appointed British commander, arrived with his wife at Fort Michilimackinac late in the summer of 1765 Rogers, secretly hopeful of finding a northwest passage, commissioned Jonathan Carver, a mapmaker, to begin westward exploration. In company with the British trader, William Bruce, and several French traders, Carver visited Green Bay in 1766 and observed abandoned Fort Edward Augustus. Carver in his journal erroneously reported that the fort and its British occupants had been captured by the Menominees after the fall of Michilimackinac.[8] In the succeeding years the British made no effort to regarrison the deserted Green Bay post, but traders maintained the friendship of the Indians. Shortly after peace returned to the upper lake country, Charles Langlade moved his family from Michilimackinac and established a trading post at Green Bay.[9]

The Langlades were joined by other French and English traders, some of them, like Pierre Grignon and Amable de Gere brought their wives. Such settlers by their steadfast behavior and fair treatment kept the Menominee Indians and their neighbors loyal to the British service. In 1767 the Menominees sent a delegation, led by Chief O-kim-a-say, to Major Rogers at Michilimackinac to again request the regarrisoning of the Green Bay fort. Rogers gave Chief O-kim-a-say a certificate of merit in recognition of the Menominee-British friendship, but he sent no soldiers. In September, 1773, the Menominees were observed by a visitor to the Green Bay area who arrived by "canue" with a "small fleat." The trader, Peter Pond, noted the presence of the Menominees in his journal, made quaint by its highly phonetic spelling and originality. Of the Menominees, Pond wrote:

> on the North Part of this Bay is a Small Villeag of Indians Cald the Mannamaneas who Live By Hunting Chefely thay Have another Resors [resource] the Bottom of Bay Produsus a Large Quantity of Wilde Rice which that Geather in Septr. for food. I ort to have Menchand that the french at ye Villeag Green Bay whare we Incamt Rase fine Black Cattel & Horseis with Sum Swine.[10]

This account is the only early record of cattle, horses, and swine being raised at the Green Bay post.

At the outbreak of the American War of Independence Charles Langlade responded to a summons to duty issued by Captain Arent Schuyler de Peyster, commander at Michilimackinac after 1774.[11] In issuing the call Major de Peyster realized that action from Charles Langlade assured the cooperation of the western Indians with the British cause. On June 4, 1777, Langlade, Chief Carron, and sixty Menominee warriors, reported at Michilimackinac en route to Montreal.[12] Rumors circulated among the Indians at the fort informed the Menominees that Spanish agents were en route to their territory. Alarmed by the news, some of the Menominees, to the annoyance of Major de Peyster, abandoned Langlade's command and hastened home. Langlade's force at Michilimackinac was augmented by the arrival of thirty-two canoes of Sioux, Sacs, Foxes, Winnebagoes, Ottawas, and Chippewas led by Langlade's nephew, Charles Gautier, from Prairie du Chien. Gautier confirmed the rumors that a Spanish belt was being passed among the tribes, and he added that an American belt passed by the Ottawa Indians had reached Prairie du Chien.

Charles Langlade with his Indian force marched to Montreal where a grand council was held in the Indians' honor. Langlade served as interpreter for the council. In Montreal he met his friend Chevalier Luc de la Corne St. Luc, who accompanied the Langlade force that joined with Major Archibald Campbell's troops and moved southward to join Lieutenant General John Burgoyne's army in New York. Langlade's troops met with Burgoyne's army at Skenesborough in July, 1777. The accounts reveal little of the exploits of Langlade's force. General Burgoyne was dismayed by the ferocity of the Indian attacks. The general was confounded when the western Indians, as was their custom, gave notice that they were returning to their homes for the winter. When forced to surrender at Saratoga, New York, on October 14, 1777, General Burgoyne futilely tried to fix blame for his disaster on the few Canadian and Indian forces amidst his 8,000 British regulars.

In the spring of 1778 the Menominees endured a hostile attack by the Chippewa Indians in which two Menominee chiefs were counted among the dead. Despite the tribal grief, a war party of Menominees accompanied Langlade to Canada that summer. The activity of this group is not known, but on August 17, 1778, Governor Frederick Haldimand presented Cha-wa-non,* grand chief of the Menominee Indians, a certificate that recognized the chief's authority over the Menominees and in dealing with the British. That same summer George Rogers Clark and the American frontiersmen captured the British posts of Kaskaskia and Vincennes. Indians in the Illinois territory and as far north as Milwaukee rallied to the new American cause as Clark skillfully negotiated treaties with the tribes at Cahokia, thereby enabling the Americans to maintain control in the valley of the Illinois. These events were instrumental

*Cha-ka-cho-kama, the Old King.

in moving the boundary of the United States from Ohio to the Great Lakes.

Major de Peyster wrote Charles Langlade and Charles Gautier in the fall of 1778 enlisting aid for Lieutenant Governor Henry Hamilton, who was in the Illinois country determined to regain the lost British forts.[13] Before the Menominees and the British-allied Indians of the north could reach Illinois, Henry Hamilton was taken prisoner at Vincennes by General Clark, and the British counteroffensive temporarily collapsed in the West. Major de Peyster quickly dispatched presents to the Menominees and Winnebagoes to hold them to their British alliance. The major held a grand council of the western Indians at l'Arbre Croche on July 4, 1779. Following the council, de Peyster put his speech to the Indians into a rhymed chronicle. To the Menominees, de Peyster said:

> The Ottagams, Pioreas and Sacks,
> Have scarce a blanket on their backs,
> Old Carminees' Weenippegoes,
> Want fuzes, powder, ball and clothes,
> And skulk in dens, lest old Langlade
> Should give their heads the batonade;
> These suck their paws, like Northern bears,
> Exposing nothing but their ears,
> To hear if Gautier de Verville
> Doth crave assistance from LaFeuille
> Or, if the Chippewas of the plains,
> Draw near to Wabashaa's domains,
> While none on earth live more at ease,
> Than Car-ong's brave Menomenies.[14]

De Peyster said he would rally all of the Lake Michigan Indians and called upon specific Indian chiefs to help him. Glode,* son of old Carron, was among the list of chiefs.

A new commandant, Patrick Sinclair, arrived at Michilimackinac late in the summer of 1779 to replace A. S. de Peyster, who was given Hamilton's post at Detroit. Sinclair again called

---

*Glode, a French name. Glode's Menominee name was Con-note.

upon the Menominees and their neighbors to join a three-pronged expedition against the American-held posts along the Illinois and Mississippi rivers.[15] In April, 1780, Menominees en route to Prairie du Chien to join Captain Hesse's force captured a large armed boat filled with American trade goods and twelve boatmen. The captured goods, owned by the St. Louis trader, Charles Gartiot, were used to provision the Indians in Hesse's command. The boat and crew, accompanied by thirty-six Menominees, were taken to Sinclair at Michilimackinac. The Menominees at Prairie du Chien continued on with Captain Hesse's troops. That group of seven hundred and fifty men set out upon the Mississippi River to recapture Kaskaskia and the Spanish post of St. Louis. Some of the Menominees at Michili-mackinac joined with Charles Langlade and proceeded by way of Green Bay to attack the posts along the Illinois River. Po-e-go-na, the Feather-shedder, Mu-wa-sha, Little Wolf, and Le Baron with other warriors joined Langlade at the Menominee village. The remaining Menominees at Mackinac joined a group assigned to watching the lead mine area between the Wabash and Illinois rivers, permitting passage through the area only to those bearing a British pass. The Hesse expedition did make an attack at St. Louis on the Spaniards, who at the time were outnumbered four to one. The British cause failed, nevertheless, when the Sacs and Foxes defected, and the remaining Indians, fearful that Clark was ready to cross the river from Cahokia, lost the desire to continue the attack. Nothing remained for Captain Hesse to do but abandon the elaborate war plan.

Throughout the war, Canadian and English traders continued to exploit the Great Lakes fur trade. One such trader, John Long, visited the western Great Lakes Indians during the summer of 1780. Long described the Menominee Indian houses as "covered with birchbark and decorated with bows and arrows and weapons of war."[16] Long's trading party, consisting of twenty Canadians and thirty-six Indians, proceeded to Prairie du Chien to collect the peltry stored there. This action was in anticipation of an invasion of the area by Colonel Montgomery

50

in retaliation for the recent attack on Cahokia and St. Louis. Long's expedition collected three hundred packs of furs and burned sixty packs that they did not have room to carry. Shortly after their departure from Prairie du Chien, Montgomery's detachment raided the post.

The cost to the British government for maintaining the peace and loyalty of the western Indians was enormous, since the Indians would respond favorably to whichever white men could best satisfy their insatiable desire for trade goods, canoes, guns, and rum. Major de Peyster in a letter to Governor Haldimand observed that "the Indians are now come to such a pitch as to make their own demands, and that the refusal of a trifle, if not done with caution, may turn a whole warparty."[17] By 1781 the Green Bay Indians repented of their recent balk in fighting the British war and appeared at Michilimackinac to renew their pledge of loyalty and to accept presents.

Vieux Carron, long an honored leader among the Menominees, died on November 3, 1782. The next spring Captain Daniel Robertson, commanding officer at Michilimackinac, sent George McBeath and Charles Langlade, Jr., as official representatives of the British to meet with the Indians at Prairie du Chien. A great council of 1,200 Indians was held there in May, 1783. The Menominees, Foxes, Sacs, Sioux, and Winnebagoes attended the council. The tribes agreed to a mutual peace among themselves and renewed loyalty to the British king. La Jeunesse was spokesman for the Menominees at the conference.

The immediate postwar years brought little change to Menominee life. Only seven white families lived at Green Bay in 1785. The community consisted of seven men, five women, eight children, ten domestic servants, and four Pawnee slaves. The Menominee Indians, themselves, held some Indian slaves, chiefly Pawnees purchased from the Ottawas. The Menominees never enslaved their war prisoners, but occasionally purchased slaves from other tribes. There existed rumors of blacks among the Menominees. According to Augustin Grignon's memoir,

Captain de Velie had a Negro servant at Green Bay, and Baptist Brunet also owned an African boy. Grignon stated that in 1791 or 1792 two Negro traders from Mackinac established a trading post at the mouth of the Menominee River. These blacks attempted to establish themselves as medicine men among the Menominees. When Menominee children became ill and several died, the Menominee Indians killed the black traders.[18] There is nothing in Grignon or in the records to support the rumor of black blood among the Menominees.

The British agreed in the Jay Treaty of 1794 to abandon the Great Lakes posts by June 1, 1796. The British, thereby, remained at Fort Michilimackinac, then located on Mackinac Island for an additional two years following the treaty. When the move did come, the fort was "surrendered to Major Henry Burbeck and his force of United States regulars, and the British moved to nearby St. Joseph's Island, where they built a new fort and waited to recapture Mackinac."[19] In the years following the American Revolution the Menominees and other Bay Indians engaged in a war with their traditional enemy, the Chippewas, and their ally, the Sioux. From the slight attention given the matter in the reports, the war must have been sporadic at best. It did not greatly disadvantage the traders, nor did it arouse the British garrison still at Mackinac. A Sioux raid on the Menominee village at the Menominee River left sixteen Menominees dead and three taken captive. The British chose to dissuade the Indians from warfare by a generous distribution of gifts among all parties in the war. Traders with gifts approached the Chippewas, Ottawas, and Sioux, and the trader Ainsee visited the Menominees, Winnebagoes, and Foxes. For the next two decades the British fur trade in the region of the northern Great Lakes flourished. After 1787 the great North West Fur Company and Hudson's Bay Company monopolized trade throughout the area. It was not until a decade later that the American Fur Company entered into the field, and Stanislaus Chappu built a trading post on the Wisconsin side of the Menominee River across from the main Menominee village.

The United States gave scant attention to her western land gains until 1800 when the Indian Territory was created in the Northwest Territory. In that year the trader Charles Reaume became the first United States official in the Green Bay area when he was named justice of the peace. Nine years later the Illinois Territory replaced the Indian Territory, and the American Fur Company purchased British fur trading interests at Mackinac. The American Fur Company established the Southwest Company at that location, and soon engaged in competitive trade with the British in the Green Bay area.

While the early American fur traders left no record of their experiences among the Menominees, the tribe received a visit from Zebulon Pike, who had been chosen by President Thomas Jefferson to trace the Mississippi River to its source. In March, 1806, Lieutenant Pike made contact with the Menominees. He called the Menominee Indians by their French name, which in his *Journal* he wrote Fols Avoins. Tomah, then an influential representative of the Old King Cha-wa-non, headed the advance Menominee welcoming delegation that met the Pike party on March 6, 1806. Of Tomah, Pike recorded:

> He is a fine fellow, of a masculine figure—noble and animated delivery, and appears very much attached to the Americans. . . . this was an extraordinary man for hunting. As an instance, he killed Forty elk and a Bear on one day, chasing the former from dawn til eve.[20]

At the initial meeting with the American scouting party, Tomah registered a complaint against the Frenchman Greignon, thought to be Augustin Grignon at Green Bay, who, he said, abused the Indians and beat them without provocation. Pike promised to report this matter to the American post at Michilimackinac.

On March 23, 1806, Pike was received by the Menominee Old King, Cha-wa-non, whom Pike called Shawanoe. Pike's report concerning the Menominees confirmed the observations of all the visitors to the tribe before him. Pike wrote:

Charlevoix and others have all bore testimony to the beauty of this Nation. From my own observations, I have sufficient reason to confirm their opinions as it respects the Males (they all being straight, well made men, about middle size, and have a certain mild, but independent expression of Countenance that charms at first sight. Their complexion's are generally fair for Savages, their teeth good, their Eyes large and rather languishing; and in fact they would pass for handsome amongst the handsomest) but I never thought the Ideas given of the Women to be correct before. In this lodge were five very handsome women when we arrived, and about sundown a pair arrived, whom my interpreter observed was the handsomest couple he knew; and in fact they were, the man being about 5 feet 11 inches, and possessing in an eminent manner all the beauties of countenance which distinguished his Nation. His companion was twenty two years old — a Dark Brown eye, jet hair, and an elegant proportioned neck, and in her figure by no means inclining to corpulency, which they generally are after being married. He appeared to attach himself particularly to me and after some time he informed me that his wife was the daughter of an American, who, passing through the Nation about twenty three years before, remained a week or two — possessed her mother, and that she was the fruit of this Amour; but his name they were unacquainted with. I had brought six Biscuit with me, which I presented her with on the score of her being my Country Woman, which raised a loud laugh, and she was called the Bostonian during my stay.[21]

Pike found the Menominees shrewd businessmen. He was entertained in the Old King's lodge where, with forty-one Menominees, he smoked the peace pipe, observed the dog dance and took part in the feast of the dead. In his *Journal* Pike recorded having visited seven villages of the Menominee Indians in the area between Butte des Morts and the Menominee River, where the major village still stood. Pike commented on the fact that although a small nation, the Menominees were respected by their "neighbors for their bravery, and independent spirit, and esteemed by the whites as their friends and protectors." He stated that "when in the country, I have heard their head chief assert in council with the Sioux and Chipeways 'That although

54

they were reduced to few in number, yet they could say, we never were slaves.' As they had always preferred, 'that their women and children should die by their own hands, to their being led into slavery by their enemies.'"[22] None of the soldiers, who accompanied the Menominees into battle, ever reported such an action by the Menominee warriors in their villages.

The relative isolation of Green Bay protected the Menominees from the first surge of America's westward movement. As early as 1807, Justice Charles Reaume notified the American post at Michilimackinac that the Green Bay Indians were badly disposed toward the Americans. He warned that they were determined to make war upon them, and had appointed a place of rendezvous from which to attack several posts at the same time.

> They have a parable, by which it seems that a Manitou or Prophet is sent to them from above to instruct them. . . . We have also made this discovery by the nation called the Folles Avoines or Wild Oats Indians. The greater part of whom refuse to go to this general Rendezvous.[23]

In response to the increasing pressures of the white advance, the great Shawnee chief, Tecumseh, sought to unite all of the old northwest and southern Indians into an all-Indian confederation. Tecumseh traveled to Green Bay in 1810 or 1811 in an effort to win Menominee support for the impending war. The Menominees with old Carron's son, Tomah, as their spokesman met with Tecumseh at Green Bay. Tecumseh related his brave deeds and accomplishments in war, promising the Menominees a great victory if they should join his cause. Tomah answered the great chief with words meant to dissuade the Menominees from taking the warpath. He acknowledged Tecumseh's exploits in war, and then, after a pause, he "slowly raised his hands, with his eyes fixed upon them, and in a lower, but not less prouder tone, continued but it is my boast that these hands are unstained with human blood!" Tomah concluded that because of the smallness of his nation he had always supported a peaceful course:

> that he was fully aware of the injustice of the Americans in their encroachments upon the lands of the Indians, and for them feared its consequences, but that he saw no relief in going to war, and therefore as a national thing, he would not do so, but that if any of his young men were desirous of leaving their hunting grounds, and following Tecumseh, they had his permission to do so.[24]

For the present Tomah's influence prevailed and the Menominees remained at home.

In 1811 Nicolas Boilvin (Boileau), transferred from the Indian subagency at Des Moines to the position of Indian agent at Prairie du Chien, began holding daily councils with the Indians in his territory. War was threatening between the United States and Great Britain, and the British traders, led by Robert Dickson, were busily infiltrating the area of the Upper Lakes with presents for the Indians in far greater quantities than the American post at Prairie du Chien could provide. Agent Boilvin reported having stopped Menominee, Fox, and Sac Indians from visiting the English at Detroit by giving them rum, tobacco, and ammunition. In the hope of enlisting the support of the western Indians for the expected war, Boilvin urged the chiefs to accompany him to Washington to cement the new American relationship. As soon as this matter came to Robert Dickson's attention, he urged the chiefs to disregard the American efforts at friendship and to remain loyal to the cause of their Father, the British king. Dickson's sincerity and past friendliness easily swayed the Indians of Green Bay to remain loyal to the British cause.[25] When Boilvin left Prairie du Chien with a Sioux and two Winnebago chiefs to go to Washington,[26] Dickson enlisted over one hundred Sioux, Menominee, and Winnebago Indians and set out for Mackinac, arriving there before July 1, 1812. The Menominees on this expedition were led by Tomah. The Old King, Cha-wa-non, entrusted Tomah with the care of his young grandson, Oshkosh, who participated in his first war party. At this time Grizzly Bear, a future spokesman for the

Menominees, also served in the Tomah command. Governor Ninian Edwards of Michigan Territory learned of Dickson's movement and warned that Dickson's Indians would be used to carry British trade goods by canoe, or overland if need be, to the Lake Michigan and western Indians.[27]

Governor Edwards' intelligence was not fully accurate, for Dickson and his Indians, including thirty-nine Menominees, joined with Captain Charles Roberts' British regulars, Canadian and British traders, and the local Chippewa and Ottawa Indians in a surprise attack on the feeble American garrison of Mackinac and effected a surrender. The fort under Lieutenant Samuel Hanks capitulated on July 17, 1812, without a shot being fired, and the Indians cooperated in the orderly surrender. Captain Roberts permitted those Americans not wishing to pledge allegiance to the British Crown to leave by boat for Detroit.[28] At this same time a group of thirty select Menominee warriors, led by Chief Wee-nu-sate, proceeded to Amherstburg, on the Canadian shore of the Detroit River across from Fort Detroit, and succeeded in defeating Major Denny's troops at the Canard River. They remained there entering into other engagements with equal distinction. From these early successes it is certain that the Northwest was geared for war well in advance of receiving the news of a declaration of war. That news reached the northern post of Michilimackinac on July 9, 1812.

By July 26 Thomas Forsyth reported that the Indians from Detroit and the lakes had formed an alliance with all of the Indians as far west as the St. Peter River on the Mississippi. He reported that the Indians had organized into four grand divisions: first, Sioux and Foxes; second, Menominees, Sacs, Winnebagoes, Chippewas, and Ottawas; third, Potawatomis; and fourth, Miamis, Ottawas, Chippewas, and Potawatomis from the Detroit area. Forsyth concluded his report by saying, "I really do not believe that there is an Indian in America that is a friend to the United States."[29]

The first summer of war proved how effective the Indian allies were to the British, as Fort Dearborn on the Chicago

River surrendered on August 13, 1812, followed the next day by General William Hull's surrender of Detroit. When Captain Heald and his troops attempted to withdraw from Fort Dearborn, an army of five hundred Indians, including Menominees, fell upon the Americans and destroyed them. Robert Dickson rewarded the Great Lakes Indians for their summer's work by sending supplies for the winter of 1812–13.

In March, 1813, Nicolas Boilvin received a letter informing him that "everything is against you Americans, all nations in general have given their word to the English traders," and the letter concluded by informing Boilvin that his property at Prairie du Chien had been taken or destroyed, including his cattle which the Menominee Indians had killed.[30] If British troops succeeded in occupying Prairie du Chien, the Mississippi River settlements and Americans throughout Missouri and Illinois would be subject to attack. To prevent this, William Clark in the summer of 1813 sent Lieutenant Joseph Perkins and one hundred and fifty soldiers to occupy Prairie du Chien. Perkins' command upon reaching their destination built and occupied Fort Shelby.

Two hundred and twenty Menominees were in the ranks of the six hundred chosen northern warriors who accompanied Robert Dickson to Detroit in July, 1813. Colonel Proctor was at Detroit with a five hundred man force. Low on supplies and waiting for relief and additional troops, Proctor found Dickson's troops a burden. Against his better judgment, but with the hope that they could capture supplies, Proctor launched offensives against Fort Meigs on the Maumee River and Fort Stephenson on the Sandusky River. Dickson's command, including the Menominees with Tomah and his young charge, Oshkosh, participated in both campaigns. Another group of fifty Menominees, led by Souligny and White Elk, joined Tecumseh's forces at Fort Meigs.[31] These assaults resulted in failure for the British and, faced with the approaching winter, the western Indians returned home. In October, 1813, Tecumseh was killed in the Battle of the Thames. Augustin Grignon reported that eight or ten Menominees, belonging to Yellow Cloud's band, fought with Tecumseh at the Thames. With the collapse of the British front in the area of Detroit, Dickson returned to Green Bay and the Fox River for the winter of 1813–14. That winter all lived in great need and on the brink of starvation. As early as December, Dickson wrote, "I hear nothing but the cry of hunger from all Quarters," and by March, "I have done what I could for them, and will in consequence starve myself."[32] Throughout the terrible winter the loyalty of the Menominees never faltered, and Dickson wrote, "the folls avoines behave with Spirit and Judgement, it is fortunate for us there are such Indians in such times."[33]

By June, 1814, Dickson and an Indian army of three hundred braves were again at Michilimackinac, where Colonel Robert McDowell was completing preparations for an assault against the newly established American garrison at Prairie du Chien. On June 28, William McKay assumed command of an army consisting of seventy-five voyageurs, Michigan fencibles, Canadian volunteers, one hundred and thirty-six of Dickson's Indians, and a three-pound cannon. At Green Bay the expedition was joined by forty-five white men and another three hundred and fifty Menominee, Chippewa, and Winnebago Indians. The Menominees were led by Ma-cha-nah, the Hairy Hand, and Tomah's son, Mau-kau-tau-pee. The British contingent reached Prairie du Chien on July 17, and the siege of Fort Shelby began that same day when American Lieutenant Joseph Perkins refused to surrender. The shelling of the American gunboat, *Governor Clark*, with the three-pound cannon forced the gunboat to make off downstream. To the surprise of both sides, the *Governor Clark* did not return but proceeded downriver to St. Louis. By July 19 the American garrison was reduced to surrender, and Fort Shelby became Fort McKay.[34]

The final encounter of the Menominee Indians in the War of 1812 saw Tomah's force joining Dickson in an attack against an American offensive on Mackinac Island in August, 1814. When Colonel George Croghan landed a force of eight hundred

Americans on Mackinac Island on August 4, 1814, he was met and overpowered by a British force under Colonel Robert McDowell. Prominent in the battle that ensued were the Menominee Indians in Dickson's command. Oshkosh and Grizzly Bear fought in this campaign, and the Menominee Indians, Yellow Dog and l'Espagnol, were credited with the death of American Major Holmes and the wounding of Captain Deshu.[35] The Menominees suffered casualties, most important of which was the death of Chief Wee-kah.

Once again the Menominees had wholeheartedly supported their white friends only to see them removed from their midst and their replacement by strangers from the East, known among the Indians as "Bostonais" or "Long Knives." After one hundred and twenty-nine years of loyalty to the French and a half-century relationship with the English, the white encounters for the Menominees had created a dependence upon white supplies, rum, and manufactured merchandise. It had resulted in the loss of many brave warriors, and it had left the Menominees with only paper certificates and worthless medals to attest to their sincere and courageous friendship to the sovereigns across the sea. It is not surprising that the Menominees viewed with apprehension the new demands that awaited them in their future effort to coexist with the United States.

Menominee Indian warrior

from a painting by George Catlin
National Collection of Fine Arts, Smithsonian Institution

61

Menominee Indian games

from paintings by Mary Irvin Wright
National Anthropological Archives, Smithsonian Institution

Indian mother and child

State Historical Society of Wisconsin

Fishing by torchlight

from a painting by Paul Kane
Royal Ontario Museum, Toronto

The Spirit Rock and a nineteenth-century Menominee cemetery

State Historical Society of Wisconsin

Indian and his bride (*ca.* 1908)

National Anthropological Archives, Smithsonian Institution

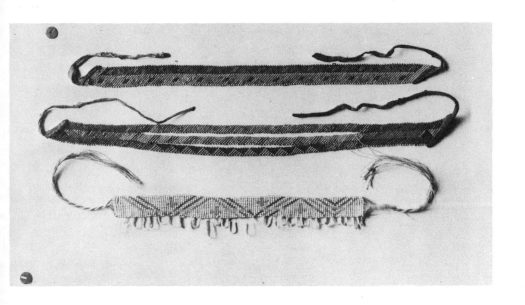

Menominee beaded necklaces

National Anthropological Archives, Smithsonian Institution

Landfall of Jean Nicolet

from a painting by E. W. Deming
State Historical Society of Wisconsin

IV

Early United States Treaties

The only time the Americans shook hands was when they wanted another piece of Menominee land.

Chief Oshkosh

Direct American relations with the Menominee Indians began with a complaint to Secretary of War William Crawford, from a United States Indian commission at Portage des Sioux in 1815. The Menominee, Winnebago, and Chippewa Indians had ignored an invitation to send delegates to Portage des Sioux to conclude treaties with the United States government.[1] The Menominees gave a pledge of allegiance to the United States at Michilimackinac on June 17, 1816. On that day William Henry Puthuff, United States Indian agent at Michilimackinac, held council with Indians en route to Drummond's Island, formerly St. Joseph's Island. In the group were five hundred and eighty-four Menominees, two hundred and two Chippewas, one hundred and sixty-one Winnebagoes, one hundred and forty-one Sioux, and thirty-nine Ottawas. Po-to-na-pack and Tomah were the principal Menominee chiefs in attendance, and Tomah was the spokesman for all the Indians at the council.[2] In his speech, Tomah, blaming the British for having induced the

71

Menominees to embark upon the late war, requested that American traders be sent to Green Bay. He pledged himself to seek a discharge from the British service and offered his support to his great father, the President of the United States. Each chief of the other tribes present endorsed Tomah's words and pledge. All agreed to return to Puthuff with a report of events at Drummond's Island.

Puthuff, since his appointment as Indian agent, August 18, 1815, had been upset by British Colonel McDowell's use of Drummond's Island in Lake Huron. The island was a depository for the semiannual distribution of annuities and presents to those Indians who could be induced to visit the island, acknowledge British supremacy, and agree to sell furs exclusively to the British. Even though William Puthuff was aware of British generosity, he expressed surprise when the Green Bay Indians returned, for every man and boy had received arms and ammunition, which, according to Puthuff, exceeded the issues made at any one time during the late war. The American agent viewed this action as an inducement to win Indian resistance to American occupation of the posts at Green Bay, Grand Portage, and Prairie du Chien. At the time this information was being recorded, two companies of riflemen and an infantry company of the Third American Regiment, commanded by Brevet Lieutenant Colonel Talbot Chambers, were already en route to Green Bay. Two companies of infantry under Colonel John Miller and a detachment of artillery accompanied the troops in anticipation of Indian resistance at Green Bay. The Winnebagoes had noticeably resisted American overtures of friendship. The four ships carrying the troops arrived at Green Bay on August 8, 1816. Despite rumors that eight hundred warriors intended to prevent a landing, John O'Fallon, captain of the riflemen, reported that no opposition occurred.[3]

The War Department's plan for Green Bay included the establishment of a military post and a trading post or factory to promote trade with the Indians. Colonel John Bowyer accepted the appointment as Indian agent at the post, and Matthew

Irwin became the first factor at Green Bay. Bowyer's first duty was to acquaint himself with the Indians in his area and, consequently, he invited the tribal chiefs to Green Bay. Writing to Lewis Cass, Michigan superintendent of Indian affairs, Colonel Bowyer requested medals with which to replace British medals relinquished by the Indians at his persuasion, and he also asked for arm bands and little flags.[4] Governor Cass had complained to the United States Indian Office concerning Indian medals. The confiscated British medals were solid metal, Cass stated, while those of the American government were hollow. He warned, "this little fact has injured us more in their [the Indians'] opinion than any other occurrence in our intercourse with them."[5] James Mason, United States superintendent of Indian trade, assured Cass that three sizes of solid silver medals were being prepared for distribution.[6]

The presence of British subjects and traders in the area posed a serious threat to the beginning of American enterprise at Green Bay. In communiques as early as April, 1816, the War Department expressed a desire to restrict trade privileges to American citizens. Bowyer notified Cass of the futility of maintaining a United States factory in the area "so long as British subjects are suffered to have intercourse with the Indians." Bowyer expressed confidence that British influence would continue and would result in wasted expenditures by the United States in attempting to maintain a factory at Green Bay.[7] Matthew Irwin wrote that of the fifty families at the post in 1817 all but one were British subjects, and many were Frenchmen with Indian wives. Irwin enclosed a list of those still active in the Indian trade. The following with their rank in the War of 1812 comprised the list:[8]

> James Prolier, Captain
> Peter Grignon, Captain
> Jacob Franks, Captain
> Joseph Kolette, Captain
> Paul Grignon, Ensign
> Augustin Grignon, Interpreter

Presch Grignon, Sergeant
Lewis Grignon, Lieutenant
Charles Grignon, Interpreter
Amable Grignon, Ensign
Laurence Filley, Sergeant
Peter Powell, Lieutenant
Robert Dickson, Indian Agent

President Madison decreed on January 22, 1818, that the trade between foreigners and the Indians living within the United States was to end. The British North West Fur Company through a generous distribution of liquor continued its efforts to attract trade and Indian migration to Lake Superior. Governor Cass suggested that the Americans counteract the threat by the same technique, "permitting a small quantity of spirits to be introduced."[9] The next years saw a drastic decline in the fur trade in the Great Lakes area and its expansion westward. In 1821 the United States abolished its factory system, and the trade became the interest solely of the Southwest Fur Company of John Jacob Astor.

The American interest in land cessions was first manifested in the western Lake Michigan frontier in the 1804 treaty with the Sac and Fox Indians, by which they surrendered their claim to lands south of the Fox River. This treaty was never accepted by the majority of either tribe, and the ill feeling engendered by the treaty sowed the seeds for the Black Hawk War. The Menominees first entered into treaty with the United States on March 30, 1817, at St. Louis. William Clark, Ninian Edwards, and Auguste Chouteau represented the United States. This treaty ceded no land, but proclaimed peace and friendship between the United States and the Menominee nation, and the Menominees acknowledged the sovereignty of the United States in the area. The Menominee Indians who signed the treaty were:

To-wa-na-pu (Soaring Thunder)
Wu-kay (The Calumet Eagle)
Mue-goo-mio-ta (Fat of the Bear)

74

Wa-ca-guon or Sho-min
War-ba-no (The Dawn)
Ie-bar-na-co (The Bear)
Kar-kun-de-go
Sha-sha-ma-nee (The Elk)
Pe-no-name (Running Wolf)
In-e-me-ku (Thunderer)[10]

Colonel Bowyer later wrote Lewis Cass that "the fellows who have signed this treaty have no influence or character with the Indians, and I am confident this treaty has been made without the knowledge of the principal chiefs, and of nine-tenths of the nation knowing or even hearing of the transaction."[11] This might have been true since Menominee leadership was on the verge of collapse. Tomah, the grand old orator of the tribe and tutor for the future leaders, died in 1818, and Cha-wa-non, who had served as chief from before 1778 when British Governor Haldimand of Canada recognized him, died in 1821 at the age of one hundred. Future leaders of the tribe, such as the Old King's grandson, Oshkosh, and Tomah's son, Josette, when the treaty of 1817 was concluded, were without power. The treaty was a formality, and for it to have been signed by the real leaders of the tribe the commissioners would have had to travel to the Menominee village.

That same year the Ogden Land Company of New York formulated a plan to remove the Indians from that state to land in the Northwest Territory. The tribes to be removed consisted of three Algonquian-speaking tribes from New York, the Stockbridges, Munsees, and Oneidas. The Stockbridge chief, Solomon U. Hendrick, believed his people to be languishing from their confinement in New York and readily adopted the removal idea. The Reverend Jedidiah Morse also endorsed this plan after having discussed it with John Sargent, the Methodist missionary to the Stockbridge Indians.[12] Reverend Eleazar Williams, missionary to the Oneidas, by 1818, seized upon the ideas of new lands and a united group of Six Nation Indians in the West. David Ogden contacted Superintendent Lewis Cass concerning the matter, and Cass decided that the forthcoming Indian council to be held near Fort Wayne provided an excellent time to propose the eastern removal. At about this same time the War Department, however, decided that the New York Indians should be moved to the country west of Lake Michigan.[13]

In the summer of 1820, Reverend Williams and a delegation of Oneidas visited the area of Green Bay in the Michigan Territory. This group had the approval of the War Department to seek a new homesite. The Menominee Indians were very upset by these visitors. Jedidiah Morse, who visited the Old King village in July, 1820, and who stayed among the Menominees for three weeks, reported that the Indians were greatly distressed at the suggestion of a land treaty. Morse defined the land claimed by the Menominees at the time of his visit to consist of that comprising the northwestern shores of Green Bay; the area sixty miles wide extending the length of the Menominee River; and, an area from the Red River to the Grand Choctaw River. In addition to these claims, the Menominees shared land in common with the Chippewa, Sac, Winnebago, and Sioux Indians that extended westward to the Mississippi River.

A land arrangement was made between the New York Indians and a group of Menominee and Winnebago Indians in August, 1821. According to the terms of the sale, $1,500 was to be paid for a small tract of land in the area of the Fox River between the Menominee and Winnebago villages. The Menominee Indians who signed the agreement were the warriors, Eske-na-nin, and A-ra-ku-taw, Chief Wee-kaw, and the war chiefs, Much-a-one-taw and Kis-ku-na-kum. The receipt of payment for the grant was signed by the war chief Skaw-won-nen, Iska-kaw (Scare All), Ocquo-ne-kaw (Pine Shooter), Yellow-Dog, A-ka-tu-taw (Spaniard), and Great Wave. All of these men at later treaty negotiations denied having signed the document.[14]

In September, 1822, another and vaster land grant was ceded to a delegation representing five of the Six Nations. This latter cession was made, according to later testimony, by S. C. Stambaugh, Indian agent at Green Bay, "with the instruction of Mr. John C. Calhoun, secretary of war, and Governor Lewis Cass, and confirmed by President James Monroe, March 13, 1823."[15] According to the terms of the treaty, the Menominees and the Winnebagoes ceded a total of 6,720,000 acres of land, covering an area one hundred and forty miles in length and seventy-five miles in width, lying between Green Bay, Sturgeon Bay, and the Fox River. In return, Stambaugh's report stated, the New York Indians paid $3,950 in goods. Nine Menominees signed this formal treaty:

Chiefs	War Chiefs
Oquo-mon-i-kan	Wik-no-saught
Pah-mon-i-kopt	Py-wee-ku-naugh
Saghkd-tat	Wyhtch-an-ig-haugh
Whpuh-kau-chywen	Ske-kaugh-my[16]
Osha-winno-kmitch	

The original New York Indians signing the transactions were the Stockbridge, St. Regis, Tuscarora, Oneida, and Munsee tribes. They in turn sold a portion of their lands to the Brothertown Indians in the new territory.

Shortly after the conclusion of the land purchase agreement, New York Indians began to migrate to their newly acquired lands in the Fox River Valley. The Menominee Indians became apprehensive about the settlement and sought to invalidate it. They correctly declared that the chiefs of the tribe had not entered into the negotiations. As a matter of fact, since the death of Cha-wa-non, the Menominees were without a great chief, and the tribe divided over the issue of New York land claim. The strongest position was that supported by the influential members of the tribe, the mixed bloods, and the French, which voided the land treaty and implored federal adjudication of the matter with the Six Nations. The general distress was confirmed in a petition written by Indian Agent Henry B. Brevoort and Judge James Doty to President John Quincy Adams on June 16, 1824. The petition stated that the tribe shared land with other Indians only to meet their immediate needs, and there was no extra land to give away. This petition, attested to by fifteen tribal leaders including Oshkosh and Josette Carron, concluded that "we are satisfied with the settlement made here with the whites, but we cannot admit any nation of Indians to settle in the country."[17] On March 26, 1825, Governor Lewis Cass transmitted a petition from the Stockbridge and Oneida Indians to President Adams. In his accompanying letter to the President, Cass referred to the conventional arrangements of the 1821–22 negotiations and concluded that the contract entered into had greater consequences than was expected by the Menominees and Winnebagoes.

During 1825 the United States government worked to settle tribal boundaries throughout the Midwest to bring about peaceful relations among the many tribes. On August 19, 1825, a federal treaty was concluded at Prairie du Chien with the Sioux, Chippewas, Winnebagoes, Menominees, and other groups.[18] Superintendent of Indian Affairs for St. Louis, William Clark, and Michigan Governor and Superintendent, Lewis Cass, served as commissioners for the United States. Article Eight of the Treaty of Prairie du Chien treated with the Menominees. It stated:

> The representatives of the Menominies not being sufficiently acquainted with their proper boundaries, to settle the same definitively, and some uncertainty existing in consequence of the cession made by that tribe upon Fox River and Green Bay, to the New York Indians, it is agreed . . . that the claim of the Menominies to any portion of the land within the boundaries allot to either of the said tribes shall not be barred by any stipulation herein . . . it is understood that the general claim of the Menominies is bounded on the north by the Chippewa country, on the east by Green Bay and Lake Michigan extending as far south as the Milwaukee river, and on the west they claim to the Black River.

The Treaty made provision for a future meeting to settle undetermined boundaries, but left the time of the gathering to the discretion of the President of the United States.

Governor Cass, on September 22, 1826, acting under authorization from the War Department, called for a meeting of the Menominee and Winnebago Indians at Butte des Morts in July, 1827. Thomas L. McKenney described Butte des Morts in a letter sent to Secretary of War Lane Barbour. McKenney reported that Butte des Morts, or Hill of the Dead, is a beautiful site located on the west end of Lake Winnebago. The Butte is a high, broad mound encircled by a "fine stand of timber," and from its top one can look across the trees at the wide river and the lake.[19]

A reluctant group of Menominee Indians arrived at Butte des Morts in July, 1827. Lewis Cass and Thomas L. McKenney served as United States commissioners to the negotiations. Governor Cass was distressed to find that the Menominees had not yet resolved the matter of a chief, and that they had come to the proceedings without a designated spokesman. In his report to President Adams, written in January, 1828, Cass reviewed the conditions that existed at the Butte des Morts gathering. He reported that after conferring with the Menominees and studying the matter of a leader with them, he placed the medal of the Grand Chief around the neck of Os'koss (Oshkosh) the Brave.[20] Having chosen a chief for the Menominees who was acceptable to all of them, including the mixed bloods led by Josette Carron, Cass turned to the task of treatymaking.

The Treaty of Butte des Morts defined the Chippewa-Menominee boundaries. It also concluded that the territorial differences with the New York Indians should be referred to the President of the United States for legal determination.[21] Trade goods to the amount of $15,682 were distributed among the Indians by the commissioners, and a stipulation was inserted into the treaty providing for an annual allotment for education for all of the tribes. The United States Senate modified the treaty before ratification in an effort to protect the claims of the New York Indians. The amendment made by the Senate said that "the treaty shall not impair or affect any right of claim which the New York Indians, or any of them have to the lands, or any of the lands, mentioned in the aforesaid treaty." Although President Adams signed the Treaty of Butte des Morts into law on February 23, 1829, the Menominee Indians refused to accept the final draft of the document. With this development, the naming of Oshkosh as chief of the Menominees became the most significant consequence of the meeting at Butte des Morts.

Oshkosh, the Brave, grandson of Chief Cha-wa-non, was born in the Old King village on the Menominee River in 1795. As a youth, he was taught by his grandfather's adviser, Tomah. A considerable friendship developed between Tomah and the boy, and because of this, the young Oshkosh accompanied Tomah to the council fires and on the warpath. It is not known how Oshkosh earned the title of the Brave, but he had already received this title by the time that he became chief in 1827. He might well have earned his title in the final encounter of the Menominee Indians in the War of 1812 at Fort Michilimackinac. After that war and through the ensuing years, Oshkosh gained in prestige within the tribe, becoming head of the Bear Clan at the death of the Old King in 1821. From the outset, he opposed the surrender of Menominee lands to anyone. Like Tomah, Oshkosh resented the American establishment of Fort Howard at Green Bay in 1817, and he was ever suspicious of the American promise, feeling that the only time the Americans shook hands was when they wanted another piece of Menominee land.

When Oshkosh ascended to the chieftainship, close ties had been established between the Indians and the white settlers on Menominee land. The census of 1824 indicated that the region of the Menominees was still a remote frontier with only one hundred and sixty white inhabitants in the Green Bay area. Of this number only seven were white women. Most of the French and English traders in the area had married women from the neighboring tribes. Felix Keesing in his study of the Menominees concluded that on the whole the Menomini had been peculiarly fortunate in the types of white men who had dealings with them; their paternalistic and personal relationships with the Indian, their sympathetic observance of custom, their utilization of the tribal leadership, and the periodic distribution of presents and honors all were well suited to win the loyalty and co-operation of the Indian.[22]

The accession of Oshkosh to his grandfather's position as Grand Chief of the Menominees is all but ignored by the writers of Menominee Indian history. The government reports merely state the fact of the selection of Oshkosh, and Phebe J. Nichols, while sympathetic toward Chief Oshkosh, recounts only that "Os'koss the Brave was the one. It was all right with the Menominees. The mixed bloods under Josette [Carron], however disappointed rallied under Os'koss." Paul Kane provides the most interesting tale of the election of Oshkosh. Kane, a wandering Canadian artist, visited the Menominees in 1845. He stated:

> when Oscosh aspired to the dignity of head chief, his election was opposed in the council by another chief, who insisted on contesting the post of honour with him. Oscosh replied, that as there could only be one head chief, he was quite willing on the instant to settle the dispute with their knives by the destruction of one or the other. This proposal was declined, and his claim has never since been disputed.[23]

If there is truth in the Kane account, one can presume that the challenger might have been Josette Carron, son of Tomah.

Just as accounts of the accession of Oshkosh are lacking, so too are physical descriptions of the chief.. Augustin Grignon remembered that

> the word Osh-kosh signified Brave, and such this chief has always proved himself. He is now sixty-two years of age, . . . Oshkosh is only of medium size possessing much good sense and ability, but is a great slave to strong drink, and two of his three sons surpass their father in this beastly vice.[24]

Phebe Nichols, quoting from the book, *A Merry Briton in Pioneer Wisconsin,* by an unknown author, describes Oshkosh's condemnation of whiskey and its evil effect upon the young men of the tribe. Oshkosh, while at a Lake Poygan treaty payment session, said: "I am resolved to preserve order in the camp, and I set my face against the whiskytraders. Caun whisky —caun whisky!"[25] The most pleasing description of Chief Oshkosh is recorded by Paul Kane, when he visited the Menominees:

> I attended a council of the Menominees on the Fox River, at which there were 3,000 Indians invited by head chief, Oshkosh—Bravest of the Brave. . . . He opened the council by lighting a pipe, and handing it to all present, each person taking a whiff or two, and passing it to the next. . . . After this ceremony the main business of the council began: it almost exclusively consisted of complaints to be forwarded to the Government.
>
> After several of the minor chiefs had delivered their sentiments, Oscosh himself rose, and spoke for about an hour, and a finer flow of native eloquence—seasoned with a good sense—I never heard, than proceeded from the lips of this untutored savage. Although a small man, his appearance, while speaking, possessed dignity: his attitude was graceful, and free from uncouth, gesticulation. He complained of numerous acts of injustice which he supposed their father, the President, could not possibly know, and which he desired might be represented to him, through the agent, accompanied with a pipestem of peace richly ornamented.[26]

The Quakers, who attended the mixed blood treaty payment at Green Bay in the summer of 1849, also recorded their impressions of Chief Oshkosh:

> . . . Head chief, wore no ornament, except the embroidered knee bands. Though his name signifies the Brave, there was nothing in his port or the character of his countenance, to indicate energy of purpose, superiority of intellect, or the dignity of rank. He had a little wrinkled face, proportioned to his stature, and small twinkling eyes, out of which there occasionally shot a ray of shrewdness. He totally lacked that high and noble bearing which we are apt to imagine in these forest kings.

The Quaker account describes the selection of Oshkosh by Lewis Cass and concludes that "whether from customary respect paid by Indians to elevated position, or from intrinsic merit, which the Friends had not acuteness to detect, he Osh-kosh exercises great influence over his people."[27]

When Oshkosh succeeded to the position of Grand Chief, he instantly inherited the problems of the tribe, not least of which was the land crisis created by the cessions of territory to the New York Indians. Before further attention could be given to the matter of land disputes, the Menominees responded to a call from the United States Army at Fort Howard to render assistance in the Winnebago War of 1827. During that summer hostile Winnebago Indians from Rock River attacked settlers at Prairie du Chien, where they murdered Registre Gaguier Gagnier and Solomon Lipcap, and scalped Gaguier's year-old child. The Indians also attacked the keelboats returning to Prairie du Chien with furs and supplies from Fort Snelling, and warred on Illinois miners and trading parties bound to and from St. Louis.[28] Determined to punish the offenders and anx-ious to prevent further aggression, General Atkinson immedi-ately dispatched troops from St. Louis northward, while Col-onel Snelling led four companies from Fort Snelling southward to the Fever River. Governor Lewis Cass, meanwhile, hastened to Green Bay where he met with the Winnebago Indians. The Winnebagoes refused to cooperate with Cass, denying any knowledge of the ringleaders in the recent uprisings. Military preparedness against the Winnebagoes continued.

Major William Whistler arrived on the Fox River opposite the Wisconsin Portage on September 1, 1827. With him were two companies of the second regiment from Fort Howard, a company of militia, and a group of New York and Menominee Indians. On September 3, two Winnebago war leaders, Red-Bird and We-Kau, voluntarily surrendered to Whistler's troops. Other Winnebagoes, including Little Thunder and Calumet Eagle, surrendered to General Atkinson. Although the Winne-bago War was bloodless, a company of Menominees was mus-tered into the United States Army and served under Captain Smith from August 23 to September 16, 1827. These were the first Menominee Indians to serve in the United States Army.[29] Foremost among the enlistees was Oshkosh, recorded by the military as O'Skash, the Fingernail.*

Upon the return of the Menominee Indians from the Winnebago expedition, they were again confronted with the question of the New York Indians, the problem of their lands, and for the first time matters of white education. Having refused the Treaty of Butte des Morts, both the Menominee and New York Indians frantically petitioned their White Father in Washington for assistance. In the midst of these treaty troubles the Menominees found themselves solicited by both Catholic and Episcopal missionaries. As early as 1823, Father Gabriel Richard, while visiting Green Bay from Detroit, began construction of a Catholic church on property donated by the Langlades of Green Bay. The little church and school addition were completed in 1825 by Father Vincent Badin, missionary to the northern Michigan Potawatomis. Father Badin promised to come on occasional visits to the mission which he left in the care of a French Canadian in minor orders, "Friar Fauvel," and in 1826 Fauvel opened the school. Bishop Fenwick came to Green Bay in May, 1829, to censure Fauvel and correct a bad situation, since Fauvel had deceived the Indians and whites by posing as an ordained priest.[30] Although excommunicated, Fauvel remained in the Green Bay school until the arrival of Father Samuel Mazzuchelli in the fall of 1830. Father Mazzuchelli returned to Green Bay in 1831 to take up residency and to operate the Roman Catholic Indian Free School. Mrs. Rosalie Dousman and Miss Elizabeth Grignon served as teachers in the new school. The object of the school was to "inculcate industry, morality, and Christian piety —and to teach the art of spelling, reading, and writing."[31]

As early as 1822, the Menominee Indians who participated in the abortive negotiations of that year with the New York Indians solicited the aid of the Domestic and Foreign Missionary

*The English translation for Chief Oshkosh's name in this instance is very unusual.

84

Society of the Episcopal church to send teachers among them. The 1827 Butte des Morts Treaty made provision for an annual government grant of $1,500 to the Menominee Indians for education. The Episcopalian missionary, Reverend Richard F. Cadle, visited Green Bay in 1827, and two years later he was named superintendent for an Episcopalian Indian school. By December, 1830, the Episcopalian school, taught by Reverend Cadle, his sister Sarah, and John V. Suydam, had thirty-one Indian students, only one of whom was a Menominee.

The Menominees must have been apprehensive over the arrival of strange missionaries, eastern Indians, and federal agents among them. As though these matters were not trouble enough, Chief Oshkosh was indicted for murder. The charge, filed with the United States Circuit Court in Brown County, was for the murder of Oke-wah, an Ottawa Indian, on June 3, 1830. On June 14, Oshkosh and the Menominee braves Am-able and Shaw-pe-tuck were tried at the Brown County courthouse in Green Bay. The court record reveals that Oshkosh, "moved and seduced by the instigation of the devil," knifed the Ottawa to death, and that Am-able and Shaw-pe-tuck aided and abetted the murder. Judge James Doty provided legal counsel for Oshkosh. The defense argued that the Ottawa had killed Mask-i-wet, a Menominee warrior, and that Oshkosh and the Menominees charged with murder had been witnesses to the killing of their tribesman. In an effort to apprehend the murderer, they had in turn killed him. Oshkosh and his associates were acquitted and the Court discharged the case.[32]

Confronted with the need of rendering a decision on the question of New York Indian claims in the Michigan Territory, President Andrew Jackson appointed John S. Mason, General Erastus Root, and James McCall as commissioners of the United States government. These men were instructed to proceed to Green Bay, investigate the controversy, and, if possible, adjust the matter satisfactorily to both parties. The commissioners arrived in Green Bay in August, 1830, and called for a general council to be held in Green Bay, commencing on August 24.

In a manner reminiscent of more recent summit conferences, the council opened as scheduled, but its chance of success was threatened immediately by dissatisfaction expressed by all parties. The Menominees objected to the interpreter, who spoke Chippewa, and who, they charged, had misrepresented them in the 1821–22 negotiations. The Menominees and Winnebagoes objected to the white men who served as representatives in the New York delegation. Among the members of the New York delegation were a Mr. Dean of New York, counselor to the Brothertown Indians; Reverend Mr. Coulton, a missionary and friend; and Mr. John Beal of Green Bay, attorney for the Oneida and Stockbridge Indians. The matter of delegates was resolved on August 26, when Judge Doty was appointed counsel to the Menominees, and Henry S. Baird was assigned to the Winnebagoes. Charles A. Grignon was appointed and accepted as official interpreter for the Menominees.[33]

On August 23 the council turned to the problem of the conference, and the New York Indians presented their demands. According to the Stambaugh report, the New York Indians requested and claimed title to 1,200,000 acres of land that contained the valuable water power sites of the Fox River. Grizzly Bear, chief spokesman for the Menominee Indians at the Green Bay council, rejected the New York request, saying the Menominees had never intended to sell their lands to the "Waubenokies." When the commissioners insisted that the tribes come to an agreement, the Menominee delegation, headed by Oshkosh, made an offer of settlement. They proposed to yield a tract of land extending back thirty miles along the Fox River from the falls of the Grand Kackalin to the Little Butte. It is estimated that this tract comprised about 144,000 acres. The New York Indians promptly rejected the suggestion. After all attempts by the Indians had failed to resolve the dilemma, the commissioners brought forth a proposal. Their suggestion called for an allotment of twenty thousand acres to the Brothertown Indians on the east side of the Fox River; six thousand acres to the Stockbridges also on the east side of the Fox River; and

250,000 acres to the remainder of the New York Indians on the west side of the river, but bordering the river for only a short distance. Both sides in the controversy were hostile to the government proposal, and the council was dissolved on September 1, 1830.

On that same day the Menominee delegation called on Indian Agent Samuel Stambaugh, and in the presence of the commissioners and others of the agency, requested that they be sent to Washington so that they could present their grievances to the President. The Menominees were aware that the Oneida and Stockbridge Indians had sent a delegation to Washington in 1827 and again in 1828. Through the good offices of the Green Bay Indian agent arrangements were made for Oshkosh and a Menominee delegation to travel to the nation's capital in the fall of 1830. A party of fourteen Menominees, headed by Chief Oshkosh, left the Menominee village for Green Bay to join Colonel Stambaugh. Upon arrival in Green Bay a surprising turn of events occurred. Oshkosh, after conversation with trader residents near the Indian agency, announced that he was not going to go to Washington, since no valid treaty could be made without him.[34] Thus it happened that, in November, 1830, the party of Menominees, minus their Grand Chief, left Green Bay, accompanied by two interpreters and Samuel Stambaugh.

The party was enlarged at Detroit when Governor Cass assigned T. A. Forsyth and John T. Mason to accompany the group as representatives of the Michigan Territory. Reverend Eleazar Williams, his wife, and two Oneidas had followed the group to Detroit, and there Governor Cass invited them to join the contingent bound for Washington. The Reverend Williams was one of the most interesting persons in this entourage, since he claimed to be the "lost Dauphin of France, Louis XVII." Williams' biographer, John V. Smith, states in regard to the Washington trip that "he was always on the lookout for little jobs of this kind, which Mr. Hanson magnifies into instances of self-sacrifice to the interests of the Indians, but anything

87

was a God to him, which would pay expenses, and furnish him with dinners."[35]

En route to Washington, the Stambaugh party stopped for three days in Buffalo to see Niagara Falls. To the Menominees, who loved their own wild rivers and sylvan lakes, the sight of the falls must have been as breathtakingly beautiful as it is to the modern viewer. The group arrived in Washington in December, 1830, and President Jackson received the delegation. Major John H. Eaton, secretary of war, and Samuel Stambaugh were appointed by Jackson as commissioners to treat with the Menominees. Grizzly Bear, the spokesman, and I-om-e-tah, son of Tomah and elder of the tribe, were the Menominee principals at the meeting. On February 8, 1831, a treaty was concluded which was promptly altered on February 17 to permit the President to determine the specific land allotments for the New York Indians. The treaty made provision for the "weaning" of the Menominees "from their wandering habits, by attaching them to comfortable homes." To initiate this, five farmers were to be sent to the Menominee land where a gristmill, blacksmith shop, and ten Indian homes were also to be established.[36] The Treaty of 1831 bears the name Stambaugh's Treaty, and was ratified by the Senate and signed into law, July 9, 1832. The Senate amended the territory provisions affecting the New York Indians and added 200,000 acres in addition to the cession originally agreed upon by the Menominees. Signatories to the Treaty of 1831 were the Menominee Indians who made the Washington trip:

> Kaush-kau-no-wave (Grizzly Bear)
> A-ya-mah-taw (Fish Spawn)
> Ko-ma-ni-kin (Big Wave)
> Ko-ma-kee-no-shah
> O-ho-pa-shah
> A-ki-ne-pa-weh
> Shaw-wan-noh
> Mash-ke-wet
> Pah-she-nah-sheu.

Chi-mi-na-na-quet
A-na-quet-to-a-peh
Sha-ka-cho-ka-no

Treaty negotiations, the nation's capital, and New York Indians were forgotten in the summer of 1831. Twenty-five Menominee Indians were murdered in the early morning of July 31 in a surprise retaliatory attack by Sac and Fox Indians at Prairie du Chien on the campground just above Fort Crawford.[37] The reprisal was for the murder by Menominee and Sioux Indians of eight Fox leaders en route to Prairie du Chien the preceding summer. The Sac and Fox had entered into a treaty of friendship with the Menominees and Winnebagoes at Prairie du Chien in July, 1830, but that pledge was ignored by the Sac chieftain Black Hawk and his British band of Indians on Rock River in Illinois. In June, 1831, T. P. Burnett, subagent at Prairie du Chien, wrote Clark that "the Winnebagoes of the Prophet's village on Rock River have united with the Sacs and Foxes," though the Wisconsin Winnebagoes remained loyal.[38] The peace of the whole Rock River area was threatened by marauding parties of Sac and Fox warriors. The Rock Island bands were distressed by threats against them from the white citizenry in the area, and by the military decision calling for their removal. Black Hawk, determined to remain with his tribe on their ancestral land, denounced the Treaty of 1804.

The band of Menominees, attacked at Fort Crawford, had been at Prairie du Chien since the early spring, 1831. They were intent upon securing Sioux help in a retaliatory attack against the Chippewas. General Joseph Street, Indian agent at Prairie du Chien, chose to feed the group in the hope of pacifying them. The morning following the brutal attack General Street wrote:

two or 3 hours before day on the morning of the 31st of July, a party, consisting of 80 or 100 Saukes and Foxes, surprised a Menominee Camp . . . killed 25 of the latter, and wounded many, who may probably recover. There were about 30 or 40 Menominies,

89

Men, women and children in the camp, most of whom were drunk, and the women had hidden their guns and knives, to prevent them hurting each other. The Saukes and Foxes though so greatly superior in numbers and attacking by surprise . . . lost several men, who were seen to fall at the onset, and retreated in less than ten minutes with only a few scalps, pursued by 4 or 5 Menominies who fired on them until they were half a mile below the village. I received information and was on the ground in 1½ hours after the murders were committed. The butchery was horrid, and the view can only be imagined by those acquainted with savage warfare.[39]

That same day General Street sent an express to Rock Island to apprehend the guilty.

The Menominees killed at Prairie du Chien were a war chief, three headmen, four warriors, six women, and eleven children. Six other persons were wounded. General Street took command of the survivors of the attack. After attending to their immediate needs, Street presented every Menominee woman and child with a suit of cloth clothing and a blanket. To the men he gave kegs of powder and one hundred pounds of lead, and he ordered that spears be made for each man by the Winnebago blacksmith at the post. The Menominees requested Street to ask the President for six guns for Chief Carron, "who lost all his family (wife, children, brother murdered) in about 10 or 15 minutes." After additional gifts were distributed to arriving Menominee hunters, the Menominees proceeded up the Mississippi for the fall hunt. At this same time the Menominees outlined a plan for retaliating against the Sac and Fox Indians. According to General Street's information,

in the spring, the whole Nation are to come out at the falls of the Black River. From thence, the squaws and children go across to Wisconsin (where they leave their canoes this fall) and thence portage on down Fox River to Green Bay. The warriors with some Chippeways proceed down Black River to the Mississippi where joined by the Sioux (and Winnebago, if they will) they will make up their war party and descend in two columns on the Sac and Fox, one by land, one by water. Meantime the Menominee and Sioux still implore the effectual interference of the Government.[40]

90

On September 5, 1831, a council was held with the chiefs of the Sac and Fox Indians at Fort Armstrong by Major John Bliss and Felix St. Vrain, United States agent at Rock Island. Keokuk, the great Sac warrior, defied the white agents with a charge that Sac and Fox attacks could be balanced by attacks upon them in the past, and he said, "I expect it is because our names are Sacs and Foxes that you make a noise about it."[41]

The council broke up after the Indians expressed their inability to apprehend the men responsible for the crime against the Menominees. Major Bliss remained confident that the murderers would be surrendered, and believing this, General Henry Atkinson decided not to pursue the culprits until spring.

The Menominees began collecting at the Black River rendezvous site early in January, 1832. They had made peace with the Chippewas, and were determined to retaliate against the Sac and Fox Indians. In the spring of 1832 General Henry Atkinson led the Sixth Regiment to Rock Island by way of the Mississippi River. Indian Superintendent William Clark hoped that a voluntary surrender of the leaders in the Menominee massacre would still be made. The troops arrived at Rock Island on April 12, 1832, and there learned that the Black Hawk band had entered Rock River the previous day and were ascending it.[42] Rock Island Indian Agent Felix St. Vrain wrote Clark that he had witnessed one of the murderers of the Menominees brandishing a lance, "saying that it had only served to kill some of the Menominees at Prairie du Chien, but he hoped to break or wear it out on the Americans."[43] Before the end of April, the Sac chief Keokuk, who had previously sought to restrain Black Hawk, surrendered three of the Menominee murderers at Rock Island.

Since Black Hawk's exact plans were unknown, Colonel Samuel C. Stambaugh sent a call for the Menominee Indians to assemble at Green Bay to prevent the movement of Black Hawk toward the Milwaukee River in the event that he came that way. Close to three hundred Menominee Indians responded to the summons. A scouting party kept watch and intercepted a messenger from General Atkinson bound for Green Bay. Colonel Stambaugh received orders to muster as many Menominees as possible and to pursue Black Hawk's war party. Two companies of Menominee Indians served in the Stambaugh command during the Black Hawk War. The two companies and the Menominee headmen who served in them were:

Captain Augustin Grignon's Company

Auskash or The Brave - 1st chief
Ko-mah-ne-kin or Big Wave
Maw Basseaux
Pow-wa-ko-ny or Great Soldier
Key-shaw or The Sun

Monsh-kau-maw-gsy - the leader

Tschi-ka-mah-ki-chin - war chief
Monse or The Moose - war chief
Chip-pan-na-go - war chief
Nah-nan-ape-to - war chief
One Hundred and Twenty-three Warriors

Captain George Johnston's Company

Grizzly Bear - 1st chief
A-ca-mot
Pe-wait-ton-etto
A-yem-a-tah
Wa-boose
Lou-le-je-nei

Ribbon - war chief
Caron - war chief
The Brave Brother - war chief
Moskett - war chief
Ma-wa-che-nai-pau-mau - war chief
Ke-sha-o-co-tee - war chief
One Hundred and Thirty-five Warriors

The Menominees served in the United States Army from July 20 to August 28, 1832.[44] The Stambaugh battalion reported at Fort Winnebago with orders to report to General Winfield

Scott's command then mustering at Chicago. Reverend Cutting Marsh saw the Menominee band on their way up Fox River and observed:

> Their painted faces, ornaments, drums, whistles, war clubs and spears, made them appear, indeed, savage and war-like. Their songs, uttered from their throat, consisting of deep gutteral songs, and the occasional whoop was calculated to make one feel darkness still brooded over this land removed so far from civilization.[45]

On July 30, 1832, Colonel Henry Dodge's force claimed a victory in the massacre of the hapless force of Black Hawk at Wisconsin Heights, thirty miles up the Mississippi from Prairie du Chien.[46] The Menominees proceeded to Prairie du Chien where a complete rout of Black Hawk's band was taking place as Chief Wabashaw and his Sioux braves pursued the fleeing Sac and Fox Indians. En route to Prairie du Chien, the Stambaugh troops followed a small party of the Black Hawk force down the Wisconsin River and brutally attacked and destroyed this group. By the time Scott arrived at Fort Crawford to take command of the war little remained to be done. Menominee Indians joined with Sioux and Winnebago soldiers to scour the countryside taking scalps and prisoners.

Even before the Menominees returned home from the war, the altered Treaty of 1831 had arrived. Agent George Boyd wrote Governor Porter at Detroit praising the assistance of the Menominees in the war and expressing his concern about the treaty changes of which the Indians were unaware. According to Boyd:

> By This treaty as it now stand, the Menominees are required to relinquish the beautiful Country set apart by the former, or Stambaugh's treaty, as their agricultural domain, the most fertile and valuable portion of all their Country, to the New York Indians . . . the poor Menominees are pushed back upon Wolf River, on lands of decidely very inferior quality, and without any equivalent for this exchange whatever.

Boyd suggested that should the Menominees adopt the treaty they be compensated by ten thousand dollars in a trust fund, the interest from which to be used to purchase corn. Boyd concluded that such annual interest would yield to the Menominees "one thousand bushels of corn—a never failing supply."

Boyd's intentions were fruitless because the trip to Washington and the treaty negotiations had been but a diversion for the Menominees. Without Chief Oshkosh the treaty was worthless. When the ratified treaty was presented for approval to the Menominee tribal council on October 22, 1832, the Menominees in one voice rejected it.[47] Secretary of War Lewis Cass had sent Governor George Porter to the Menominees with the treaty. Porter worked to find a solution to the old dilemma. In council with the tribe a new treaty, the Treaty of 1832, was worked out. This was something of a victory for the Oshkosh forces, since the new treaty, which was proclaimed on March 13, 1833, while granting 500,000 acres on the southwest side of Fox River to the New York Indians, secured title to 500,000 acres for the Menominees in the area northeast of the Fox River. The Treaty of 1832 bears the marks of the brave Menominee leaders who had recently returned from the Black Hawk War, including Grizzly Bear, Fish Spawn, Big Wave, and Oshkosh's mark made by his brother, who was fully empowered to act in his place.

The Menominees desired to be left in peace, free from the pressures of white encroachment. They did not want their treaty money spent to hire farmers and teachers. They had hoped to free themselves from white supervision by cooperating in the 1832 treaty negotiations. However, forces were even then mobilizing against them. The Rock River Winnebagoes had been forced into a treaty in 1832 which ceded even the Wisconsin Winnebago land in the Fox River Valley to the United States government. The treaty put the hapless Winnebagoes on neutral ground in the midst of the Sioux Nation across the Mississippi River. In accord with President Jackson's policy of Indian removal, such a plan would soon be applied to the Menominees.

Grizzly Bear, orator and statesman for the Menominees, died in the fall of 1834, and that same year the tribe had been

ravaged by smallpox so severe that the epidemic is still remembered. It is estimated that one-quarter of the tribal membership
died of smallpox that year. George Catlin, just beginning the
career that would distinguish him as a portraitist of the Indians,
visited the Menominees shortly after the Black Hawk War and
described the Indians as being "reduced and enervated by the
use of whiskey and the ravages of smallpox." Mah-kee-me-tew,
Grizzly Bear, and his wife, Me-chee-toe-meu, were the principal Menominees who posed for Catlin portraits. Ko-man-ne-
kin, Big Wave, and Coo-coo-coo, the Owl, also had their portraits painted. Catlin described Coo-coo-coo as being a very
aged chief of more than one hundred years. Like most men who
visited the area of the Menominees, Catlin was attracted by
the natural beauty of the land. In this instance he became a
harbinger of the future events which affected not only the
Menominees but all of the Indians in the area. He wrote:

> During such a Tour between the almost endless banks, carpeted
> with green, with one of the richest countries in the world, extending
> back in every direction, the mind of a contemplative man is con-
> tinually building for posterity splendid seats, cities, towers, and
> villas, which a few years of rolling time will bring about, with new
> institutions, new states, and almost empires; for it would seem that
> this vast region of rich soil and green fields, was almost enough for
> a world of itself.[48]

In 1835, George Featherstonhaugh, an English geologist and
surveyor, who passed through the Fox Valley en route to the
"Minnay Sotor" River, met Menominee Indians in the Fox Valley. He stated that upon leaving Butte des Morts he "met several
canoes with Menominey Indians in them, all the men having
their faces entirely blackened over with charcoal, which is their
mourning for the death of a relative." Featherstonhaugh described the Menominee men as having good teeth and the
women wearing their hair in long, thick braids. He too was
fascinated by the land, which he described by saying "a more
perfect wilderness could not be imagined."[49]

In the years following the Treaty of 1832, the Menominees

grumbled about the small annuities provided by the treaty and became so desirous for money and supplies that they decided to sell land for additional revenue.[50] Soldiers, who had participated in the Black Hawk campaign, had seen the Great Lakes area, and many wished to return to the new land to live. In July, 1836, the Wisconsin Territory was organized, and Henry Dodge, as territorial governor, hoped to treat fairly with the Indians even though he was instructed to purchase Indian lands wherever possible within the territory for white settlement. If possible, Dodge was to lure the Indians into ceding all of their Wisconsin lands in exchange for land west of the Mississippi River.[51]

At the 1835 annuity payment Chief Oshkosh and the Menominee headman Silver reported to Agent George Boyd that the tribe was ready to sell land north and west of Lake Winnebago. Secretary of War Lewis Cass sent an agent to appraise the land throughout Wisconsin, and he also reported that the Menominees would sell. In March, 1836, Lewis Cass reported the matter to President Jackson and suggested the removal of the Menominees west of the Mississippi. Governor Dodge called for negotiations for Menominee land to be held in August at the Cedars on Fox River opposite the present town of Kimberly, Wisconsin.[52] Green Bay and Prairie du Chien traders, Louis and Augustin Grignon, John Lawe, Joseph Rolette, army officers from Fort Howard, Brigadier General George M. Brooks and Lieutenant Robert E. Clary, attended the negotiations that got under way on August 19, 1836. The Menominee half bloods Charles A. Grignon and William Powell served as interpreters. In addition eight missionaries and a large delegation of mixed bloods were at the meeting. Since there was immediate hostility to talk of removal west of the Mississippi, Governor Dodge quickly turned his attention from this matter to that of a land purchase. Dodge reminded the Menominees of a clause in the 1831 treaty by which the Menominees were permitted to hold the land north and west of Lake Winnebago until such time as the President deemed it expedient to extinguish their title. The

96

Menominees received this announcement with shock and hostility. Oshkosh, spokesman for the Menominees at the negotiations, announced that "we always thought that we owned the land that we occupied; but yesterday, we heard that our Great Father had a right to take it when he wanted it—we did not so understand the treaty." Aya-ma-taw spoke on behalf of the Menominees who went to Washington in 1831. He said:

> our great father told us at Washington that the balance of our land on the west side of Fox River should remain to, and be ours as long as we should live, and that we should have the right to give a piece of our land on the west side of the river to the half broods of Menominee blood—that the President would not want to purchase any more land.[53]

On August 31, 1836, Oshkosh offered three million acres east of Wolf River, and Dodge asked for an additional twenty-four miles of white-pine timberland along the Wisconsin River. The whole was estimated at four million acres for which the Menominees asked nearly two million dollars. Dodge scaled down the financial request to a total of $700,000, which at the time was satisfactory to all concerned. This payment actually yielded the tribe about seventeen and a half cents an acre. According to the settlement in the treaty, annuities were to be $23,500 annually for twenty years; trader claims of $99,710.50 against the Menominees were to be paid by the government; half bloods were to receive $80,000; and, an annual gift of salt, tobacco, and clothing was to be furnished the tribe.[54] In addition the treaty canceled all unpaid compensation from the previous treaties in return for a $76,000 investment by the United States government on behalf of the tribe. This was one of the largest settlements made to date for the cession of Indian land. It is thought that Dodge would have paid more, except that he feared the Senate would not ratify the treaty if the payment were increased. The traders and mixed bloods urged the Menominees to sign, and on September 3, 1836, in one of the swiftest treaty negotiations on record, the chiefs of the tribe signed the Treaty of the Cedars, ratified officially in February, 1837.

That spring the Menominees in accordance with the treaty moved from their age-old homeland. They departed from the Old King village on the Menominee River and sites on the Oconto River, and moved to the land between the Wolf and Wisconsin rivers. Since Madison was chosen over Green Bay as the Wisconsin Territorial capital, major traffic in the area moved south of the traditional Menominee homeland, but lumbermen eagerly established themselves on the old Menominee lands in the area of Menominee, Michigan, and Marinette, Wisconsin.

The Menominees retained the hope that they could hold onto a remnant of their original land. In the years ahead, as the people of Wisconsin with the encouragement of the United States government attempted to wrest the remainder of the land from the Menominees, no one paid much attention to the little Menominee chief who spoke so quietly. If they had, they would have realized that behind the quiet voice of Chief Oshkosh was a strong will, aided by a shrewd mind, that had already determined that the Menominees had yielded all they intended to give, and that they would remain in the land of their origin. In the years to follow, the Menominees would cede additional land, but throughout the period and in the final settlement of 1856, they were to stand stubbornly by the firm decision of Oshkosh. The white negotiators would apply great pressure, but, in the end, they would admit that in Chief Oshkosh they had met their match.

V

Menominee Land

The poorest region in Wisconsin was better than the Crow Wing.

Chief Oshkosh
September 4, 1850

The Menominee plight following the Treaty of the Cedars was described by Governor Henry Dodge in the 1839 Wisconsin Superintendency Report to the Commissioner of Indian Affairs. According to Dodge, the Menominees, still a wandering tribe, depended heavily upon their annuities, hunting, and fishing for sustenance. Dodge urged that removal of the Menominees to the country southwest of the Missouri River would be beneficial to the tribe, since "the Menominees derive but little advantage from that portion of their annuities which is paid in specie," most of it ending in the pockets of traders who extended credit to the tribal members. Efforts to teach the Menominees agriculture resulted in failure, and Dodge concluded that it would be well to remove them "afar from the influence of their white friends," among agricultural and stock raising Indians on the frontier.[1] Menominee unrest was caused by the insufficient annuity payments, which left the tribe borrowing corn against next

99

year's payment; the removal of neighboring tribes like the Winnebagoes and the so recently settled Oneida and Stockbridge Indians; and surprise raids by marauding parties of Fox Indians. Attempts to remove the Winnebago Indians from the Wisconsin Territory provoked trouble for the Menominee Indians, when the dispossessed Winnebagoes persisted in squatting on Menominee land. George Boyd reported murders by both tribes and concluded, "It is full time that the Menominees should be protected in their just rights, and the Winnebagoes driven from their grounds."

Discontent over the handling of treaty payments in 1838 and 1839 generated serious charges against Indian Subagent George Boyd. The specific charges against Boyd were that he employed his son James as interpreter for the Menominee Indians, even though James Boyd did not speak Menominee and spoke a very imperfect form of the Chippewa language. Also, he hired Charles R. Brush and James Boyd to assist him with the 1839 annuity payment, paying them one hundred and fifty dollars of the annuity money. Upon the closing of the farming enterprise after 1836, it was charged that he took the cattle and farm implements for his own use, giving inferior beef at the annuity payment and charging $500 of annuity money for it. He held the annuity check for 1839 an inordinate length of time, and then sent to Galena for specie, charging $400 against the annuity payment for the transfer of the specie. In addition, he paid claims from the annuity money that the tribe had rejected. It was further charged that Boyd's son, Robert, employed as striker and blower in the blacksmith shop at Winnebago Rapids by his father, collected his wage, but did not work at the job. Of the $7,000 from Galena in the 1839 payment, half was in Illinois state bank notes which were discounted at 10 per cent less than specie. Boyd appropriated money for the claim of Moody Mann, a payment that the Menominees had approved.[2]

On order from the Brown County court, Justices of the Peace Joseph G. Knapp and David Johnson subpoenaed witnesses and gathered affidavits as testimony to the charges. Since the testimony gathered came principally from dissatisfied traders, the case against Boyd was quite clear. The traders all swore that they could provide larger cattle at less cost, could better serve and did serve as Menominee interpreters on the treaty grounds, and that Boyd was rude and generally gruff in his dealings with the Indians. George Boyd testified in his own behalf, asserting that "every Treaty made between the United States and their people the Menominees clearly prove that in order to negotiate with the Tribe, it is only necessary to conciliate some dozen of Traders and half broods." He further charged that only six chiefs had signed the charges against him, and he knew eighteen other Menominee chiefs who would support him.[3] In the memorial of the six Menominee chiefs was the request that the Grignons be assigned as permanent agents among them. Boyd concluded the defense of his actions in a letter of appeal to Governor Henry Dodge in which he stated: "From the foundation of this government in 1776 to the present time, a more deliberate and cold blooded attack on a public office has never been recorded." Henry Rowe Schoolcraft, Indian agent at Michilimackinac, seemed to seal Boyd's fate, when he wrote:

> the negligence and imbecility of the old gentleman are becoming every year more apparent, and the tone and manner in which he writes would be cause of offence in any agent who was less habitually wrong headed in his official business, and less profoundly ignorant of the fiscal questions presented for his action, than he is.[4]

New dissatisfactions arose at the treaty payment of October, 1840, when, after counting out several boxes of silver dollars, Agent Boyd discovered that the remaining boxes were found to contain French five-franc pieces,[5] which were counted into piles of ten pieces, as were the silver dollars, and paid to the Indians as dollars. The value of the five-franc piece at that time was ninety-six cents so that the Indian did not lose much in real value,[6] although the Menominees were not convinced of this.

Governor Dodge, increasingly concerned as reports of continuing dissatisfactions, depredations, and dishonesty were presented to him, concluded that the Menominees should be removed south of the Missouri River. He said, "It is difficult to keep them in their own country without a mounted force of regular troops."[7] In February, 1841, Henry Dodge met in Madison with a delegation of Menominee chiefs, headed by Oshkosh. Oshkosh, as spokesman, repeated the age-old Menominee complaints at delay in being moved to their own defined lands; lack of gunsmiths; late annuity payments; neglect by the Indian agent; squatters on Menominee lands; uninvited Potawatomis and Winnebagoes among them; and his intention as chief to lead a war party against the Sacs and Foxes. Governor Dodge also discussed old issues that included warnings against killing pigs and heifers belonging to the white settlers; against making war; and he urged the Menominees to bury the hatchet, "bury it deep in the ground, not again to raise it." It appears from the recorded conversation that the Menominees still flew British flags to which they had ready access at Drummond's Island, and that as of 1841, they still had not received large United States flags to fly over their villages.[8]

Oshkosh was involved in an obvious disputation with Agent George Boyd. He supported the charges made by Morgan Martin on behalf of the tribe, and signed the memorial asking that the Grignons replace Boyd at the agency. George Boyd in return complained against Chief Oshkosh, calling him the Chief of Traders and "the biggest scoundral" within the whole tribe. In March, 1841, the War Department reviewed the charges against George Boyd and acted in accordance with recommendations from Governor Henry Dodge that found Boyd guilty as charged on three of the accusations against him.[9] The conclusion indicated that George Boyd was to be removed from the position of Indian subagent at Green Bay. On April 25, 1842, Governor James D. Doty of Wisconsin announced that Colonel Boyd left the Green Bay Agency, and the next month the War

Department approved Doty's appointment of George W. Lawe as interpreter and subagent to the Menominees.

The Menominee Tribal Roll, compiled in fall, 1842, identified eight bands of Menominee Indians with 2,464 Indians permanently residing at the locations indicated. The census stated that the roaming Menominees and the one hundred or more Potawatomis, Winnebagoes, and Chippewas among the tribe, were not counted. The bands, their chiefs, population, and location included:

Band on the Upper Wisconsin: Oshkosh, Chief, 105 families, 411 persons.

Band on the Wolf River: Sho-ne-nieur, Chief, 51 families, 167 persons.

Band on the Little Chute: I-au-me-tah, Chief, 93 families, 288 persons.

Band at Lake Winneconne: Little Wave, Chief, 85 families, 406 persons.

Band at Lake Shawano: Wau-ke-cheon, Chief, 68 families, 202 persons.

Band at the Bay Settlement, Green Bay: Wau-bun-o, Chief, 94 families, 258 persons.

Band on the Oconto River: Cha-me-bom-me, Chief, 89 families, 313 persons.

Band on the Peshtigo River: Shaw-won-na-pen-acce, Chief, 46 families, 154 persons.

Of all of these persons eight hundred and seventy-five were under the age of ten years, and only one hundred and eighty-five were over the age of forty. Chief Oshkosh's family with twelve members was the largest. Of these twelve, five were under ten and two were over forty, and the Oshkosh family had eight male members.[10] Walter Hoffman presents a genealogy of the Menominee chiefs in his work *The Menomini Indians*. According to the genealogy, Oshkosh was married three times. His first wife was Bamba-ni (Flying About the Sky), who bore him three sons, A-kivine-mi (Ahkonemi), Neopit, and Koshka-noqne (Koskano-knieu). Following the death of Bamba-ni, he married

Shaka-noni-u (Decorated with Plumes), and after her death, Tomo-ko-um, by whom he had a daughter, Kino-ke.*

The public sale of former Menominee lands in the area of Lake Winnebago and Green Bay began in the fall of 1843. That summer the Menominees had again resumed their removal to the lands between the Wolf and Wisconsin rivers. Not satisfied with the gains of Menominee territory already secured, the Wisconsin legislature sent a petition on July 6, 1843, to President John Tyler, asking for the extinction of the Menominee claim to the land northwest of the Fox and Wolf rivers.[11]

Subagent Lawe's stay at Green Bay was of short duration. He completed the 1843 treaty distribution at Lake Winneconne, where he seized six hundred dollars worth of whiskey and goods belonging to Ebenezar Childs which the trader had proposed to sell to the Menominees without a license. Lawe blamed his dismissal in the fall of 1843 upon Morgan L. Martin, for whom he had secured money from the 1843 annuity.

In 1844 the Menominees were complaining that white men were lumbering along the upper Wisconsin River in Menominee territory. David Jones, the new subagent, reported that the area was posted against trespassers. Like his predecessors, Jones constantly fought unlicensed traders, and in 1845 he was replaced by Arthur G. Ellis, a long-time white settler at Green Bay.

In the 1845 annual report Ellis described the condition of the Menominee Indians, who had left their Green Bay locations and moved inland:

> Their present Territory embraces a great variety both of soil and climate, extending from the beautiful prairies on the Fox River to the more rugged and mountainous regions between the waters of Lake Superior, and those flowing into the Fox River and Green Bay. The Southern part of their land is very desirable as a farming

---

*Felix Keesing prepared a comprehensive genealogy of Menominee leaders. Typescript MSS, 7 E, Wis. State Hist. Society.

country. The Northern portion equally so for its immense forest of
pine timber and (as is reported) for its minerals.

The Menominees are making but indifferent advancement toward
civilization. . . .

But a small portion of them give their attention to agriculture,
and there is *no school* in the Menominee country! 'This latter fact
is deplorable. These poor people seem surrounded by influences
operating to keep them in darkness. It is the policy of those who
prey upon them to keep them in ignorance, and especially to prevent them from acquiring the English Language.[12]

Ellis heard Menominee complaints against the government
and the tribal demand for an annual interest payment on the
$26,000 of the Treaty of the Cedars money invested in Kentucky
bonds. He counseled Governor Dodge to propose to the Menominee chiefs at the treaty payment of 1846 the purchase of their
entire Wisconsin territory. He stated that at that time "they
would be compelled to reply before the malign influence could
organize itself to defeat the government." Ellis continued, "The
whole authority of the nation will be assembled there, and the
subject not taking them by surprise, for, as I said before, they
are aware that the thing is contemplated—the Indians would
be prepared to act."[13] Henry Dodge instructed Ellis to proceed
with such an inquiry at the Menominee annuity payment of
1846. He advised that any impending treaty concerning such a
matter be made in Washington, away from the influence of the
traders and other interested parties.

In the same report Ellis denounced the failure of Reverend
Van der Broeck in his newly established Indian school at Lake
Poygan. The report claimed that the agent could not find one
Indian "either adult or child, that can read a word of English,
except for a few that were educated some years ago at the Green
Bay Mission school." I-au-me-tah's band at Little Chute on the
Fox River were the most attentive of all the Menominees to the
influence of Reverend Van der Broeck, although Ellis ignored
the priest's former good work at Little Chute, where his school
had sixty Indian pupils. It was there that he induced the Menom-

inees to celebrate the feast of Corpus Christi, a practice preserved among the Catholic Indians until 1960. The Father also taught his parishioners to cultivate the land and to build log cabin houses for themselves. Ellis continued his hostility toward Father Van der Broeck. Early in 1847, Bishop Henni informed Ellis that the elderly Father Van der Broeck was to be replaced by Father F. J. Bonduel as teacher and minister among the Menominees, and that he would be aided in his teaching duties by Mrs. Rosalie Dousman. George Ellis quickly conveyed the news of the appointments to Governor Dodge, adding that "the truth is that the Indians charge distinctly, that for the last five years in consequence of his neglect of them, they have greatly declined in religious knowledge and made no improvements whatever in letters."[14]

The Menominee request for an annual interest payment resulted in an inquiry by the War Department into the affair, and President James K. Polk observed that the principal already amounted to $115,686.58, and that henceforth the interest would be paid to the Indians annually. This executive order was rescinded because it was ruled that the President did not have the authority in the matter.

The treaty payment of 1846 answered the question of whether the Menominees would cede the whole or part of their country. Albert Ellis reported:

> the traders and whites had anticipated the question, and counciled the Indians. The Chiefs had their answer ready: their country is small, they could not go further west.[15]

Ellis' own attitude, however, remained that of removing the tribe south of the Missouri River, since he foresaw nothing but annihilation for the Menominees in the face of the rapid white advance upon them. In the early winter of 1847, the Indian Department recommended to Ellis that the Menominee chiefs journey to Washington for the purpose of concluding the desired treaty of cession. This plan was abandoned when Congress

106

refused to appropriate expenses for a delegation. In July, 1847, Colonel L. A. Verplank and Governor Henry Dodge were commissioned to negotiate a treaty with the Menominee Indians. Verplank became ill en route to the negotiations and abandoned the project. Both commissioners were convinced that the Menominees could not be induced to sell, and the plan was temporarily abandoned.

Early in 1848, Chief Oshkosh reported that he had refused to accept a war-belt passed by the Winnebagoes urging a war against the Sioux. Oshkosh had refused also to pass the belt on among the Chippewas. The United States Indian Commissioner William Medill recommended that Oshkosh be given a message of commendation for his refusal to take part in the plan and for promptly reporting the circulation of the war-belt.[16]

Wisconsin statehood in May, 1848, increased attempts to obtain Menominee lands. Memorials and petitions flowed from the Wisconsin legislature demanding a new treaty with the Menominees. With statehood the Wisconsin superintendency was abolished, and subagent Ellis at Green Bay was directed to communicate directly with the Office of Indian Affairs in Washington. William Medill, United States commissioner of Indian affairs, in October, 1848, journeyed to Wisconsin to preside at the treaty payment of that year. In reality, he intended to secure the remaining Menominee tribal land and to relocate the Menominees in the West. Medill expressed his intentions to the press, and the *Green Bay Advocate* reported, "It is the determination of the Government to delay no longer in throwing open the Indian lands to settlers."

At the historic 1848 treaty payment, Colonel William Medill was the dominant figure. He cajoled, threatened, and flattered the Menominee chiefs and the mixed-blood leaders into agreement on a new treaty. Threats and charges were made aimed at destroying the influence of the American Fur Company and the Ewing, Chute Trading Company from Fort Wayne, Indiana, in the Menominee territory. Although the agents of the companies objected, Medill won Menominee support for a federal treaty. The conference extended over ten days and concentrated chiefly on the amount of land still claimed by the Menominees. While Chief Oshkosh claimed land totaling eight million acres for the tribe, Medill used the United States government figure of slightly in excess of three million acres. Medill succeeded in convincing the Menominees that he would pay them $350,000 plus at least 600,000 acres of ceded Chippewa land in the Crow Wing River area of northwestern Minnesota for their new home. Medill actually had been authorized to go as high as $571,840 for the land. As Oshkosh and the Menominee chiefs voiced opposition to the offer, William Medill threatened no funds and a forcible removal from their land. He went so far as to have a false clause of cession inserted into the old Treaty of the Cedars and had that clause of cession read to the tribe, thereby claiming that the Menominees had already given the government title to their land.

In vain did Oshkosh and Silver object. There was no one to help them, and so the chiefs on October 18, 1848, accepted the proposal by which "the Menominee tribe of Indians agree to cede, and do hereby cede, sell, and relinquish to the United States all their lands in the State of Wisconsin, wherever situated."[17] By the terms of the treaty the Menominees were given two years in which to remove, and provisions were made whereby the United States would pay the expenses of a delegation of Menominees to explore the Crow Wing River territory in Minnesota. The sum of $350,000 was to be paid as follows:

$ 30,000 to settle debts and prepare for removal
  40,000 to the mixed bloods, named by the Chiefs
  20,000 upon removal
  20,000 the first year after removal
  15,000 for a manual training school, grist and saw mills
   9,000 for mill operators
  11,000 for the blacksmith shop to continue its work after the expiration date of 1857 fixed in the Treaty of 1836

    5,000 for individual improvements upon the land ceded
    200,000 to be paid the tribe in ten equal payments when the 1836
    annuities ceased.

Twenty-eight Menominee leaders, headed by Oshkosh, affixed their marks to the Treaty of 1848. For the moment all of their homeland seemed lost, and the future appeared very uncertain.

Perhaps no event in all of Menominee history received more complete or careful recording than the initial treaty payment of 1848. It was the subagent's duty to supervise implementation of the treaty and the ultimate removal of the Menominees. Clearly no move would be made until a tribal delegation explored the newly assigned lands, and such would not happen until the tribal debts and the mixed bloods were paid. President Zachary Taylor ordered Secretary of the Treasury Meredith to name a commissioner to settle with the Menominees. The position fell to the abolitionist Thomas Wistar, Jr., a Philadelphia Quaker. Wistar's companion in the treaty payment venture was Alfred Cope. These men kept diaries of their experience, and Alfred Cope submitted a series of twenty-seven articles entitled "Visit to the Menominees" to *The Friend* literary journal. The Quaker commissioners arrived in Green Bay aboard the steamer *Michigan* on June 4, 1849. After surveying the many taverns that sprawled along the waterfront, with ragged Indians staggering in and out of them, Thomas Wistar observed that Green Bay certainly did not look like a town "founded ten years before the Commonwealth of Penn."[18]

The two commissioners held council with the Menominee chiefs at Green Bay from June 16 to June 20, 1849, where they compiled the list of half bloods and traders to receive payment.[19] At first the Indians were reluctant to leave their Lake Poygan meeting grounds for the abandoned Fort Howard meeting room. The agents insisted on the protection of the old stockade to ward off the whiskey peddlers and those who might try to influence or bribe the Menominee delegates. In selecting this site Alfred Cope observed that it was "a pleasant circumstance, that

109

a building, erected in hostility to the natives, should, at the close of its existence, afford them shelter and protection against evil." The sobriety and businesslike manner of the Menominee delegation throughout the conference greatly impressed the Quaker agents. To help the Menominee chiefs in the task of compiling the list of mixed bloods, a notice was inserted in the *Green Bay Advocate* urging such persons to report to the Astor House in Green Bay, where a daily list was made and presented to the Indians at the fort for consideration and acceptance. Oshkosh's band was the last to arrive at the meeting, coming in to the fort on June 15, 1849. From the descriptions given of the Indian delegates, it appears that Oshkosh's seventeen-year-old adopted son was one of the few in attendance who attempted to adorn himself with decoration:

> A son of the Sachem, about 17 years of age, a tolerably stout and handsome youth, with a smooth oval face, was the most of a dandy. Red, green and white streaks traversed his visage, and broad red knee bands, inwrought with white beads in curious devices, edged with parti-coloured fringes, drew the attention of the beholder to a goodly pair of legs. On his muscular arms were displayed glittering bracelets of tin, and a plume of dyed feathers surmounted his head, the raven locks of which were glossy with grease.[20]

The description given of Antoine Gauthier, the Menominee delegation's own interpreter is interesting. The account states:

> and, along with them, a silent interpreter of their own, one Antoine Gauthier—a half-breed, French and Menominee—a tall, gaunt figure, with long shaggy locks, and the face of a bandit, whose office seemed to be listen and store in his memory, for the future use of his superiors, the remarks which might fall from the white men, and to report to them, privately, any misinterpretation, should there, unhappily, be cause.[21]

After five days of deliberation during which the Menominees worked diligently to screen the "foreign mixed-bloods," that is persons with Indian blood other than Menominee, a list of eli-

110

gible mixed bloods was completed so that on June 20 the roll was closed, and the apportionment decision, having been signed by the chiefs and other Menominee delegates, was attached. Alfred Cope described the method of inscribing the official copy of the document:

> The name of a chief is written down for him, he then advances, touches the top of the pen with the tip of the forefinger and at once walks off, after which an upright cross is appended to the name, by the person holding the pen. . . . It is obvious, that by a little management, these poor, unlettered beings might be made to appear to sanction any thing.

The finished document declared:

> We, the Chiefs of the Menominee Nation, in council assembled with Thomas Wistar, Jr., Commissioner of the President of the United States, do hereby declare that the above list of the names of the persons of the mixed-blood of our people, entitled to the $40,000 appropriated for them by the Congress of the United States, in conformity with the Treaty concluded at Lake Powawhaykonnay [Poygan], in October, 1848, has been agreed upon in council, and is to the best of our knowledge and belief, correct.
> And in conjunction with the Commissioner we hereby award to each and every person, man, woman and child above enumerated, the sum of fifty dollars.
> We further award to each of the following named persons — fifty in number — an equal part of the remainder of the aforesaid $40,000 after the award above agreed upon, shall have been first set apart.[22]

Although the Menominees anticipated about five hundred names on the list, a tally revealed seven hundred and seventy-seven names which at fifty dollars a person absorbed $38,850, leaving only $1,250 for the favored fifty. The council agreed that each of the fifty should receive an additional twenty-five dollars.

Before the council adjourned Oshkosh petitioned Thomas Wistar as official commissioner could do nothing in regard to and to request "a mitigation of the cruel sentence which was to tear them from their native country and banish them to one which they believed was little better than a desert." Although Wistar as official commissioner could do nothing in regard to this matter, he did offer to bear a letter from the Menominees to Washington. The interpreter charged that such an act would be an insult to the Indian agent who was the official representative of the Indians.

It was necessary for Wistar to leave for New York to secure the specie so that the mixed bloods could be paid the money awarded to them by the council. Alfred Cope spent the time until Wistar's return visiting the Oneida and Stockbridge settlements in the area of Duck Creek. While Wistar was away, the mixed bloods, especially the traders, sought to awaken discontent over the paltry seventy-five dollars assigned to most of them. Commissioner Wistar returned to Green Bay on July 7, 1849. The gold brought by Wistar was placed in the vault of the United States land agent. Cope reported:

> In the same vault was a large sum of specie, just boxed up and ready to be forwarded on the morning of the 9th overland in a light vehicle to be driven by the agent without companion or guard down to Chicago, there to be added to a larger sum and transported to New York for government account—the very spot from which the Commissioner had just come with his valuable cargo. The wisdom of this method of circulating the precious metals is hidden from common eyes. The inventors of the Sub-Treasury system are entitled to the credit, whatever it may be.[23]

Two hours before the payment of the mixed bloods began on July 9, 1849, a hastily convened council was held with the Menominee chiefs to consider the names of eighty-one claimants previously overlooked. I-au-me-tah, then seventy-six and the eldest of the Menominee chiefs, attended this council, sitting in the place of honor next to Oshkosh. At the original council Silver had sat beside Chief Oshkosh. Of the eighty-one claimants reviewed, twelve were found to be already on the roll, and eight others were admitted. The payment of the additional twenty-five dollars awarded those signified for special favor was not paid until the next day, July 10. Dissatisfaction arose from the extra twenty-five dollar awards, and hostile suspicion led to charges of embezzlement against the honest Quaker commissioners. Morgan L. Martin and Stephen R. Cotton were prosecutors for the plaintiffs. A hearing was held in the presence of Justice of the Peace John W. Dunlap on July 10, 1849, and Indian Agent Bruce exonerated Thomas Wistar by informing the court that not only did the commissioner give him the $1,000 of unclaimed awards, but had donated $500 of his own expense money for relief of the poor among the Menominee Indians. The hapless Wistar upon his return to Washington was confronted by the commissioner of Indian affairs, who requested the return of the $500 of expense money that he had saved and given away. The commissioner, however, allowed a perdiem eight dollars a day expense budget and ten cents a mile for travel, which used up the allotted $2,000 fund from which Wistar had saved $500. All of this trouble seems like small reward for a job well administered.[24]

Indian Subagent Bruce reported the completion of the payment, and urged that the exploring expedition to the Crow Wing reservation be made at once. Ebenezar Childs had been appointed by Secretary of Interior Thomas Ewing to lead the Menominees on the exploring expedition. Childs arrived in Green Bay on July 2, 1849, and secured a promise from the Menominee chiefs to meet on July 17 at Lake Poygan to select a delegation for the journey. No chiefs arrived at the Lake Poygan campgrounds until July 24, 1849, and the next day they announced that even though Childs had all in readiness for the trip, it was better to wait until spring before departing. Ebenezar Childs had no recourse but to return to Green Bay, where he discharged the horses and supplies and began a waiting game.[25]

After refusing to leave for the Crow Wing River area until spring, the Menominee chiefs held several meetings with friends of the tribe, including Luke Laborde, John Battese, Oshkosh's

son-in-law John DuBay, Charles Carron, and the white traders
F. F. Hamilton and Alexander Spaulding. The chiefs were led
to believe that Spaulding could perhaps keep the Menominee
Indian homeland.[26] To compound the confusion for the Menominees, David Jones, former subagent, offered to sell the Indians
their former land in the area of the Menominee and Peshtigo
rivers, suggesting that the Indians use the $30,000 allotted by
the Treaty of 1848 for paying debts as the purchase price. In his
letters William Bruce expressed his contempt for "those evil
persons" who had been instrumental in advising the chiefs "by
tampering with them."

During the fall of 1849 the Menominees were afflicted by a
cholera epidemic as well as general fear caused by the threatened removal. Chief Oshkosh charged that the tribe had been
drawn into their present trouble by the Catholic portion of the
tribe,[27] who since 1846 had been under the influence of Father
Florimond J. Bonduel, Capuchin missionary to the Menominees
at Lake Poygan. Throughout the fall of 1849 Father Bonduel
worked with the Christian chiefs in an effort to thwart the removal of the tribe. The chiefs petitioned the President of the
United States, and Father Bonduel sought help for the Menominees from Bishop John Martin Henni. These actions evoked
sharp criticism from Indian Subagent William Bruce against the
priest.

Relations between the Menominees and their white neighbors worsened in 1850, when on January 1, 1850, Oshkosh's
adopted son, the colorful young warrior at the 1849 council,
was stabbed to death by Joseph Cayau in front of the home of
Maxine LeBreche at Grand Rapids in Portage County.[28] At the
inquest on January 23, Joseph Cayau pleaded self-defense,
saying that when he pushed the Indian who had confronted
him, the boy fell upon his own knife. When Justice Joseph Wood
released Cayau for lack of evidence, the Menominee warriors
held a council of war. Only Oshkosh, himself, prevented an
actual outbreak. He commanded his band to disperse into the

114

woods to hunt and await the sugar-making season. He also asked that Agent Bruce be prepared to meet with his warriors in the spring when they returned. That spring of 1850 one thousand Winnebago Indians returned from their designated home on the Crow Wing River of Minnesota, where they were actually starving, to the Black River to hunt for game. The bands that returned were those of Chiefs Dandy and Little Hill.[29]

George W. Lawe was named to replace Colonel Childs on the exploring party, but when the Menominees objected, Childs made the trip as originally planned. On May 29, 1850, Agent Bruce notified the Indian Office that the chiefs allied to Oshkosh were ready to explore the new territory, and the Christian chiefs were also expected to be ready. The group left Lake Poygan by wagon on June 7, 1850, arriving "in good spirits and perfect health" at Blue Mound, and then Prairie du Chien. According to the Prairie du Chien *Patriot*, that community had "never seen a body of Indians so well and neatly dressed and behaved as this delegation of the Menominee." Eighteen persons comprised the party. The Indians were led by Chief Oshkosh, accompanied by ten chiefs and headmen, and two Indian cooks. In addition there were William Bruce, Ebenezar Childs, William Powell, interpreter, and two friends of the Menominees, Charles Tullar and Talbot Prickett.[30]

This group proceeded by steamer to St. Paul and then by wagon to the junction of the Mississippi and Crow Wing rivers. They journeyed up the Crow Wing by canoe to the junction of the Leaf River and on to Leaf Lake. One group, headed by William Bruce, proceeded by canoe along the Leaf and Long Prairie rivers. The other members of the party, led by Childs, went overland into the Partridge River country. The exploring party rejoined on July 10 at Long Prairie village on the Winnebago Indian reservation. Eighteen men made the trip to the Crow Wing River, and what each saw was dependent upon what each sought. The Menominees, realizing their need for game, wild rice, and a peaceful environment, kept silent throughout the expedition. The whites and mixed bloods sought those things that would promote the swift and peaceful removal of the Menominee Indians from Wisconsin.

The reports prepared by William Bruce and Ebenezar Childs spoke in glowing terms of the clear lakes, abundant fish, swampland for waterfowl, interspersed with large areas of "rich, black loam," excellent for farming. Bruce observed that there were ample maple groves to assure an abundant sugar supply. Childs endorsed the fact that it was beautiful country, "which to a sportsman . . . would be enchanting." The others expressed doubt that the Crow Wing would be a good home for the Menominees. Big game was scarce, there was no wild rice, and, contrary to Bruce's observation, they felt that the neighboring Chippewa and Sioux Indians threatened the peace of a Menominee move.[31] Charles Tullar noted the maple groves, clay pits, and hay meadows, but he also observed the scarcity of wild rice and big game, so essential to a tribe dependent upon the chase for its existence. Tullar's view was shared by William Powell on behalf of the Menominees.

The Menominees remained silent on the trip, saying they must first report to their nation. Bruce believed that the Indian report would be unfavorable, and that the chiefs still hoped to remain in their homeland. The expedition returned to Lake Poygan late in July, and Chief Oshkosh promised to meet William Bruce at Lake Poygan on August 12, 1850. At the meeting the Menominees refused to give their answer to removal, demanding instead that they consult first with the President of the United States in Washington. The Indians agreed to pay their own expenses. They would later petition for government payment on the basis that a party of Chippewas had visited the nation's capital expense free, even though they went without permission. A fifteen-man delegation made the trip to Washington, D.C., leaving the agency late in August, 1850. The Menominee nation was represented by their most distinguished tribesmen. Oshkosh was accompanied by the pagan chiefs, Shawanno (Shawano) and Kee-cee-naw (Keshena), and the tribal Christian chiefs LaMotte and Carron. In addition Wau-ke-cheon, Sho-nee-niew, Sage-took, and Chee-que-tum were in the party. The Indian Department's representative was Subagent William Bruce with the interpreters Charles Grignon and William Powell. Father Bonduel, John Jacobs, and Archibald Caldwell represented the special interest groups among the Indians, traders, and mixed bloods.

Father Bonduel was probably the most controversial figure in the delegation. William Bruce for six months prior to the Washington trip sought Bonduel's removal because of the priest's disruptive influence over the Indians, whom he encouraged to resist removal. Before the Crow Wing expedition, Father Bonduel threatened that the Christian Indians would join the British if the government attempted to enforce removal.[32] While in Washington, Charles Grignon in support of Bruce's stand addressed a letter to the Office of Indian Affairs recommending the instant recall of Father Bonduel because

> every act he does is marked by ambition and selfishness. He has already divided the Tribe into factions, and those opposed to him he designates as Pagans. He works against the best interest of the United States and has gained influence over the dispersal of annuity payments and the credit payments.[33]

Although Father Bonduel sought his salary each year at the annuity payment, he was a good friend to the Indians, and worked to promote the well-being of his flock. The influential priest continued his work among the Menominees until 1853, when Bishop Henni replaced him with the Franciscan Father Otto Skolla.

In Washington, Richard W. Thompson offered his legal services to the Menominees, representing himself as a lawyer acquainted with Washington politics. He originally requested one-half of the money that he would help the tribe receive, later changing this figure to one-third. In 1855, when Thompson demanded that the Menominees compensate him for his services, his fee was $40,000, and the Menominee tribal council rejected his claim. The Menominees who employed Thompson in Washington were Carron, Shawano, LaMotte, and Wau-ke-cheon.[34]

Prior to the arrival of the Menominee delegation in the nation's capital, a series of letters had been sent to various offices including President Millard Fillmore's on behalf of the Indian cause. The letters sought permission for the tribe to remain in Wisconsin or, if they were removed, that a more favorable location than the Crow Wing River area should be found. Through R. W. Thompson the Menominees petitioned and received an interview with President Fillmore on September 4, 1850. Oshkosh's speech was interpreted by William Powell. Oshkosh expressed the tribe's dissatisfaction with the Crow Wing territory, stating that the resources of the land had been misrepresented, and that there was danger to the Menominees in the proximity of the Chippewa and Sioux Indians. He reminded the President that late fall was too cold a time for the tribe to move. Finally, Oshkosh requested that the Menominees be assigned a home somewhere in Wisconsin, proclaiming that "the poorest region in Wisconsin was better than the Crow Wing."[35]

President Fillmore on the day following the interview granted the Menominees the right to remain on their land until June 1, 1851.

The Menominees returned home, and friends of the Indians and traders began working to aid the tribe in retaining their homeland. R. W. Thompson, who accompanied the delegation to Keshena, and Father Bonduel went to Madison to seek legislative help. James Doty wrote President Fillmore that the Christian Indians complain that "it was by false representations and menaces on the part of Commissioner Medill that they were induced to sign the Treaty of 1848."[36] The Christian chiefs signed a petition requesting land on Lake Pepin in Minnesota Territory away from the Pagan Indians on the Crow Wing reserve. Indian Commissioner Orlando Brown answered Doty's letter stating that the Treaty of 1848 with the Menominees was a legitimate treaty, now the law of the land. He also advised that the "Lake Pepin land is Sioux Indian land which when purchased will be required for our own population."[37] Petitions were sent to the President from ninety-one citizens of Little Chute in Outagamie County and ninety-two residents of northern Wisconsin declaring the Crow Wing unfit for Menominee occupation. The petitions' plea was that the Menominees be permitted to settle "about the headwaters of the Wolf, Wisconsin, and Menominee Rivers, or, that they be permitted to select another site west of the Mississippi."[38]

A series of complaints had been sent to Washington against Agent Bruce. The charges against Bruce were made by friends of the Stockbridge Indians and Menominee traders. In May, 1851, William Bruce was replaced by George Lawe as subagent at Green Bay. At this time the Menominees received two additional extensions of time before removal, one until June 1, 1852, and then until October 1, 1852. In the meantime, President Fillmore ordered the Indian Office to send a representative to look over Wisconsin land as a possible home for the Menominees. Elias Murray, the northern superintendent of Indian affairs, visited the Menominees, and with William Powell, and Chiefs LaMotte, Wau-ke-cheon, and Osh-ke-he-na-niew, explored the east side of Wolf River. Murray concluded that the country was generally sandy, with some pine timber, numerous lakes and swamps, and evidence of bountiful game. The agent reported "the chiefs are highly pleased with the country."[39]

The Menominees were temporarily distracted from their removal problem in March, 1852, when Frederick Partridge of Vinland township claimed a Menominee child, Oakaha, belonging to the Indian woman, Nah-kom, as the long-lost child of his brother, Alvin Partridge. The Partridge boy had been lost in the woods near Plymouth, Wisconsin, during sugar-making time in 1847. He was two years old at the time. In 1852 the case of the missing boy was heard in the circuit court in Winnebago County

119

before Judge Edwin S. Buttrick. After testimony from many Menominee Indians and Augustin Grignon, Archibald Caldwell, and Mrs. Rosalie Dousman, asserting that they knew the child to be Nah-kom's, the court ruled in favor of the Menominee woman.[40] Partridge relatives, however, unwilling to surrender the boy, had him abducted and sent to the family homestead in Trumbull County, Ohio.[41] It was northern Superintendent Francis Huebschmann who found the boy, not in Ohio, as expected, but in McHenry County, Illinois. Before the case could come to trial again the child was kidnapped a second time and taken to Tennessee, leaving the Menominee Indian mother bereft of her son.

Throughout the spring of 1852, new petitions on behalf of the Menominees remaining in Wisconsin reached the President. These memorials prove that the Indians had the confidence and sympathy of the white population in their vicinity. Four hundred names appear on one petition recommending that the Menominees remain in the area of the Oconto and Fox rivers.[42] Continued pressure brought reward, and in October, the Menominees received permission to move to a temporary site along the upper Wolf River. Father Bonduel assisted the Christian Indians in the removal, while Oshkosh and the pagan bands came by canoe. On November 3, 1852, Oshkosh and the Menominee chiefs addressed the President: "We are now at our new home on the Wolf and Oconto river and we feel happy."[43] A total of 2,002 men, women, and children made the migration to Kaw-kaw-peh-kaw-toe, the first falls of the Wolf River. Father Bonduel described the disorder and misery at the new site as each family moved over the snow-covered ground in search of a winter campsite. On November 6, 1852, Father Bonduel completed a hastily constructed bark building and opened a mission at the falls, naming it St. Michael's in honor of the patron saint given the Menominee Indians by Father Claude Allouez two centuries earlier. Shortly after the arrival of the tribe, a memorial was sent to northern Superintendent Elias Murray stating the tribal decision not to occupy land along the Oconto River, but to hopefully remain at the Wolf River location.

> We believe that the tribe will be more likely to be concentrated at this point than any other, and that our young people would be less exposed to the evil influences of the whites, than they would be on or near the shore of Green Bay.[44]

The future for the Menominees brightened when the Wisconsin state legislature gave its consent "to the Menominee Nation of Indians to remain on the tract of land set apart for them by the President of the United States on the Wolf and Oconto rivers, and upon which they now reside."[45] This decision resulted in the federal government's confirming the Menominee reservation in the Treaty of 1854.

Besides the arrival of Father Skolla in 1853 among the Menominees, John T. Suydam became the new subagent at Green Bay, and Francis Huebschmann assumed the office of the northern superintendency at Milwaukee. That spring the Indians broke ground with hoes and planted crops, but without success. The dry summer and sandy soil failed to produce a crop, and Superintendent Huebschmann notified Indian Commissioner George Manypenny that the Menominees were left with game and wild rice, the government pork and flour being depleted. Huebschmann concluded:

> that the Menominees should suffer from want caused by circumstances beyond their control while the Government is owing them a very large sum under the Senate amendment to the Treaty of 1836 ($76,000 with compound interest since 1836) I do not believe to be the intention of the present administration.[46]

Huebschmann urged the payment of a semiannual interest to the Menominees, and suggested that the first payment be made in February before the Indians went to their sugar camps. The request for cash interest payments was again ignored by the federal government.

In the midst of the depredations on the timber lands, requests for opening areas of the temporary Menominee reserve to public sale, and complaints that the Menominee Indians were inclined to leave the reserve to fish in Green Bay, the federal government authorized Francis Huebschmann to negotiate a new Menominee treaty. By the terms of the Treaty of 1854, signed at the Falls of the Wolf River, on May 12, the Menominees ceded the land assigned to them on the Crow Wing River in 1848 for the tract of land on the Wolf River in Wisconsin. This was the land

> commencing at the southeast corner of township 28 north of range 16 east of the fourth principal meridian, running west twenty-four miles, thence north eighteen miles, thence east twenty-four miles, thence south eighteen miles, to the place of the beginning—the same being townships 28, 29, and 30, of ranges 13, 14, 15, and 16, according to the public survey.[47]

The treaty guaranteed salaries for a miller, blacksmith, and teacher to staff a manual labor school. For the difference in the quantity of land ceded and paid for in the Treaty of 1848, the government allowed $242,686 to be paid in fifteen installments beginning in 1867. Although Chief Oshkosh and Keshena did not sign the treaty on May 12, the treaty was amended on August 22, 1854, to include their signatures. Francis Huebschmann concluded that if Oshkosh had really opposed the treaty, none of the pagan chiefs would have signed the original document. The ink had not dried on the treaty before the traders and mixed bloods, who had been excluded from the treaty, began enlisting the aid of Indians to protest the treaty. Old Chief I-au-me-tah and Oshkosh were prevailed upon to sign a letter of protest, but Subagent Suydam dissuaded the Indians from further action.

According to Felix Keesing, who collected the information from old-time Menominee residents, the tribal leaders chose locations on the new reservation for their bands. Some families lived away from their parent group, and others formed new groups, so that the group membership in no way resembled the prereservation bands. The Christian Indians, led by I-au-me-tah, Carron, LaMotte, Kinepoway, Osh-ke-he-na-niew, and Wau-tas-au, settled along the east bank of the Wolf River. The followers of the Indian religion divided into the Bear and Thunder people as of old. The Bear people, followers of Oshkosh and Shawano, chose the west bank of the river, while the Thunder people under Chief Weke settled farther up the Wolf River on Weke Creek. The Menominee River band, led by the young Keshena, made their home at the 1854 treaty site near the falls, and the village was named Keshena for the young chief. Still other groups settled at Poshtigo Lake and at the South Branch of the Little Oconto River.[48]

A United States post office was established at Keshena in 1855, and that fall, Superintendent Huebschmann recommended that a new census of the Menominees be taken. Throughout the summer the tribe was embroiled in a controversy involving R. W. Thompson's claim for $40,000 in payment for his part in keeping the Menominee Indians in Wisconsin. At a Menominee council on September 7, 1855, Thompson confronted the Menominee chiefs, declaring that he had gained for them $242,000 "but you made no provision to pay me!"[49] He told the Indians that the government would pay him, and that the Menominees could repay the government over the next twelve years. Thompson ended his plea by asking, "When did I cheat the Menominee? Who has been his friend? Who has told the Great Council about his wrongs? You have spoken through my mouth!"

Efforts were made to bribe the chiefs in favor of Thompson's claim. G. W. Ewing offered one hundred dollars to any chief who voted in favor of Thompson. Ewing threatened the Menominees with removal to the Mississippi River if they denied the claim. The traders, mixed bloods, and a few white men like Father Bonduel and G. W. Ewing, themselves having claims against the tribe, supported lawyer Thompson. The dramatic vote on the matter occurred on September 10. Carron, spokesman for the young warriors, declared, "You may get my bones, but you cannot get my soul. That will go up, where all the good spirits go." Oshkosh hoped to have the issue settled in Washington. His frustration over the matter is reflected in his statement, "I am a chief and I am no chief. I am weak; thinking one way and then the other. . . . We can come to no decision. I would rather resign." Before the council ended, Oshkosh led the chiefs in signing the paper that denied the Thompson claim, and the tribe stood firm against an appeal of the claim to Washington. By this action the Menominees assumed the cancellation of other claims, including $15,000 owed to Charles Grignon.[50] Francis Huebschmann supported the Indians' decision, and in a letter to the Indian Office announced, "These men have piled up so much mud to be thrown at me, and have raised such clouds of dust to cover their iniquities that it is no pleasure to wade through them."[51]

Preemption claims also concerned the Menominees in their new home. The Menasha Land Office reported that they did not know of the Treaty of 1854 until May, 1855, and that land sales had been made during that time on the Menominee reservation. The land office acknowledged eighteen preemption claims in ranges 13 and 14 of townships 28, 29, and 30. The United States General Land Office decided to return the purchase money to the eighteen land buyers.

A final treaty was made with the Menominee Indians on February 11, 1856, at Keshena. Francis Huebschmann negotiated this treaty in which the Menominees gave a tract of land not to exceed two townships in the western part of their reservation on the south line, as a home for the small groups of Stockbridge, Munsee, and New York Indians who had avoided removal. The Menominees were to receive sixty cents an acre for the land, and the money was to be used to promote the welfare and improvement of the tribe.[52] The Quinney Party of the Stockbridges, and the Orchard and Christian parties of Oneidas, had received permission from the Wisconsin legislature on April 1, 1853, to remain within the state.

The long quest was at an end. The Menominees had sought a home since the day the settlement of Green Bay first threatened the serenity of their woodland existence. With the signing of the recent treaties, the Menominee Indians were satisfied and "thought the business finished with us; and that we had only to make our homes as comfortable as we could, and expected no other calamity than sickness and the calamities that are common to us all."[53] Indian Superintendent Huebschmann expressed hope for the Menominees:

> The leading idea is that as much as practicable all the work to be done for the Menominees is to be done by them, and the whites are to be employed only to superintend the work and to teach them how to work, so as to enable them in time to be their own mechanics and their own farmers.[54]

It appeared that the Menominee dream of peace needed to fulfill their destiny was about to come true. Only one tragedy remained to close out the decade of the 1850's in the Menominee story. That was the untimely death of the brave little leader, Chief Oshkosh, whose determination and perseverance on behalf of his people had swayed the thinking of the white men in Madison and Washington. Oshkosh's death was announced to Subagent A. D. Bonesteel at Fond du Lac by Keshena on September 11, 1858. According to Keshena's report as recorded by Bonesteel, Oshkosh had purchased liquor from a trader:

> He and his two sons, the oldest and the youngest, drank freely and became intoxicated. Oshkosh who is very cross when drunk got fighting with his sons. They, getting exasperated, tied him, beat and floged him so severly that he died from the effects of it.

Agent Bonesteel concluded that Oshkosh's death was to be greatly regretted since "he could always command respect and yield a powerful influence over his Tribe."[55] Oshkosh, the Brave, who as a small boy had sat at the council fires beside his grandfather and Tomah, who fought beside Menominee warriors in the early wars, and who won favorable treaties for the

Menominees in the face of adverse conditions, lived to see a dream come true. He died knowing his people would continue to walk on the land of their ancestors, and that "even the poorest region in Wisconsin was better than the Crow Wing."

Menominee Dream Dance drum

State Historical Society of Wisconsin

Chief Oshkosh, the brave

from a portrait by Samuel Marsden Brookes
State Historical Society of Wisconsin

Ah-co-ni-may or "Subject to have in the mouth to talk about," called
Reginald A. Oshkosh

State Historical Society of Wisconsin

Ah-Ke-Ne-Ba-Wae Dancers
Gerald, LeRoy, and Richard "Rocky" Sanapaw perform a traditional
dance in the Woodland Bowl, a natural amphitheater situated among
tall white pines.

from a painting by Fred A. Schmidt

Supmahkit

Jerome and Merciline Sanapaw make syrup and sugar in their sugar
camp every spring as did earlier generations of Menominee. Mrs.
Sanapaw whisks the boiling sap with a branch of hemlock just at
the right moment after having stirred the sap with a wooden spoon
while it boiled down. Her husband approaches with two buckets
of sap balanced on his wooden shoulder yoke.

from a painting by Fred A. Schmidt

Maple sugar making

from a painting by Mary Irvin Wright

National Anthropological Archives, Smithsonian Institution

Making a bark canoe (*ca.* 1892)

The bark covering has been folded around a canoe framework, and stakes have been driven into the ground to hold the bark in place while it is stitched to the framework.

National Anthropological Archives, Smithsonian Institution

Menominee Indian Reservation

Gebr Studio, Shawano, Wisconsin

Government boarding school

National Archives

VI

Reservation Days

*Ten years hence the Menominee will only be known
as a people that once lived.*

Chief Keshena
February 23, 1870

The Menominees, following the death of Chief Oshkosh, re-
quested assistance in selecting a new principal chief. Subagent
Augustus Bonesteel attended a tribal chiefs' council at which
Ah-kon-emi, Oshkosh's oldest son, testified: "My Father had
intended that I should succeed him . . . but in late years my
Father told me that he had lost all confidence in me, . . . and,
therefore, he would bestow his chieftainship to my youngest
Brother Ne-wah-pet [Kosh-o-ano-niew]." The younger Oshkosh
objected, saying, "I am nothing but a child and I am foolish."
The boy requested that his eldest brother be recognized as
chief.[1] Neopit, the middle son, was not considered in the line
of succession, since he was a Christian chief. No decision was
reached at the council, but for the next two years old Chief
I-au-me-tah, oldest of the Menominee chiefs, was recognized
as tribal leader. In 1860 Carron, who had usurped I-au-me-tah's
role as band chief many years before, was replaced by I-au-
me-tah's son, Sha-boi-tuck, and Ah-kon-emi, with I-au-me-tah's

135

consent, became the acknowledged head chief of the Menominee tribe.[2]

Menominee dissatisfaction with their situation, made even more precarious by continued crop failures, manifested itself in two unauthorized visits to Washington, D.C., one in February, 1859, and the other in March, 1860. On this latter trip key leaders formed the delegation, including Ah-kon-emi, Keshena, Osh-ke-he-na-niew, Sho-ni-on, and John Gauthier as interpreter. Subagent Bonesteel repeatedly sought permission for a Menominee delegation, since, as the Menominees said, "Oshkosh was the only one of the tribe that really understood all about these affairs with the government."[3] When the Indian Office refused the requests, Agent Bonesteel urged that the Menominee delegations be refused a hearing while in Washington, since they had gone without permission.

The rebellious spirit of the Indians led not only to illegal travel parties, but to the refusal of their 1858 annuity money, as a pretext to force a Washington hearing, and in 1860, they refused seed for the spring planting. Ignatius Wetzel, the Menominee reservation blacksmith, lost his position for conspiring with John Gauthier in persuading the Indians to refuse the seed unless Menominee complaints received a hearing. In addition to these actions, the Christian Indians, encouraged by the Capuchin missionary, Father Anthony Gauche, who had succeeded Father Menard in 1860, insulted Mrs. Rosalie Dousman, proctoress of the Menominee female school. In a midnight raid, the Indians burned Mrs. Dousman's house. Agent Bonesteel reported that after thirty-two years as the Menominees' "faithful, self-sacrificing benefactress," Mrs. Dousman was determined to leave.[4]

Fortunately for the future of the Menominee reservation, by 1861 conditions began to improve. The crop yield for the year was five thousand bushels of threshed wheat and rye, and the schools operated without incident. According to the annual report, there was a male and female school, and a sewing- and garment-factory school that produced trousers, shirts, skirts, and dresses. In 1861 the school also made twenty-eight shrouds for the dead, and twenty sunbonnets for the little girls. The next year Mrs. Dousman was put in charge of a coeducational classroom for primary aged boys and girls, and Kate Dousman was given charge of the older students. During these years the teachers received a salary of three hundred dollars a year.[5]

The great Minnesota massacre by the Sioux Indians in 1862 triggered a reaction throughout the Northwest. In the Green Bay agency area, while the local resident Indians remained loyal and were as terrified as the white settlers, roving parties of Winnebagoes and Potawatomis stirred the countryside. The Menominees were approached by Winnebago messengers from Chief Dandy, and the Menominee Indian, Katch-ko-na-niew, met Chief Dandy on Yellow River. Dandy sought to organize the northern lake Indians in a confederation to help the South in the Civil War. The Winnebago chief threatened the Menominees with destruction along with their white neighbors if they did not cooperate. The messengers warned that the war would result in the defeat of the North, since the western and southern Indians were already fighting for the southern cause.[6] Governor Juneau Solomon of Wisconsin advised Agent Moses Davis to arrest Chief Dandy and his cohorts if they appeared within the agency. The Menominee chiefs, headed by Ah-kon-emi and Keshena, sent a letter, written by interpreter William Powell, protesting the continued intrusion of unwelcome Winnebago and Potawatomi Indians on the reservation.[7] Although an Indian war in Wisconsin did not materialize, Indian skirmishes were waged in Indian Territory, Kansas, Colorado, and Texas, and many soldiers fought Indians instead of Confederates during the Civil War.

The Menominees overwhelmingly supported the Union cause in the Civil War, and one hundred and twenty-five of the reservation population volunteered for service.[8] While the youth enlisted in the United States Army, the Menominee chiefs as token of their loyalty surrendered six highly prized British

137

medals to Agent Davis. They asked for Lincoln medals to re-place them. A 1740 silver crescent medal received at Quebec was the oldest medal in the group.

Louis Kak-ush-ka was one of the first Menominees to enlist, and his service record is among the most interesting of those of the Menominee Indians. Kak-ush-ka enlisted on September 5, 1861, and was mustered into Company H of the Ninth Wisconsin Infantry Regiment. Private Kak-ush-ka was wounded in the battle of Newtonia, Missouri, on September 30, 1862, and he served as a nurse in hospital units at Little Rock and Princeton, Arkansas. He was taken prisoner at the Battle of Jenkins Ferry, Arkansas, April 26, 1864. At the time of capture, Private Kak-ush-ka was working in the regimental hospital at Camden, Arkansas. On May 7, 1864, he escaped from the hospital, but was recaptured by the rebels on May 10, nine miles from Pine Bluff. Kak-ush-ka was sent to Tyler, Texas, as a war prisoner on June 16, 1864. He was paroled at Red River Landing, February 26, 1865, and sent to New Orleans. Louis Kak-ush-ka was discharged at Madison on March 17, 1865.[9]

Dennis Turkey enlisted in the United States Army on January 1, 1862, at Green Bay. He was mustered in as a member of the newly formed Company K, Seventeenth Regiment, Wisconsin Infantry Volunteers. The next month, Joseph Antoine, John and Alexander Kitson, John Law, and Jackson Corn were mustered into the unit at Benton Barracks, Missouri. At least twenty-two Menominee men served in this regiment, which distinguished itself at Corinth, Mississippi, in May, and again in October, 1862. Moving northward, the Seventeenth Regiment of Wisconsin Infantry Volunteers joined General U. S. Grant's central Mississippi campaign, fighting at Fort Gibson and Champion Hill, before engaging in the siege on Vicksburg from May 18 to July 4, 1863. The Kitson brothers both suffered wounds at Vicksburg. The regiment continued in the war, fighting at Mechanicsburg, in the Atlanta and Savannah campaigns, and the Raleigh and North Carolina campaigns.

The Seventeenth Wisconsin Regiment was present at the

surrender of General Joseph E. Johnston and his army, April 26, 1865, and it marched in Grand Review in Washington on May 24, 1865.[10] Among the Menominees in the unit, Joseph Macotoquet and Louis Shesick were wounded at Marietta, Georgia. Joseph Waupeno died in action at Kenesaw Mountain, Big Shanty, Georgia, on June 25, 1864. Joseph Keshena, wounded at Rome, Georgia, died in a railroad accident at Kingston, Georgia, June 25, 1864. John B. Wau-ke-chon also was severely wounded at Rome, Georgia. John Kitson, first injured at Vicksburg, was killed in an accident at Columbus, South Carolina, on February 17, 1865. Three Menominees, Peter Corn, Joseph Antoine, and Charles Grignon, died of disease during the campaigns. John Law served in the regimental color guard after the 1864 campaign, and Henry Pegram achieved the rank of corporal in the regiment.

The largest group of Menominees served in Company K, First Battalion, Thirty-seventh Regiment, Wisconsin Infantry Volunteers. At least forty-four Menominee men volunteered for service in May and June, 1864, and were assigned to the newly formed Thirty-seventh Regiment at Madison. This unit, attached to the Army of the Potomac, engaged in assaults on Petersburg, Virginia, June 16–18, 1864, and in the siege against Petersburg, June 19, 1864, to April 2, 1865. Eleven Menominees of Company K were wounded in the Petersburg campaign, nine were killed in action, and four died in prisoner-of-war camps. The wounded included Isaac Ah-pa-kee, Jerome Kah-to-tah, Henry Ka-wah-to-wah-pa-o, Meshell Mah-ma-ka-wit, John B. Pah-po-quash, Joseph Pay-ye-wah-sit, Jacob Pe-quack-e-kah-nien, Meshell Sha-boi-shah-kah, Sr., Edward Sha-she-quen, John B. Sha-pah-ka-sic, and Antoine Wa-ba-no. Killed in action near Petersburg in July and August, 1864, were Sergeant John Garllaino, Corporal Semour Hah-pah-tah-wa-no-quette, James Ah-she-tah-yash, Meshell Ken-no-sha, Barney Mosh-che-nosh, Amable Nah-she-kah-ap-ah, Joseph Nah-wah-quah, Joseph Pah-po-quien, and Joseph Wah-sha-we-quen. Peter Pa-po-not-nun, reported missing in action near Petersburg on July 30, 1864, died in the

139

Danville, Virginia, prison camp on October 5, 1864. Augustus Pe-ah-wah-sha also died in the Danville camp on March 20, 1865. Paul Wier-is-ka-sit, prisoner-of-war, died of his disabilities in Salisbury, North Carolina, August 8, 1865. Teco Domineekie and Meshell Sha-boi-shah-kah, Jr., were both captured in the Petersburg campaign and sent to the Danville prison camp. Both were paroled from the prison in March, 1865, because of illness.

The Thirty-seventh Regiment took part in the pursuit of General Robert E. Lee's Army of Virginia, April 3–9, 1865. In mid-April, the unit was ordered to Washington, D.C., where it participated in the Grand Review on May 23, 1865. The First Battalion, to which the Menominees were attached, was on duty at Arsenal, Washington, during the trial and execution of President Lincoln's assassins. The unit was mustered out at Delaney House, Washington, D.C., on July 27, 1865.

Four Menominees are known to have served as substitutes in the war. Simon Paya-wackie of Company K, Eleventh Wisconsin Infantry Regiment, was a "substitute before the draft" for William B. Noyes of Janesville, Wisconsin. The Menominee Indian Ka-ka-sha also served as a substitute in the Thirty-eighth Regiment. Each substitute received the regular enlistment bounty and an extra one hundred and fifty dollars from the man whose place he took. A legend surrounds the third Menominee substitute, Joseph Davis, a mixed blood on the reservation, who was said to be the son of the Confederate president, Jefferson Davis. Wy-no, the Indian mother, was supposed to have first met Jefferson Davis at Fort Howard and later in Chicago. There might also have been a meeting at Prairie du Chien. At the time of the Civil War Joseph Davis took the Indian name Wau-kau-kau-ma-haut, meaning "son-of-President of the South."[11] A Menominee Indian named Joseph Kah-ke-ma-hot served in Company F, Thirty-eighth Wisconsin Infantry Regiment, as a "substitute before the draft" for John Wiley of Richmond, Wisconsin. Private Kah-he-ma-hot was wounded while on the picket line near Petersburg, but lived to return to the Menominee reservation, where he was honored as the Fourth of July speaker for many years.[12]

Abraham Oshkosh served in Company F, Third Wisconsin Cavalry, from February 12, 1864, until September 29, 1865, when he was discharged because of an unidentified physical disability. Oshkosh saw duty at Fort Scott, Arkansas, and he was discharged at Fort Leavenworth, Kansas.

Doctor Horace O. Crane, the military medical examiner at Green Bay in 1863–64, reported:

> Of the Indian race I have examined about 130 men, embracing half breeds of the Stockbridges, Brotherton, Chippewa, Oneida and Menominee tribes; of these men only about 10% were rejected as physically disqualified, and most of these for extensive cicatrices from burns or incised wounds. Only one case of hernia occurred, but neither varicoule nor varicose veins of the extremities. There were three or four cases of scrofula and secondary syphilis. I learn from officers commanding these men that they were good soldiers, being unsurpassed for scouting or picket duty, but quite unable to stand a charge or artillery fire.[13]

The valor displayed by the Menominees at Vicksburg and Petersburg seems to belie the doctor's final statement.

Before the Menominee veterans returned home the reservation was hit by a severe epidemic of smallpox. In response to the outbreak, the health authorities at the nearby town of Shawano placed a guard between their town and the reservation to prevent anyone leaving or entering the Indian land. At Keshena the schools, mills, and stores were closed. Yet, the disease spread rapidly. The danger was increased as Father Mazeaud insisted upon public funerals in the church for the victims of the disease. Dr. Charles Barrows of Shawano went to Keshena with Subagent Davis and vaccinated those Indians who accepted his service. Both Dr. Barrows and Moses Davis protested the holding of public funerals. When the priest refused to cooperate, Dr. Barrows had the sheriff of Shawano County arrest him and remove him from the reservation. Mr. Davis, meanwhile, persuaded many Christian Indians to move

141

into the wilderness to escape the disease. The Pagan Indians had moved at the outbreak of smallpox among the Menominees. Bishop Henni objected to the removal of the priest until he could investigate the charges, but Subagent Davis defended his action in the matter on the basis of the urgency of the situation. Over one hundred cases of smallpox occurred in the outbreak and at least fifty deaths.

The Menominee veterans organized Post No. 261 of the Grand Army of the Republic, the only such chapter to exist on an Indian reservation. This group remained active in tribal affairs until the turn of the century. In 1883 eleven Menominee families qualified for Civil War pensions ranging from two to eight dollars monthly. Four widows received the maximum payment of eight dollars.[14] The war and its aftermath did not greatly disturb the Menominee way of life at Keshena. A considerable number of Menominee men had traveled and mingled with other men under the totally unique circumstances of a war, but the veterans seemed to return easily to the routine of the reservation.

The Treaty of 1854 made provision for the erection of a sawmill on the Menominee reservation. This provision introduced the Menominees to the most valuable resource on their land—timber. The lumbering interests by 1861 were intent upon securing access to Menominee white pine, as anxious as they were in 1959 to buy timberland in Menominee County. A small sawmill had existed since 1846 at Keshena Falls, in the area where the Indians had created sugar camps before moving there to reside. The sawmill was purchased for tribal use in 1854, and the making of maple sugar became a major cash product in the early days of the reservation. The earliest existing contract granted by the Menominee chiefs to cut timber on the reservation was that granted Robert A. Jones, August 22, 1854. The contract granted Jones timber rights for ten years in return for one hundred barrels of flour annually. The United States Office of Indian Affairs investigated the contract in 1861 and discovered that Jones was living on the reservation, but to that time had not engaged in cutting timber. The Office of Indian Affairs declared Jones a trespasser, and the Department of Interior voided the contract on July 15, 1861.

While Robert Jones did not take advantage of his contract, there were men who cut Menominee timber without regard for a contract or property rights. Early in 1854 Subagent John V. Suydam complained to the northern superintendent about the timber depredations on Menominee lands. Suydam contended that three to five million feet of logs had been cut during the winter and thrown into the Oconto River. He urged the superintendent to take immediate action, because the ice would soon break up and "in a short time these logs will float down the River and all evidence will be obliterated."[15] Yearly, the agency reports to the commissioner of Indian affairs contained complaints of further intrusions on Indian timberlands. In 1865 Agent Davis reported:

> Recently I have discovered a trespass on the pine on the east side of the reserve. I have just had a surveyor run the line, and he reports the line of trees cut, and estimates six hundred thousand feet of pine cut and removed from the reservation.[16]

The Menominees cut logs and sent them by water to the mill, where they were peeled, cut, and prepared for building. In 1857 the Indians used 228,300 board feet of timber in logs and planks for building houses, a church, and two stores on the reservation. In addition, the mill provided fuel, pickets, fence rails, "and all products necessary to human occupation and the transition from a hunting and fishing economy to a more civilized one." The effect of the cuttings upon the forest was negligible. The significant result was in clearing land in the areas of the Keshena and South Branch settlements, and the accompanying maple sugar industry. The fact of human occupation created an additional fire factor in the forest, in some areas recurrent fires resulted in barren or treeless areas for occupation.

Eight Menominee chiefs protested by petition to activities

of the "Pine Ring," a lumbering association headed by A. B. Knapp and Company, and James Jenkins, which since 1866 had secured the right to clear and sell "dead and down" timber on the Menominee reservation. The chiefs charged that the Pine Ring secured their contracts by bribery, and had used the plea that the timber cut was partially destroyed by fire. The lumbermen were charged with plundering Menominee timber stands. The chiefs requested that no future contracts be issued without their consent.[17] Again, the Menominees sought permission for a delegation to visit Washington to settle the matter of timber rights. The Pine Ring also took action against the Indian complaint. Their representatives took the Menominee chiefs Ah-kon-emi and LaMotte to Washington. The allegations and events in the dispute seriously split the tribal leadership.

A major fire in 1868 led to the prediction that "a few more years will in like manner destroy what is left."[18] During these years the Menominee population also had declined to an estimated low of 1,400 people. In 1870 Chief Keshena grimly stated:

> But a few years ago, less than my age, the Menominee people occupied much of the rich valley of the Wolf and Fox rivers. We were prosperous and happy. Twenty-five years ago we numbered near 4,000 warriors, today, where are we? Within the limits of these few barren gameless townships of land, our numbers growing less every year, until our pay roll now numbers less than 1,400 souls. Ten years hence the Menominees will only be known as a people that once lived.[19]

It has been said that the first Indian cutting of timber for market was begun by the Menominee women, who cut hop poles and tied them in bundles of twenty-five to seventy-five poles. The men hauled the bundles to Shawano and Green Bay where they were sold.[20] In 1867 the sawmill was completely renovated, but according to the agency reports, the major governmental concern at the time was to convert the Indians to an agricultural economy. In 1868–69 Agent Morgan Martin's concern was to achieve the individual allotment of Menominee land. Martin believed that

144

whenever any individual of the tribe was sufficiently educated to commerce life for himself, he should be supplied with a necessary outfit, and should have an allotment of land secured to him and his descendants, inalienable except with the approbation of the government. In this manner one after another would become weaned from his tribal relations, and feel and know that he was independent of tribal authority.[21]

Alarmed by Martin's words, a Menominee delegation, consisting of Keshena, Wau-ka, and Shu-ne-an, went to Washington in June, 1868, with complaints against the agent. That fall the Menominees petitioned for a formal hearing of their grievances. Their major concern centered in a request to modify the Treaty of 1854, which they claimed they had been forced to accept under the threat of removal. The chiefs also vowed that Chief Keshena's name had been forged to the treaty, and that he had never sanctioned the settlement.[22] The next year Agent Martin advocated the sale of Menominee timberland, and the confinement of the Indians in two or three agricultural townships. He urged an end to bands and chiefs, and the payment of annuities only to those Indians who used the money to improve their condition. Finally, Martin stated:

> the land should be given them in severalty, as soon as they shall have learned by proper education and training to appreciate its productive value, and they should be taught to depend each upon his own unaided efforts to procure the necessaries of life.[23]

The Department of Interior in response to the tribal unrest refused to honor the contracts for the sale of timber cut on Menominee land during the winter of 1869–70. The pine cut by Charles Bagley and Daniel Crawford was impounded by the United States marshal, and the whole issue was entered in the United States Circuit Court in Brown County.[24] Meanwhile, other lumbering companies, such as A. G. Rockwell and C. M. Upham, and A. B. Knapp and James Jenkins, sought a direct settlement with the government. At the instigation of the Pine Ring, another Menominee delegation, consisting of Sam Teko and Wau-pa-no, with William Johnston as interpreter, went to

145

Washington in February, 1870, against the will of the Menominee chiefs.[25]

While in Washington, Sam Teko and Wau-pa-no made many suggestions contrary to real Menominee sentiment. They asked that the government sell illegally cut timber to the highest bidder, and that the proceeds be distributed among all persons on the reservation including the mixed bloods and traders. They claimed that the Menominees desired to have their land surveyed and subdivided into forty-acre lots, and urged that present tribal leadership be replaced by a permanent council. The delegation spent from February 1 to April 15, 1870, on their mischievous business, and they submitted a bill to Commissioner Ely Parker of $1,286.80 for expenses before leaving Washington. The expense account was paid, and the next year, William Johnston and Sam Teko tried to engage another delegation to accompany them on a return trip to the capital city.

By midsummer, 1870, the United States Department of Interior was convinced that the sale of Menominee pine timber remained as "the only thing which will protect the interests at once, the interests of the Indians, and of the government. It would appear that the systematic stealing of the timber cannot otherwise be stopped."[26] The matter was settled to the satisfaction of the lumbermen, and the impounded logs were released for sale at the rate of one dollar and fifty cents per thousand feet. Lieutenant William Bourne, new subagent at Green Bay, was put in charge of collecting the payments.

Encouraged by agency reports, and the open desire of the lumbermen for pine land, Congress on February 13, 1871, authorized the sale of six townships of Menominee reservation timberland. This action was contingent upon the consent of the Menominee Indians, which they steadfastly refused. Instead, 1871 marked the beginning of commercial lumbering operations for the Menominee tribe. In that year Subagent William T. Richardson made application for permission to enable the Menominees to cut and sell a portion of their pine timber. Richardson submitted a plan and believed that

146

this lumbering plan, wisely managed, will prove of vast good to this tribe. It will not only furnish many of them work during the winter season, but the timber thus converted into money will furnish funds to be used under the approval of the Department for an increase of their agricultural and educational facilities.[27]

Under William Richardson's direction the Menominees established and manned a regular lumber camp that cut and marketed two million feet of pine timber the first year. The timber sold for $23,731. The Indians received $3,000 for labor and the tribal fund was credited with five dollars per thousand feet. The prices were better than those received in the area up to that time by any of the Indians. The Menominees had thus added a considerable profit to their other money-making activities. At this time the tribal sugar-making industry was producing sixty tons of maple sugar a year. During the 1870's this sugar sold on the Shawano and Green Bay markets for about eight cents a pound. One thing was certain, the Menominees liked lumbering better than farming, and for the first time since arriving on the reservation, they expressed a hope for the future. Richardson requested permission to purchase a shingle-making machine for the mill so that otherwise worthless pine timber might be utilized. This initial success in timber was short-lived as Subagent Richardson was replaced by Thomas N. Chase of Georgia. Subagent Chase was interested in making farmers out of the Menominees. Chase thought that a million dollars could be made quickly by cutting and selling all of the timber and converting the whole reservation to agriculture.[28]

Menominee dissatisfaction was heightened in 1872 when Chief Ah-kon-emi was indicted in the United States Circuit Court in Shawano County for the murder of Augustin Grignon on June 21, 1871. The trial was held in July, 1872, and the chief was found guilty of third-degree manslaughter and sentenced by Judge Ellis to three years at hard labor.[29] In the interim Neopit became the recognized chief of the tribe. Meanwhile, the rebel group, led by Sam Teko, gained strength when Chiefs Keshena and Carron joined an unauthorized delegation

147

to Washington in August, 1872. Without proper authorization, this delegation, like many before it, only succeeded in antagonizing the Indian Office. That fall Neopit was suspended from his chieftainship for striking and seriously injuring Chief Carron.

In 1873 Agent Chase, insisting that he knew nothing about timber cutting, urged the Office of Indian Affairs to name William Richardson special agent to "close up the Menominee pine timber business." That year E. S. Hammond, E. H. Galloway, G. H. Weed, Erick McArthur, George Hunter, and associates received a charter from the State of Wisconsin authorizing the creation of the Keshena Improvement Company. The new corporation planned to improve the whole distance of the river. Subagent Chase questioned the authority of the state to empower a private company to improve a river within the borders of a reservation or to collect a toll on reservation logs driven down the river through the reservation. According to the charter permission was given for the collection of twenty cents per thousand feet of logs sent down the Wolf River. This meant that the Menominees with 1,748,620 feet of logs to be marketed in 1873 would be assessed $349.72 on the use of their own river.[30] Thomas Chase urged that Washington authorities decide upon the legality of the improvement company, since federal officers in the area, including United States District Judge Philetus Sawyer, were associated with the company.[31]

Subagent Thomas Chase in 1874 decided to move the Green Bay Agency to temporary headquarters at Keshena so that he could supervise repair and road construction on the reservation. In the midst of this activity the reservation was surveyed and plotted into forty-acre lots, and Subagent Chase sought permission to assign the land to individuals engaged in agriculture or willing to become so. After studying the improvements on Wolf River and the use of the river by the Menominee Indians, Subagent Chase concluded that damage had occurred in the reservation hay marshes as a result of the Keshena Improvement Company's project. He also believed that no toll should be charged the Indians on logs floated downriver below the

148

rapids, and only ten cents per thousand feet on logs cut by the Indians above the rapids.[32] During the summer of 1874 the United States Department of Interior authorized that the Green Bay subagent settle the company toll claim against a damage settlement for the Indians and put an end to the matter. Before the argument over the toll could be settled, Thomas Chase resigned and was replaced by Joseph C. Bridgeman. In December the Keshena Improvement Company was still making "loud demands for a settlement of their logging account with the Menominees."

In the spring of 1874 Chief Tomah Sacot and fifty-five Menominee Indians petitioned the government seeking citizenship and "equal rights with the white man." The petition stated:

> We have labored for the white man some time and now wish to labor for ourselves. We do not wish to be government paupers any longer. . . . We wish to sell our reservation to the government and buy lands that suite us best.

Despite such modern declarations, and agents' letters describing Menominee progress, a rather revealing petition reached Washington in September, 1874. The petition from the majority of Menominee chiefs read:

> We want our Great Father to give all of our people five dollars apiece next February just before sugar-making time from our money that he has. We want him to promise to do so now so that we tell our trader about it and get him to let us have things that we need for our fall hunt. He knows that we will pay him if we have the money, but he wants to be sure that we shall have it. We hope that our Great Father at Washington will hear us and do as we ask him.[33]

During these years of successful lumbering experimentation, neither the farms nor schools fared as well. In 1869 the Dousmans left the reservation school, and Alexander Grignon was hired as teacher, but the school failed to attract many students. Mr. and Mrs. J. W. Stryker were employed to conduct day schools at West and South Branch. Agent Chase maintained that the Menominee children could learn even though they

149

were reluctant to study. Efforts were made to attract pupils to the schools by offering clothing and soup dinners, but to little avail. For the first time, Agent Chase made the suggestion that a boarding school be established for the children. This suggestion was to be repeated in the ensuing years. In 1869 the Menominees also lost the services of Capuchin Father Steinauer and his assistant, Brother Vincent, who had served at Keshena following the smallpox episode and its aftermath. This left the reservation without a resident pastor until 1875, when Father Amandus Masschelein was appointed to St. Michael's Mission.

In 1877 Subagent Joseph C. Bridgeman reported that among the Menominees

> wigwams are fast giving place to comfortable log and frame houses; stables are built for their stock and crops. The rifle and rod are laid aside for plow and hoe, and while they have not much land under cultivation as could be desired, yet in this they are only partially at fault. . . . Could this tribe have six to ten wide-awake farmers to follow them up closely, . . . they thus might be induced to care for their crops till gathered.[34]

To aid in Menominee progress toward civilization, at the suggestion of Indian Inspector E. C. Watkins, the day schools on the Menominee reservation were closed in 1876, and a boarding school was established at Keshena. Father Masschelein strenuously disapproved of the operation of the school, since there were no Catholic teachers. His antiboarding school campaign was so successful that only two boarders remained in the school at the end of the first term. That spring the new boarding school closed, and only a day school was operated until 1879.

In these years of social and economic unrest the Dream Dance made its appearance among the Menominees. As early as February 6, 1872, Reverend Edward Daems, vicar general of the Green Bay Diocese, wrote the Catholic Menominee chiefs threatening them under pain of excommunication to refrain from all ceremonial dancing.

150

On account of the terrible consequences which dances in your tribe have had, and surely still will have, which lead to certain spiritual and temporal destruction of your people, it is hereby strictly forbidden, under pain of refusal of the sacraments and Christian burial to have in the future any kind of dances.[35]

In spite of the threat the Dream Dance cult received impetus in 1881 when Chippewa and Potawatomi Indians brought a great "Grandfather Drum" to the Menominees with the ritual of the Plains Ghost dancers.[36] According to Felix Keesing's informants, a number of Dream Dancers from the Thunderer clan, when confronted by Catholic opposition to the dances, moved northwest of Neopit into the dense forest and established the Pagan community of Zoar. It was of these Indians that Agent D. P. Andrews wrote in 1883, "Many of the Menominees of the Pagan Party clothe themselves in buckskin and subsist principally upon the chase."[37]

In 1880 a modern cultural revolution occurred on the Menominee reservation, as the Indians became interested in their schools, law enforcement, and health care. In 1880 the day school of Keshena was again turned into a government boarding school. In 1883 a new schoolhouse was authorized. Trouble developed over the school program when Franciscan Father Zephyrin Engelhardt complained that the school children were not attending religious instruction classes at the church. He sought permission to give religious instruction at the school. When permission was refused, the priest secured the aid of the Catholic Indians in demanding that a Catholic boarding school be provided on the reservation. Bishop Francis X. Krautbauer of Green Bay and Father Vincent Halbfas, Provincial of the Order of St. Francis, gave approval for a Catholic boarding school, construction of which began in May, 1883. That fall a parochial day school was opened until the two-story boarding school was completed.

Three Sisters of St. Joseph of Carondolet arrived at Keshena on November 10, 1883, with two others who followed in Decem-

151

ber. Just three months after its opening, the mission school burned in a night-time fire on February 22, 1884. Fortunately, the Sisters rescued the children from the burning building, but the school and St. Michael's mission church were destroyed by the blaze. Once again, a temporary mission day school opened under the supervision of the Sisters in the Dodge family home. Within a year, the Catholic boarding school was again in operation, and in 1887, it accommodated one hundred and fifty children with a staff of two priests, five lay brothers, and seven Sisters of St. Joseph. The United States government, using Menominee revenue, underwrote the contract for the St. Joseph Industrial School, as it was called, and paid one hundred and eight dollars a year per student. Both the government and Catholic boarding schools maintained a notable standard of academic achievement for primary grades, enabling a number of Menominee students to enter Carlisle and Haskell Indian schools. In addition the schools taught sewing, carpentry, and shoemaking. The government school operated a three-hundred-acre farm which was a model for the whole reservation.

In 1879 an Indian police force, consisting of a sergeant and five privates, was organized on the Menominee reservation, and a court of Indian offenses, composed of three chiefs, was created at Keshena. The court heard cases involving breach of promise, trespass, assault, and intoxication. The usual punishment for the latter was ten days' labor in the sawmill. In 1890 Neopit, Chickeny, and Ne-ah-tah-pa-ny were the judges on the court. Agent Kelsey reported that

this court exercises a salutary influence in helping control the restless and disorderly elements among the Indians. The worst influence to contend with and most difficult to control comes from the use of liquor, so easily obtained by Indians from saloons near the reservation.[38]

Another organization, composed of one hundred and twenty-six members, that helped discourage the use of alcohol on the Menominee reservation was the Catholic Total Abstinence Society. In 1891, when branch mission churches opened in South and West Branch, each parish sponsored a temperance society.

On January 25, 1886, a hospital opened in the old school house at Keshena for the sick, orphaned, and aged members of the tribe under the charge of the Sisters of St. Joseph. Agent Jennings reported that the hospital filled a long-felt need of the Menominee people, and that it "has a good effect in showing the Indians the good effect of proper care and treatment of diseases by a regular physician and attendants, in contrast to their medicine charms, so prevalent."[39] In 1891 a new hospital building was completed.

Lack of leadership and opposition from the Pine Ring brought an official halt to the Menominee Indian timber enterprise in 1880. Subagent E. Stephens complained that the Indians "have nothing to do for a large portion of the year except to engage in their old custom dances, hold council, or go outside to look for work." Agent Stephens made an eloquent plea for the Indians in his report.

> If there is a general desire among the people of the United States to "civilize the Indians" of Northern Wisconsin for the sake of humanity, justice, and common sense, let them all join in our general chorus in urging Congress to rend asunder the bonds that hold them in their imprisoned and morbid condition. They are not allowed under existing laws to cut a load of wood from the dead timber wasting on their reserve and sell it at the nearest market nor can they legally cut a few hoop-poles from the dense undergrowth on their reserve and sell them wherewith to buy the necessaries of life for the hungry children. Is this not a national disgrace?[40]

Renewed lumbering began on the Menominee reservation during the winter of 1881–82, with a year's renewal by the Office of Indian Affairs for the Menominees to make and sell sawlogs from the dead and down timber on their land. That winter's project was a financial success, but it had a bad effect on the tribe, since "the farm was entirely neglected and their fields became desolate, and the money which they received for their logs, in most cases was entirely gone at the approach of a long winter again."[41] The effect of logging was also reflected in a marked decline in sugar making. From a normal thirty tons a year, that industry produced only three tons in 1887. In the same year the Menominees realized a $4,000 profit from the sale of wild blueberries.

As logging continued, the agency reported in 1887 three million feet of logs cut and sold from a land clearing project alone. The federal report for 1887, however, pointed up a new dilemma for the Menominee timber enterprise. "The cutting of green timber, and their firing of the woods, to the great injury of standing timbers, necessitated issuance of a Department Order prohibiting the marketing of timber by Indians."[42] This order was rescinded to permit the continued cutting of "dead and down" trees. In the next two years the Menominees logged 43,909,230 feet. A fraction of these logs consisted of hemlock and basswood, but the vast majority was pine.[43] During this time the agents at Green Bay endeavored to reassure the Department of Interior that the Menominees carefully utilized their lumber money and never willfully destroyed the green timber, since "they knew that green timber is much more valuable than dead timber."[44] The agents also urged congressional action to enable the Menominees to realize the full benefit of their lumber fortune. Subagent Stephens requested the immediate harvest of the timber. He wrote:

> their valuable timber is surrounded on all sides by old choppings and dead undergrowth, that are liable in dry seasons to carry destructive forest fires into their pine and cause its total destruction. Besides the heavy winds are continually blowing down great quantities of the most valuable of said timber.[45]

In 1884 Agent D. P. Andrews estimated that there were three hundred million feet of standing green pine on the reservation that was exposed to damage and destruction by fires.

The Menominees opened a new sawmill, run by waterpower, in 1886, with a capacity of 15,000 feet of lumber a day. The mill produced all lumber used for building on the reservation. A shingle machine, planer, and lath mill adjoined the sawmill and served the building needs of the Indian community. In response to appeals the Department of Interior sought congressional help, and on February 10, 1889, Congress passed a law authorizing the President to grant permission annually to Indians "to fell out, remove, sell, or otherwise dispose of dead timber standing or fallen on such reservation or allotment for the sole benefit of such Indian or Indians."[46] On February 10, the Department of Interior recommended that the President grant the Menominees permission to market the dead timber on the reservation. On March 2 and 8, 1889, President Benjamin Harrison again authorized the Menominee Indians to log "dead and down" timber. Since the permission was received too late for that season, the President on September 20, 1889, renewed the permit for the next year.

In that year the first legislation conducive to a systematic control of the lumbering enterprise of the Menominees was enacted. Public Law 153 was passed by the Congress on June 12, 1890.[47] It permitted the annual cutting of green timber as well as downed timber on the reservation, but limited the quantity to twenty million feet annually. The bill provided a reimbursable cash loan of up to $75,000 and stipulated that one-fifth of the revenue from the business was to be placed on deposit in the United States Treasury as a stumpage fund for hospital and poor relief. Four-fifths of the money was to be lodged in trust in the Menominee Log Fund at 5 per cent interest. Although it took two ballots by the Menominee General Council to confirm the legislation, this action launched commercial timber operations on the reservation on a scale equal to those of the present. The first year under the plan yielded $232,262.78 in sales, and the Menominees repaid $68,668.22 of their government loan.[48]

Coupled with the new cutting program under the Act of 1890 was administrative and congressional concern to eliminate wasteful cutting practices. Agent Thomas H. Savage's report in 1894 charged that only the best and most readily available timber was logged. Savage urged the "relumbering" of cutover land, and in 1895, the federal instructions admonished "the

155

cutting on new ground is to be clean. No timber suitable for a log, standing or fallen is to be left behind as was the case in other seasons."

In the almost two decades that the Act of 1890 governed the lumbering operation in the land of the Menominees, the total production was 301,569,560 feet of timber. Menominee economic efforts, formerly directed into farming, maple sugar making, and berry picking, became increasingly centralized in tribal lumbering enterprise. Lumbering provided employment in fall, winter, and spring, and left the Indians free to enjoy the pleasures of a leisurely summer. Treaty annuity payments had ceased by 1886, and during these years of early lumbering, the Menominees shared a small per capita payment from the interest of their vested profits, and they also provided the government with the revenue needed to maintain the reservation, its schools, hospital, and poor fund. At the turn of the century the timber stands showed no signs of exhaustion. The Menominees greeted the new century with the hope of continuing prosperity.

Birches and evergreens in Wisconsin woods

State Historical Society of Wisconsin

157

Chief Grizzly Bear

from a painting by George Catlin
National Collection of Fine Arts, Smithsonian Institution

Wife of Grizzly Bear

from a painting by George Catlin
National Collection of Fine Arts, Smithsonian Institution

Stand of white pine

State Historical Society of Wisconsin

160

Wisconsin forest

State Historical Society of Wisconsin

Girls working in Menominee forest

State Historical Society of Wisconsin

Menominee Indian Reservation, near Shawano, Wisconsin

Wisconsin Conservation Department

National Anthropological Archives, Smithsonian Institution

Gebr Studio, Shawano, Wisconsin

National Archives

Menominee logging activities

Logging on Menominee Indian Reservation

National Anthropological Archives, Smithsonian Institution

Menominee forest

National Anthropological Archives, Smithsonian Institution

Wolf River

Gebr Studio, Shawano, Wisconsin

Wah-Pon-Niqut (Morning Cloud)
Sitting high on the Dalles of the Wolf River, twelve-year-old Earl
Westcott, Jr. represents the Menominee of today who holds dear his
Indian heritage, yet looks with hope and determination to the future.

from a painting by Fred A. Schmidt
Hortonville Public Library, Hortonville, Wisconsin

VII

Lumbermen of the North

The quiet, industrious tribe of Indians goes un-chronicled, but the ones who made trouble are al-ways talked about.

Chief Reginald Oshkosh

Menominee Indians volunteered once again for service in the Spanish-American War as they had during the Civil War. At least nine Menominees served in the four Wisconsin regiments outside the state. These men were Thomas Boyd, Joseph Counard, Augustus Lafromboise, Edward Pecor, John Wannebo, Olef Wannebo, R. H. Westcott, Frederick Wolf, and Martin C. Wolf.[1] The Menominees saw duty in companies in the First, Second, and Fourth regiments. Three men, Martin C. Wolf, R. H. Westcott, and Edward Pecor, who served in the Second Regiment, saw the greatest action. The Second and Third Wisconsin regiments trained at Chickamauga, Tennessee, and debarked from Charleston, South Carolina. Both regiments suffered losses from typhoid fever at Chickamauga, and from lack of food and inadequate housing in Charleston. Conditions were so poor at the Charleston depot that a War Department investigation was launched against Generals J. H. Wilson and O. H. Ernest, the commanders of the operation. Slated to go to Cuba, the two regiments were instead sent to serve under General Nelson

169

Miles in the Puerto Rican campaign. The units participated in the capture of Ponce, the surrender of Coano, and action at Asoninate Pass on the route to San Juan. The First Regiment, in which Thomas Boyd served, was stationed at Jacksonville, Florida. This group suffered severe losses from tropical fevers. The Fourth Regiment, to which Augustus Lafromboise, Joseph Counard, John Wannebo, and Olef Wannebo belonged, was stationed at Anniston, Alabama, and was still held at that point at the time that the Wisconsin *Roster* was published.

It was neither the war nor the reservation system, but an act of nature that projected the Menominee Indians into the twentieth century. On July 16, 1905, a cyclone passed through the western part of the reservation overturning and breaking off thousands of trees.[2] The timber damage was estimated at twenty to thirty million log feet. Hardwood so broken deteriorates rapidly. Within two years, if left in the woods, the timber becomes unfit for sale. The timber in the 1905 blowdown was completely uprooted only in strips with islands of undamaged timber left standing. Waste resulted from the salvage operations, which left tangled tops and high stumps. In addition, the delay in the salvage added to the loss. Congressional permission, required to salvage the blown-down district, since the quantity was in excess of the 17,500,000 board feet already authorized, took over a year to obtain. Shepard Foreman, superintendent of the Menominee Agency, recommended that the blown-down timber be sold on stumpage, which would have left the cutting and clearing to the buyers. Instead, the Act of 1906 turned the whole problem over to the Indians.[3] In the course of the emergency, Senator Robert M. La Follette became interested in the Menominee timber enterprise. He proposed that the Menominees be permitted to mill their own lumber. The La Follette Act, March 28, 1908, the result of the senator's interest in the Menominee situation, provided that the Menominees sell lumber sawed in their own mills to be erected on the reservation by the United States government with Indian funds.[4]

170

For fifty years wealthy lumbermen from Oshkosh and Oconto, Wisconsin, had purchased Menominee logs "keeping the price down by not bidding against each other." To remedy this problem, Agent Thomas Savage had suggested as early as 1896 that the Menominees operate a commercial sawmill. Such a mill would give employment to the tribal members and bring much more money for finished lumber than raw logs. The arguments of Agent Sawyer were used by Senator La Follette in winning passage of the 1908 law.[5] Debate on the bill centered around the matter of the federal government's role in business enterprises. La Follette argued on behalf of the Indians, stating:

> The aim of the proposed legislation is to give to Indians on reservations in Wisconsin practical instruction and experience in the management of their own business, and thus to prepare them against the time when their land shall be allotted, their restrictions entirely removed, and they be compelled to assume the complete management of their own affairs.

Senator La Follette embellished his plea to fellow senators with this fine rhetoric:

> The forest is the natural home of these men. They are what is known as "Timber Indians." Their every instinct teaches them to seek a livelihood from within the forest. The care, the preservation, of these forests should be the Indian's interest and his work. What the white man has in other places destroyed, the Indian should be taught here to preserve. This does not mean that the forest shall be permitted to remain in its wild state and contribute nothing to the industrial life of the community and add nothing of economic value to our country. It does mean that the harvest of the crop of forest products should be made in such a way that the forest will perpetuate itself; that it shall remain as a rich heritage to these people from which, through their own labor, they may derive their own support, and that, too, without ruthless destruction. Under the bill as proposed . . . these Indians shall be made a factor in our industrial life. In this way they will become self-reliant, learn to know the value of their heritage, and master the best methods for its preservation.[6]

The Act of 1908 put the United States Forest Service in charge of the Menominee lumber business. The Service undertook its task of starting a Menominee lumber operation just in time to prevent private contractors, in collusion with influential Indian partners, from the execution of improper and fraudulent contracts with the Menominees. Thirty-eight contracts for utilization of the 1905 blowdown were involved. The contract situation aroused the tribe. Active enmity of tribal leaders and the natural suspicion of the Indians led the tribe to protest the arrival of Forest Service personnel. Governmental officials decided upon a plan of compensatory payment to the contractors in settlement. The Indians in the meantime reacted with violence to the Forest Service's arrival. A fire was set in the woods near Keshena, Lake Dam was destroyed by a dynamite blast, and personal threats were made against Forest Officer E. A. Braniff and Logging Superintendent W. E. LaFountain.[7]

The La Follette Act retained the annual sustained yield limit of twenty million board feet of timber. It made provision for the timber to be cut into commercial lumber in reservation sawmills, and it created the Menominee 4 Percent Fund for all proceeds from the lumber operation.[8] This fund was to be kept in the United States Treasury for the benefit of the tribe. Instead of the three mills anticipated in the law, one large mill was constructed at the Norway dam on the West Wolf River, where the new Wisconsin and Northern Railroad line crossed the river. The town of Neopit grew up around the Menominee mill which opened for business in January, 1909. It was as modern as technology permitted. It was rigged with two band saws, a horizontal resaw, edgers, trimmers, a lathe, and shingle and picket machinery. The plant was powered by a battery of six large boilers that furnished steam for a Corliss engine. The boilers and Corliss engine were housed in a large brick powerhouse which was dominated by a smokestack eight feet in diameter and one hundred and twenty-five feet high. A hot pond permitted the handling of logs throughout the winter, and an electric plant, operated by a turbine wheel in the dam, lighted the mill and the town.

Originally the Neopit townsite consisted of a sawmill board-inghouse capable of housing two hundred men, a central ware-house, four executive houses, an office building, three company houses for rent, and a number of private residences built by the Indians. On April 4, 1911, a special meeting, called by Reservation Superintendent A. S. Nicholson, created a tem-porary town government for Neopit. Superintendent Nicholson with permission, appointed C. H. Woodcock as chairman, with Peter LaMotte, vice-chairman, H. C. C. Ashford, secretary, and Bert Chevalier, recorder, as the first town officials.[9]

The advent of railroading on the reservation enlarged the lumbering operation. Ten miles of logging rail were constructed by the Wisconsin and Northern Railroad and put into service in June, 1911. The line charged five dollars per car on logs transported from the woods to the mill. The railroad spur, used to haul logs that would not float or were far from the main streams,[10] tempted the loggers to clear-cut the land. Recog-nizing the danger, the United States Forest Service urged the careful marking of trees so that both the log and the stump would show which trees had been selected for cutting. Assistant Forester E. E. Carter defined the goal of the Forest Service on the Menominee reservation:

> The aim which . . . must be the prevalent one, is to make an im-provement cutting which will leave enough trees on the ground, sufficiently close together to protect them against windfall, to form in themselves a sufficient basis for a second cut, and at the time to reseed the ground for future crops with the most valuable species on the Reservation.[11]

This goal became the basis for the sustained yield cutting and reforestation program that originated on the Menominee reser-vation and is still championed by conservationists throughout the nation.

Forest fires and blowdowns continued to be the major threat in the Menominee forests. The Indians, led by the Forest Service personnel, fought to keep back the fires that roared beyond control at the reservation boundaries.

173

On horseback, in wagons, by handcar, by special train, and afoot, men were rushed to the scene wherever a fire had broken out, usually in the day time, but several times at midnight. No expense was spared to suppress fire, and nothing was allowed to interfere with this work.[12]

Ogden Brooks, who hauled provisions from Neopit to the lumber campsites, was caught in a night-time storm. He vividly described the experience.

About 9 o'clock the men came in from fire fighting because the wind was so bad they could not keep the fire in line. The camps were on a little knoll and the fire crept entirely around these camps until nearly 100 men were boxed up, and everything began to look as if it were all over with us. Along about this time I certainly began to think about the future.

Imagine the scene. A bunch of old camps on a little knoll overlooking acres and acres of burning pine slash. Fires on all sides, roaring, crashing, crackling, fanned to fury by a periodically shifting gale. See in the frequent glare of lightning a group of men huddled together, praying, cursing, crying and laughing hysterically. And all this time not a drop of rain, the air hot as a furnace, and all the while the roar of the flames punctuated at intervals by the fall of a tree.

Presently a few big drops of rain are felt, then more and more until it is pouring down in sheets. Sheets, torrents, volleys of rain! At last the drought is broken! And the reservation and the lives of men are saved. But a new peril comes. The dark clouds in the east are forming into one compact mass and as time drags on, the roar of a tornado is heard, first low and indiscreet, like the roar of an express train, then louder and louder until at last it is upon us. The cry of joy expressed at the rain have changed to curses once more, and in the incessant glare of the lightning, see the form of strong men huddled together in abject terror.

Flying treetops and branches fill the air. Howls of fear are heard amid the din, from the Pollack camp and over it all the deep boom of the thunder.

At last it is over. It seems as if it has been of hours' duration but in reality it was but a few minutes. As the roar gradually dies away and the thunder grows less frequent, rain falls again steadily and the wind dies down. Voices are raised to almighty God in thanks, voices that have not used that name, but in vain, for years, lifted in thanksgiving.[13]

On the Menominee reservation the deep snows of winter prevented the burning of slash during the logging operation. Slash piles were a distinct menace to the safety of the forests, since they provided a source for high fires and flying sparks. Forestry Superintendent Angus S. Nicholson introduced the practice of scattering the brush from the cutting operation so that it would lie close to the ground and absorb moisture. Small, low rows of slash restricted any outbreak of fire to ground fire, which could be contained easily. A foreman and twenty-five men worked on the original slash crew. Carefully cleared logging roads on the reservation provided fire lanes for added control.

Although the practice of silviculture was well advanced on the Menominee reservation, vestiges of the old ways remained. The pagan Medicine Lodge and its dance posed "the chief obstacle and helper in the survival of old customs." The Medicine Lodge dancers were elderly tribesmen, and it was believed that upon their death only memory and tradition would remain for the Menominees. As late as 1915, it was reported that "the influence of the medicine man with his herb roots, decoctions, and mysterious incantations is still felt in the tribe and in instances makes itself apparent among the more educated and 'advanced members.'"[14] The Menominees did not engage in blanket weaving, lace making, or pottery work so common on other reservations. Some fine ornamental basketry work was done. Early spring and summer days were reserved for fishing, though little of this activity was for profit.

Thirty-three Indian chiefs from the western reservations were guests of the United States at the inauguration of President Woodrow Wilson. Reginald Oshkosh, a chief of the Menominees and brother of Ernest Oshkosh, first chief, Peter Pamonicutt, descendant of a former chief, and Mitchell Waukau, nephew of a former war chief, represented the Menominees.[15] En route to Washington the Indians received an enthusiastic welcome from the city of New York, where they shared in ceremonies at the laying of the cornerstone for the National Memorial to

175

the American Indian at Fort Wadsworth on February 23, 1913.[16]
The chiefs visited the American Museum of Natural History
and the Bronx Zoo. Chief Reginald Oshkosh received special
attention in the *New York Times* account of the visit:

> Two or three of the chiefs, had been East before, and to one New
> York is by no means a new story. This experienced Indian is Osh-
> kosh, hereditary chief and actual head of the Menominee Indians.
> . . . Oshkosh is of the purest Indian blood and a superb type of
> redman. He is thin and keen. It is doubtful if any garb could con-
> ceal the ancestry of which he is so proud. But on Saturday after-
> noon, dressed in the buckskin and beads and eagle feathers of his
> tribal costume, and with vermillion and indigo shining from his
> face, he looked like a composite picture of all the chiefs whom
> it took the flower of the Federal Army to subdue.

The story recounted Oshkosh's days at Carlisle, Class of '79,
and his quiet ability to confound those who asked him foolish
questions. Besides sharing stories, Oshkosh also talked about
the Menominees.

> Beneath his talk, one caught a note of regret that the name Menom-
> inee was not so familiar as Sioux or Chippewa. "It is always so,"
> he said, tolerantly. "The quiet, industrious college boy passes un-
> noticed. It is the wild college boy whom everyone talks about. The
> quiet, industrious tribe of Indians goes unchronicled, but the ones
> who made trouble are always talked about. The Menominees, who
> conquered for their own the land about Wisconsin, were always
> loyal to the government under which they lived. They were loyal
> to the French until the English won; they were loyal to the English
> Government and when their land passed under the dominion of
> the United States they were loyal to this government. They fought
> for the government during the civil war, furnishing two companies
> . . . and in the Menominee reservation which occupies ten town-
> ships in Wisconsin today, is the only Indian G.A.R. Post in existence.
> The Menominees have always been a self-supporting people and
> their lumber business, equipment and all, is now worth some
> $2,000,000. There are 1,300 of us, but that is a slight increase
> from a few years ago. However, I remember the day when there
> were thousands on the reservation. I suppose that in a few years
> there will be no pure Menominees left. It is better so, perhaps.
> Inbreeding is bad for the tribe and the intermarrying with the

whites is better for us morally, mentally, and physically. I believe that and urge the bringing of the whites into our work."[17]

Forty "blue-blooded" Indian chiefs, accompanied by thirty braves, participated in the inaugural parade on March 14, 1913. On the day before the parade western chiefs expressed their reluctance "to take part in this mysterious ceremony." The Indians marched in the fourth grand division of the parade which consisted of civilian organizations. They were positioned just ahead of 1,500 Tammany Hall members, wearing Indian dress, in the line of march. Dressed in full feathered regalia and war paint,

> the Indians were headed by Chief Hollow Horn Bear . . . as they marched up in front of the President's stand the chief took off his sombrero and exclaimed dramatically: "White father, white father, white father!" Then, in the concealing night, the Indians with a shrill war whoop marched on to the tune of "Tammany" and disappeared. The effect was startling.[18]

The three Menominees who attended the inauguration received an allowance of one dollar and fifty cents a day for expenses. Their total for the trip was seventy-six dollars and fifty cents. Difficulty arose on the reservation in securing tribal consent for this expenditure. A factional fight had developed among the members of the tribal council, and no action could be secured for the payment of the travel costs. The Office of Indian Affairs authorized the payment on September 24, 1914, without the consent of the council. The dispute arose from a renewed effort by the white lumbermen and their Indian partners to secure payment for the annulled contracts made subsequent to the 1905 blowdown.[19] It was then and continues to be the plan of those who crave after Menominee white pine to use dissatisfied mixed bloods and dishonest attorneys to penetrate into the Indian land and destroy the tribe's protective power. By preaching misrepresentation of their affairs by the government, they hoped to induce the Indians to open their reservation and divide their resources so that one by one their shares could be "purchased" from them. D. F. Tyrrell, Attorney at Law, from Gillett, Wisconsin, represented the timber interests in this renewed pursuit of Menominee timber in 1914, but the attempt failed once more.[20]

In an effort to encourage farm production on the Menominee reservation, Superintendent Angus S. Nicholson inaugurated the Menominee Agricultural Fair, originally held on the first weekend in September, but now held as a homecoming in mid-summer.* The early fairs attracted viewers from as far away as Chicago. By 1917 the Agricultural Fair was recorded as a financial loss, and the blame was put upon the Indians who organized the event. The 1917 fair was the last of its kind for the duration of World War I, and no fair was held again until 1920, when the annual event was resumed.[21]

A new school was built at Keshena in 1915 at a cost of $44,000. At that time there was also concern over a much-needed old folks' home and a newly launched "save the babies" campaign. A more serious problem reached the reservation when representatives of the Winnebago Indians introduced the use of peyote among the Menominees. Within one year, fifty peyote users were reported on the reservation.[22] Although not subject to the draft in World War I, twenty Menominee Indians volunteered for service. These men were reported to have acquitted themselves with honor.

A destructive factor of new dimension appeared in the Menominee forest during the summer of 1918. On August 12, 1918, the white pine blister rust disease was discovered to be infecting the pine on St. Joseph's hill near Keshena. The disease spread rapidly, so that by 1921 infected pine appeared in practically all areas of the reservation.[23] Blister rust, technically known as *Cronartium ribicola*, is spread by wind-blown spores which are nurtured on alternate host plants, especially gooseberry and currant bushes. The best control for this tree killer is the destruction of the ribes bushes within nine hundred feet of

*After 1908 the Menominee reservation was directed by a superintendent. A. M. Riley was the first Indian Office superintendent, 1908–10, followed by Angus S. Nicholson.

the pine.[24] The battle against blister rust has been an ongoing affair since its discovery in the midst of Menominee white pine in 1918. Since 1943, when the Indian women went to work in response to the war effort, "the searching and grubbing job of ribe eradication" has been performed by Menominee women.

In 1924 the status of the Menominee Indians and citizenship was under question as on every other reservation in the country. Superintendent E. A. Allen clarified the Menominee situation in a prepared statement, which ascertained that the Menominees as a tribe were dependent upon federal legislation for their citizenship. Mr. Allen believed that, if the land had been allotted, the Menominees would have received citizenship, as other tribes had. Menominee war veterans and their descendants were citizens, as were some Indians who had moved from the reservation originally and later returned or were still residing in urban centers.[25]

The only federal Indian legislation that never became effective on the Menominee reservation was the General Allotment Act of 1887. Periodically, the matter became an issue of concern to the Indians as guardians of Menominee tribal lands. Urged by Reservation Superintendent Edgar A. Allen, the Menominee Council voted in January, 1919, with only one dissenting vote, for the allotment of the reservation. Not since the days of Agent Thomas Jennings, when the allotment act was a new approach to the Indian "problem," had the topic been discussed on the Menominee reservation. In the annual report of 1920, Edgar Allen observed that Menominee progress had not kept pace with the white society surrounding Keshena, and that the Indians would never be able to keep pace "until allotment was accomplished." At this same time, while the allotment plan languished in congressional committee, dissension arose among tribal members, and opposition to the renewed concept of allotment quickly organized. Mitchell Oshkenaniew led the opponents of allotment, and he solicited and won the support of United States Representative Schneider of Appleton, Wisconsin, to their cause.[26] Once again the young, more progressive

179

element of the Menominees was stopped, and the allotment issue receded into the background. As late as 1933, the Indian superintendent still pressed the issue:

> Individual allotments of this reservation must eventually be made. It is believed this demand will come from the Indians themselves as soon as the majority of them have reached that degree of education where they will appreciate individual ownership secured to themselves and their posterity. History has proven that communal life does not tend to progress, either industrially or financially.[27]

Allotment actually became a dead issue in 1928 as a result of the Meriam Commission report.[28] Nine members of this ten-member commission, chosen by the Institute of Government Research to study American Indian problems, visited Keshena, and their findings were presented in a short socioeconomic report prepared by Phebe Jewell Nichols in 1928. The report revealed that conditions among the Menominees were similar to those observed by the commissioners on reservations throughout the nation. The poor quality of government relations with the Indians was especially deplored. Inadequate diet and the long period of federal neglect in health needs were cited as weakening the Menominees to a point that made them very susceptible to disease, particularly tuberculosis. State health services for the reservation, state responsibility for acceptable schools with standard quality educational opportunity, special attention to the needs of the people in the Zoar community, and and state responsibility for the welfare of the Menominee Indians were urged in the report. Regarding special Menominee problems, the Meriam commissioners recommended that the Indians receive proper training to operate the lumber business by themselves, and that in the future tribal leadership should be consulted before either federal or state action might take place on any matter directly affecting the tribe.[29] The most important contribution of the Meriam Commission's investigation of Menominee conditions was the recommendation that the allotment program be replaced by the incorporation of the tribe so that its white-pine resource would be protected. This recommendation was made by the commission on behalf of all reservation Indians having the economic advantage of a natural resource.

Following the Meriam Commission's recommendation, the Menominees quickly issued a press release, prepared by Chief Reginald Oshkosh: "Appeal to the public is made on behalf of the Indians to abolish the Indian Bureau that is a stumbling block to the Indians' progress at the present date. The tribe is going to reorganize into a corporation instead of a tribe." Chief Oshkosh announced the plan of the Menominees to develop their own water resources and park, tourist, and resort facilities along streams and lakes "as pretty as paradise." He said:

> The Indians with their own money will open highways in the reservation. . . . They will establish camps for the Boy Scouts. They will build log camp homes with their 2,000,000,000 feet of timber. They will build fish hatcheries and stock the streams with trout. They will utilize land not given to campers as an Indian community center. . . .
>
> Too long have whites of Wisconsin been fed on Buffalo Bill and wild west and bad Indian types of stories. Its wrong to shut us up on a reservation. We have found recently that contact with good white people educates us more than anything else. . . .
>
> It's just as the Constitution says, all men are born equal and color is only skin deep.[30]

Incorporation for the Menominee Indians was first attempted in 1931, when Congressman Edward R. Browne introduced such a measure in Congress. Congressman Browne's bill, however, died in committee, and the great plan for tribal development of the Indians' natural wealth was postponed for another twenty-five years.

A small power struggle occurred among the Menominees in March, 1929, when Chief Ernest Oshkosh died. Menominee hereditary leadership passed into the hands of Ernest's fourteen-year-old daughter, Princess Kenoke. The succession was ordered by the girl's grandfather, Chief Neopit Oshkosh. This action took many Menominees by surprise, because they anticipated that the chieftaincy would be assumed by Ernest's brother

181

Reginald.[31] Regardless of the hereditary title, Reginald Oshkosh was the family member who wielded influence over the tribal council.

There is nothing to indicate that the "roaring twenties" made any impact on events on the Menominee reservation. There was a movement to close the boarding school for a state supported public school, but no such change occurred. A ban was passed by the tribal council denying permission for whites to hunt and fish on the reservation for a five-year period. The latter decision elicited a quick protest from neighboring fish and game clubs and some concern on the part of the Bureau of Indian Affairs over the loss of revenue from the licensing of white sportsmen.[32] Complaints were filed urging the enforcement of prohibition on the Menominee reservation and citing Indian absenteeism from work as a major result of negligence in this matter.[33] During the fall months many Menominees engaged in gathering fern. It was reported in 1931 that the fern-gathering industry brought in an annual income of $30,000 to the reservation.

Joseph Scattergood, the assistant commissioner of Indian affairs, visited the Menominee Indian Reservation in 1931, the first commissioner to do so. His visit was prompted by tribal unrest over the construction of a shaving plant and water system without tribal consent. The Indians were so agitated over the matter that they insisted upon "complete control of their affairs." Commissioner Scattergood's visit convinced the Menominees for the moment that the government was well disposed toward their needs, and his report commented upon the success of selective cutting since 1926. The area clear-cut during the years 1911–26 was reported to be covered with a growth of new poplar "under which there has already started a good growth of new hard woods, pine and hemlock." Scattergood also concluded that the outlook for sustained yield of the Menominee forest was very reassuring. "Conservative calculations . . . indicate that the total stand of merchantable timber now available for cutting exclusive of the trees that would be left in selective logging, is approximately 800,000,000 log feet."[34]

Commissioner Scattergood's visit resulted in the dismissal of those whites in the mill and lumberyard against whom major complaints had been filed. Indians were hired to replace white men, and within six weeks of the visit, only nine of sixty men employed in the entire milling operation were from outside the reservation. This kind of ratio was not maintained in the jobber camps, but still every Menominee desiring work was employed. This was true at a time when neighboring white communities were suffering because of the depression.

The Menominees attracted national attention early in the New Deal when they sent representatives Ralph Fredenberg and Aloysius Dodge to Washington to refuse a $30,000 public road building project. The delegates were quoted as saying that the money was rejected because the Menominees "were proud of their eighty year record of independence and believed that people should stand on their own resources so far as possible in times of stress."[35] Since it is never easy to return federal funds once allocated, the Menominees found in the fall of 1933 that they still had the Public Works award of $30,000. John Collier, New Deal commissioner of Indian affairs, wrote Superintendent William Beyer, assuring him that the money was for Indian use and would not be charged as a tribal debt.

A serious mill fire in 1924 had necessitated the rebuilding of the mill, a project that was completed in 1927. The cost of the repairs led to a reevaluation of the entire lumbering operation on the Menominee reservation. The Menominees concluded that their affairs had been mismanaged. In 1931 a Menominee enabling act permitted the tribe to hire attorneys to represent them in a lawsuit against the United States government for losses sustained through the maladministration of their lumber operation. The firm of Hughes, Schuman, and Dwight of New York City was engaged, and the Hughes Report, July 20, 1932, substantiated the Menominee position that

> the tribal moneys in the United States Treasury should be defined; the government was responsible for the cutting of timber without designation by the Department of Agriculture;

183

operations since July 1, 1926 were unsatisfactory;
investment in the plant and inventory were improvidently increased;
clear cutting without reforestation was unlawful on the reservation and that the tribe had suffered damages to the extent such a practice had been carried on;
an independent cruise of the clear-cut land be made to determine the damage.[36]

Lee Muck, assistant director of forestry, United States Indian Service, prepared the federal refutation of the Hughes Report.[37] The Muck statement refuted each of the charges made by the Menominee attorneys. Muck concluded that the Menominee losses, incurred in 1931 and 1932, were slight in view of conditions prevalent at that time throughout the lumber industry. In answering the charge of an improvident increase in investments, Lee Muck pointed out that only 14 per cent of the increase was caused by the reconstruction of the mill after the 1924 fire, and that other investment represented long-term contracts for new Indian homes sold to the workmen, new roads, sidewalks, electric lighting, a sewage disposal plant, and the continued operation of the mill in the time of national depression.

Congress, on June 15, 1934, made provision for a per capita payment to the Menominees of the fair market stumpage value of the fully matured and ripened green timber cut on the reservation each year, provided that the amount paid out did not exceed the actual income from the lumbering operation during the previous year.[38] Initially, the plan was not successfully utilized because of a lack of a method for determining the stumpage value, and the Menominees began requesting an annual per capita payment of fifty to one hundred dollars. In 1942 Forester R. Delaney worked out an acceptable formula for determining stumpage rates. Thereafter, the per capita payment was dependent upon the stumpage valuation. Congress also granted to and conferred jurisdiction on the United States Court of Claims "to hear, determine, and adjudicate, and render final judgement on all legal or equitable claims of whatever nature the Menominee Tribe of Indians may have against the

United States."[39] In all, thirteen suits were initiated against the federal government by the tribe. Most of the claims were for damages allegedly caused by the government-directed cutting of timber in violation of the Act of 1908. The cases were undertaken on behalf of the Menominees by the expanded firm of Dwight, Harris, Koegel, and Caskey of New York City. The Menominee suits were to become of major interest to the nation's foresters because of the comprehensive testimony and findings bearing on silvicultural practices in virgin forests.

During this period when Menominee claims were initiated, serious discussions occurred on the reservation with Robert Marshall of the Office of Indian Affairs concerning the merits of tribal reorganization under the Wheeler-Howard Act of 1934. The Menominees voted in 1935 to accept the Reorganization Act, but the tribe never organized or operated under provisions of the act. The Menominees decided instead to keep their ten-member elected Advisory Council and the General Tribal Council as the official decision-making and governing bodies.[40] At the time of the discussions on reorganization, the subject of the effect of the mill operations was considered. It was generally concluded that a highly technical business could not be run successfully by the democratic process. The need, however, of training Menominee Indians for positions of leadership in the lumber business was reiterated.[41]

Payments to mixed bloods raised interesting questions at the General Council in May, 1938. The decision on excluding some of the mixed bloods from the tribal roll was based upon Menominee oral history passed down to the council by the Menominee chiefs. At the same time it was concluded that Menominee traditions, ceremonies, and oral history had been guarded best by the pagan people of the tribe, who treasured the ancient customs and preserved the heritage which the 1848 mixed bloods had rejected. The Menominees did hold a new enrollment under provision of the Reorganization Act, and adhered to the principle that only those Menominees with at least one-quarter blood be admitted to the roll. Once again, the descen-

185

dants of those who had participated in the mixed blood payment of 1848 continued to be denied participation in Menominee affairs. It was also decided that no persons already on the roll would be removed from tribal membership.[42] The 1935 Indian population statistics revealed 2,112 enrolled Menominee Indians, of whom 1,998 lived on the reservation.

Some New Deal rehabilitation money enabled the Menominees to build a community center in Keshena, and in 1937 eighty pairs of roller skates were purchased and a popular roller rink opened at the site. W.P.A. adult education funds enabled the tribe to undertake the presentation of a pageant in conjunction with their Annual Fair, but World War II put an end to these activities. After the war the Menominee fair was revived, but without the pageant.[43]

World War II produced a patriotic response on the Menominee reservation as fervent as that appearing anywhere else in the nation. Within the first year of the war sixty Menominee men had volunteered for service, and over two hundred Menominee men were in uniform by the end of 1943.[44] Many other Menominees left for the shipyards and war plants from Lake Superior to Chicago. The depletion of the labor force on the reservation could have threatened the log and lumber industry, if Menominee women had not joined to work for victory. Fifty women went to work at the mill, and others engaged in the fight against blister rust in the pine forest.[45] Transportation and truck maintenance problems distressed the Indians during the war. The trucking of logs had been begun on the reservation in 1935.[46] The difficulty of securing gasoline, tires, parts, and drivers caused the people of Keshena to request and to be granted a grocery store for their town. The shortages also resulted in delays in the logging business, when trucks, bulldozers, and machinery broke down.

The Menominee honor roll for World War II included the name of Lieutenant William R. Fredenberg, who was awarded the Distinguished Flying Cross. Staff Sergeant David E. Kenote earned a Bronze Star for "meritorious service in connection with military operations against an enemy of the United States in France from 1 August 1944 to 31 October 1944." Fourteen Menominees received the Purple Heart for wounds incurred on the European front. These were Charles Beauprey, Frank Dodge, Joseph Duquain, Gust Kinney, Mose Neosh, Lloyd Gauthier, John O'Kachecum, Joseph L. Pecore, John Shawanapenass, Joseph Smith, Mitchell Sturdevant, Edward Tucker, Benedict Warrington, and Gilbert Wauposse. Lloyd Tourtillot and Peter A. Tucker were wounded in action in the Philippines, and three Menominees, Earl J. Pecore, George Tomow, and David Whoolock, suffered wounds in the Pacific Theater of Operations. A grateful nation also pays undying honor to the Menominee dead of World War II, Joseph Matchoma (Matchokema), Thomas Soldier, and Joseph Kamanekin, who died in France, and Arnold Tepiew, who gave his life in Burma.[47]

In addition to the war effort, the Menominees were concerned about their federal lawsuits. On July 5, 1945, after more than ninety years of intermittent litigation, the Menominees received title to 33,870.23 acres of swampland for which the federal government paid $1,590,854.50 to the State of Wisconsin. The swampland had been lost to the Menominee tribe in 1854, under provision of the Swampland Act of September 28, 1850. The award also allowed $13,666.50 to the tribe in compensation for timber removed by the state from the swamplands on the reservation.[48] The final Court of Claims decision was rendered on June 5, 1944, but the conclusion of the matter was delayed until 1945 by an initial refusal of the Wisconsin secretary of the treasury and the secretary of state, both members of the State Land Commission, to sign the transaction.[49]

With the taste of a victory over the state government in the swampland case and the joyous return of the war veterans, the Menominees optimistically faced the future. Early in 1947 an education committee was established by the Menominee Advisory Council to supervise a newly instituted program of Menominee scholarships for higher education. This program, using tribal funds, was designed to encourage students to continue study in order to raise the educational level of tribal members and to train technical and professional personnel within the tribal membership.

A recreational problem in 1947 brought a rush of summer visitors to Keshena, many of them for the first time. Frank and Sarah Skubitz opened the Arrowhead Restaurant on May 1, 1947. Their menu featured native trout, venison, and pheasant. Dancing and slot machines at the establishment were an added attraction for the general public.[50] The Menominee Advisory Council, in August, 1947, banned the sale of fish and game by Indians to the restaurant owners. While the council had no objection to public dancing, it hedged on the matter of slot machines, a possible gold mine in the heartland of Wisconsin. James Arentson, superintendent of the Menominee reservation, sought government advice in this matter. Arentson received notice that Mr. Skubitz was subject to loss of his trading license and prosecution for violation of state law.[51] While no immediate action was taken in regard to the slot machines, the Arrowhead Restaurant, in June, 1948, received permission to sell hatchery trout. The slot machine served as a drawing card until 1950, when the machines were eliminated because of federal pressure.[52] By midsummer, 1951, the Skubitz business again petitioned for the right to sell native fish and game. In the testimony offered on behalf of the proprietors, it was stated that "the little gravy in the restaurant business went out when the machine went out." Despite the plight of the Arrowhead, the Menominee Advisory Council denied the restaurant use of local fish and game.[53]

The Menominee Advisory Council secured a loan from the Federal Industrial Assistance program in 1949 and established a garment factory to manufacture ladies lingerie in the Keshena community building.[54] The initial investment of $30,000 remodeled the hall, purchased thirty-five sewing machines, a cutting table, and pressing table. The Menominee garment factory operated until December 31, 1955, but never realized a profit.

The Menominee lawsuits became the focal point of tribal interest as five of the thirteen Menominee suits were dismissed, and the remaining were consolidated into Case No. 44304, *The Menominee Tribe of Indians* v. *The United States.*[55] This suit was pursued in the United States Court of Claims until March, 1951, when the Department of Justice, due to general criticism by Congress, concerning large recoveries in Indian cases, broke off its negotiations. After special appeal, the Department of Justice, because of the merit of the Menominee claims, agreed on March 29, 1951, to offer $8,500,000 to the Menominees on condition that the tribe release the government from all claims to that time.[56] On February 5, 1952, the law firm of Dwight, Royall, Harris, Koegel, and Caskey was awarded $850,000 of the judgment money for their work in the case.

The Menominee award swelled the tribal 4 Percent Fund in the United States Treasury to over ten million dollars. The tribe looked forward with great expectation to a large per capita distribution of a portion of the judgment fund. As the Menominees rejoiced in their good fortune, they were unaware that at that very time a new word, "Termination," loomed on the horizon of their sunrise. Within a few months the whole world of the Menominees was again threatened as surely as in the days of Chief Oshkosh.

VIII

Menominee County

The Red Man wants to stay on this reservation so long as the sun rises in the East and sets in the West, and so long as the water is in our river beds.

Ernest Nekonish
Neopit, 1953

The victory in the Court of Claims became both a boon and a disaster for the Menominee Indians. By spring, 1952, a Menominee delegation returned to the reservation from Washington, D.C. John B. Kelliiaa, spokesman for the group, informed the Menominee Advisory Council that the whole political atmosphere in the nation's capital tended toward ending federal supervision over the Indians. Mr. Kelliiaa optimistically reported that this might mean "the outright abolishment of the Indian Bureau."[1] Menominee tribal leadership learned at this meeting that as early as 1948 the Republicans in Congress had prepared a list of ten tribes deemed "ready for release," and that the Menominees were among those tribes. In the selection of the tribes qualified for termination four factors were considered: the degree of acculturation; the economic condition of the tribe; the willingness of the tribe to end federal aid; and the willingness of the state concerned to assume responsibilities for "their" Indians.* The Menominees mistakenly paid little attention to this changed political attitude.

190

Another tribal delegation left for Washington in December, 1952, to seek legislation for a $1,500 per capita distribution of a portion of the Menominee award money. Congressman Melvin R. Laird worked with the tribal representatives in drafting a simple per capita payment bill.[2] Congressman Laird withheld the introduction of the measure until after Indian Commissioner Dillon Myer, the outspoken critic of "wasteful" Indian spending, had left office. The Laird measure, calling for the distribution of approximately $4,700,000 to tribal members, passed the House on May 19, 1953.[3] The bill, however, encountered serious opposition in the Senate Committee on Interior and Insular Affairs, where Senator Arthur V. Watkins of Utah exercised control.

According to Congressman Laird's testimony, Senator Watkins refused to consider the matter of a per capita distribution of Menominee tribal funds unless the Menominees "committed themselves to a program of withdrawal of Federal supervision."[4] Alarmed by Senator Watkins' unreasonable position, the Menominee delegation, consisting of John Fossum, Aloysius Dodge, and Gordon Dickie, insisted that they had no authority to commit their tribe to any proposal other than the simple payment bill. They suggested that Senator Watkins visit the Menominee reservation to discuss his proposal with the tribal leadership and to see for himself the problems faced by the Menominees. Senator Arthur Watkins, accompanied by Rex Lee, associate commissioner of Indian affairs, Donald Foster, area director, Glen Wilkinson, Menominee attorney in Washington, John Jex, Watkins' aide, and Assemblyman Robert G. Marotz, arrived on the reservation on Friday, June 19, 1953.[5]

Senator Watkins met with the Menominee Indians in General Council with over two hundred Menominees present on June 20. The historic session found Watkins arguing before the In-

*Tribes other than the Menominees on the original list for termination included the Flathead, Montana; Klamath, Oregon; Osage, Oklahoma; Potawatomi, Kansas and Nebraska; Chippewa at Turtle Mountain, North Dakota; Six Nations, New York; Hoopa, California; and the Sacramento, California Agency.

dians that "self-government" was inevitable because the Menominees were tired of being "bossed" by a government that had done a "bad job" of managing their affairs. Senator Watkins proclaimed the reservation one of the most productive reservations that he had visited and announced that the government was ready to give the Menominees, not the small per capita payment they requested, but the whole reservation and their complete ten and a half million dollar treasury deposit. The Menominees, led by Gordon Dickie, James Dick, Jennie Weso, Ray Lawe, and Gordon Keshena, accused the senator of denying the Menominees their much-needed money and of being in too big a hurry in the matter of releasing the government from its obligation to protect the sovereign rights of the tribe. When Gordon Dickie asked what the result would be if the tribe refused to take action on the matter of self-government, Watkins called such a position "unwise," since the Congress and the President favored his proposal.

A handful of Menominees, headed by Tony Waupochick, chairman of the Advisory Council, voted 169 to 0 that fateful afternoon following Senator Watkins' visit to accept eventual termination of federal control. The General Council measure asked for a three-year planning period to prepare for tribal control of the reservation, the mill, and the forest. The time was to be used also to allow for the proper disbursement of tribal funds and to provide for the adoption of the inheritance laws of Wisconsin.[6] It is doubtful if any Menominee Indian fully realized the significance of that vote. A small percentage of Menominees, who spoke only their native language, did not understand either the senator or the vote, others believed that they would lose their per capita payment unless they cooperated. There was a general naive feeling that if the Menominees discovered that they were not able to go on their own, the whole idea would be amended.

By action of the Senate Committee on Interior and Insular Affairs, namely Senator Arthur Watkins, the Menominee measure presented and passed by the Senate, July 24, 1953, permitting a per capita payment, called for "complete termination of Federal supervision over the property and members of the Menominee tribe."[7] With even greater finality, Section 9 of the Senate bill, stated that when title of Menominee lands and assets were transferred, "the statutes of the United States, the rules or regulations of any agency of the United States or any State, Territory or the District of Columbia, applicable to Indians because of their status as Indians shall no longer be applicable to the members of the tribe." By act of government the Menominees were going to lose their Indianness and become white Indians!

When the House of Representatives, urged by Congressman Melvin Laird, rejected the amended Senate bill, the measure was sent to a joint conference committee. Joint hearings on Menominee termination were held in Washington, D.C., on March 10, 11, and 12, 1954. On the first day of hearing five members of the appointed joint subcommittees were present, but the number declined to two on the second day, and only Arthur Watkins was present on the last day. Watkins not only dominated the hearings, but was the designer of the Menominee termination plan. Representative Laird was successful in blocking the Watkins bill by a simple objection to placing the bill on the unanimous consent calendar. This action forced the calling of another conference committee and a compromise. The new bill allowed for four and one-half years before final termination, thereby changing the date from December 31, 1956, to December 31, 1958. The bill, Public Law 399, was passed June 17, 1954.[8] The law required the Menominees to present a termination plan by the end of 1957 with final termination the next year. It closed Menominee tribal rolls as of June 17, 1954, and authorized a $1,500 per capita payment. Upon final termination, state laws would apply over all aspects of the Menominee members and their lives.

The preparation of a final Menominee roll caused great tension on the reservation. There was fear that persons already on the roll might be removed, and there was the problem of adding

193

children not yet enrolled. The Act of June 15, 1934, served as the basic Menominee enrollment act.[9] This act had been amended by Public Law 175 in 1939 to allow children whose parents met the reservation residency and enrollment requirements to be enrolled "irrespective of the derivation of their Menominee blood." This special provision was to secure enrollment for children born between 1934 and 1939, because during those years a special Interior Department Hook Commission worked to determine the blood degree of all enrolled Menominees.[10] The law of 1939 allowed descendants of relatives who had accepted the mixed blood payment of 1848 to be enrolled. During World War II, a special allowance was made to have children's names added to the roll if their parents were temporarily living off the reservation because of wartime employment.

In accordance with the Menominee Enrollment Act of 1934, it was required that to be enrolled one must possess at least one-quarter Menominee blood and have been born of parents one of whom was enrolled and residing at the time of one's birth upon the Menominee reservation. Enrollment was denied to any direct descendants of the mixed blood payment of 1848. Four hundred and ninety-four persons submitted petitions for enrollment to the Menominee Enrollment Committee. Only sixteen of that number qualified for admittance to the Menominee roll. The tribal roll with 3,254 members on June 17, 1954, increased to a final roll of 3,270 when approved for publication by the Secretary of Interior on November 26, 1957.[11] Each petition was reviewed by the enrollment committee under the direction of James G. Frechette, Sr., and presented to the General Council for a vote. Each case was further reviewed at the Bureau of Indian Affairs with the right of final appeal to the Secretary of Interior. The petitions were recorded in the Menominee General Council minutes and under individual names at the National Archives. Many of the cases evoked an emotional response from council participants. This was especially true in the denial of the petition of the thirteen children of Jane Martin Adams.

Mrs. Adams was identified as seven-eighths Menominee blood, and her husband, Irvin Adams, as full-blooded Oneida Indian. Research revealed that nine of their thirteen children were born in St. Joseph's hospital, Keshena, but the parents resided in De Pere, Wisconsin, not on the reservation. Nor could the children be adopted into the tribe since their maternal great-great-grandfather, Jean Baptiste Macaby, had accepted the 1848 mixed blood payment. Many people spoke on behalf of the children, the grandchildren of Joe Corn, a seven-eighths blood Menominee Indian. The fact remained, "they were born there, and look like Indians," but human folly and the law ruled them out. Challenges of an equally distressing nature were made against several enrolled Menominees who held positions of leadership within the tribe. In these cases, while bitter feelings were generated, affidavits from the early 1934 enrollment confirmed their membership rights.[12]

At the time of the passage of Public Law 399, there were five hundred Menominee families with 2,677 Menominee people living on the reservation, and one hundred and three enrolled families living off the reservation. The reservation in 1953 yielded $115,189 from its wild life resources, $1,321,797 from tribal enterprises, including the mill, and $1,551,635 in income from stumpage payment, agriculture, the tourist trade, and cedar-bough and fern sales.[13] The paramount issue on the reservation after June 17, 1954, became the unanswerable question of the fate of the enrolled tribal members, their resources, and their reserved land.

The per capita payment of $1,500 secured at the price of termination was mailed to the eligible Menominee Indians in early August, 1954, from the Chicago disbursing office. Checks were sent to all tribal members over eighteen years of age or married. Shares of minors and persons declared mentally incompetent were consigned to the custody of the First Wisconsin Trust Company of Milwaukee, Wisconsin. Persons planning to help the Menominees spend their $1,500 payment were advised that the law required a license to trade. Violators of this requirement faced possible confiscation of their goods and a fine of five hundred dollars.

The major concern became the plan under which termination would occur. Such planning took more time than provided for in Public Law 399. Amidst heated arguments between Melvin Laird, the champion of the Menominee cause, and Senators Robert Newberger of Oregon, who failed to secure assistance for the Klamath Indians of Oregon in their termination struggle, and Clinton P. Anderson of New Mexico, extensions of time to 1961 were awarded. The government also finally agreed to pay $275,000 of the cost of Menominee termination.[14] Despite the extended time, the Menominees believed it was still "too soon" when the 1961 termination date arrived.

When the Bureau of Indian Affairs refused to assist in formulating a termination plan, the Menominees sought help from the State of Wisconsin. A Menominee Indian study committee, headed by the Wisconsin Attorney General, Vernon W. Thompson, with State Senator Reuben LaFave, two assemblymen from counties adjoining the reservation, county board members, and three Menominee Advisory Council members, was established. This committee had the expert advice of a specially created University of Wisconsin advisory board under the direction of Professor Burton R. Fisher of the Department of Sociology. The Menominee tribe established a coordinating and negotiating committee, composed of the chairman of the Menominee Advisory Council and three other tribal members. The Menominees elected George W. Kenote, a tribal leader who left his Washington position as assistant director of law and order with the Bureau of Indian Affairs, to head their committee. Assisting Kenote in Menominee planning were Mitchell A. Dodge, Gordon Dickie, and Advisory Council Chairman James G. Frechette, Sr. It was this Indian committee that bore the tribal burden of termination programming and planning.[15]

Termination planning became a race with time as ideas were put forth and arguments developed over what should be done. Outright fear of the intention of the State of Wisconsin arose

during the 1956 election campaign, when the successful guber-
natorial candidate, Vernon W. Thompson, announced that the
state should purchase "the whole Menominee reservation" for a
state park. Beneath the surface of this proposal lurked the state's
interest in Menominee white pine.

Public Law 399 required a plan for both governmental and
business operations of the Menominee reservation. The reservation's ten townships were divided with seven in Shawano
County and three in Oconto County, Wisconsin. The question of
governmental organization presented a variety of alternative
suggestions, including the continued division of townships between the two counties, giving all ten townships to Shawano
County, creating a state or federal forest area out of the reservation, or establishing a new county in Wisconsin. Although
inclusion in adjoining Shawano County appeared to be the most
efficient solution for the Indians, the cost in services to the
county would exceed the tax revenue it would receive. The matter of turning the reservation into some kind of public park was
discarded as impossible, since the land, owned in common by
3,270 individuals, was considered as private property. The estimated cost for its purchase was set at $40,000,000, and neither
the state nor federal government was inclined toward such an
expenditure.[16]

A Menominee General Council meeting, April 20, 1958,
attended by about one hundred tribal members, voted 50 to 0
for a referendum election on the matter of reservation organization. The referendum ballot, mailed to all enrolled adults, provided three choices. These were to form a new county, to attach
the whole reservation to an adjoining county, or to divide the
reservation on the seven-three township ratio between Shawano
and Oconto counties. The referendum election date was set for
September 9, 1958. Seven hundred and twenty-one of 1,716
eligible Menominee voters cast ballots at the polls or by mail in
the election. Six hundred and twenty-two voters favored the
creation of a new Menominee county at the time that the tribe
should sever its one-hundred-and-thirty-year-old relationship

197

with the United States government.[17] The hope of the Menominees was to create a "form of self-government, and to protect ... [the] people and property as far into the future as possible."[18]

General reaction to the whole procedure reflected great distrust and should have been a warning of future trouble. Mrs. Irene Dixon Mack expressed Menominee uneasiness:

> We should do everything in our power to retain our right to the land. . . . I do not like Public Law 399, to me it means "extermination" instead of "termination" of Menominee people and they want us to lose our title. The tribe does not thoroughly understand taxation and operation of their own affairs and business.[19]

The sentiment of the old Menominees was best voiced by Ernest Neconish:

> This is my land, you have no right to discuss any of our business. I am going to us, my Menominee people for help. They cannot just throw us out. . . . the Secretary did not ask me what is in the bottom of my heart. He should have come and asked the Menominee people, what is in their heart instead of people that do not belong here. When the white people first took hold in this continent and this nation, and after they established themselves, they promised that they would help the Indian people. That is the real law between us and the white people.[20]

The most vocal organization against the termination plan was that of the Rightfully Enrolled Menominee Indians (REMI), led by Mrs. Constance W. Deer, registered nurse and white wife of Menominee Indian Joseph Deer. The REMI group carried on a vicious campaign to discredit Menominee leaders on the negotiating committee. The organization went so far as to charge that 2,500 enrolled Menominees were on the roll illegally, while the "real" Menominees were being deprived.[21]

The task of creating a new county became the major concern of the State of Wisconsin and the Menominee-appointed law firm of Fairchild, Foley, and Sammond of Milwaukee. Mr. Frederic Sammond acted as the central agent in directing and informing all parties, Indian, state, and federal, regarding the progress of the new plan. The tribal lumber business was the second major problem that needed a solution. Five proposals were made to the Indian Study Committee and the Menominee Coordinating and Negotiating Committee concerning tribal business activities. The initial possible plans were: ownership and operation by the tribe; ownership by the tribe, operation under a private management trust; ownership by the tribe, operation by a semipublic developmental agency; ownership by the tribe, operation under a concessionaire or conditional-lease arrangement; or ownership by the tribe and continuation as a special reservation under state auspices.[22]

A complete wood cruise and a real and personal property study of all property on the reservation set the value at $35,432,-251, of which $34,431,126 was listed as tribally owned property. The figure gave each Menominee Indian on the final roll an interest of $10,529 in value. The Menominee Coordinating and Negotiating Committee warned the tribe that "no business man or firm would pay full value for the Menominee property." In support of this, the Menominee committee called attention to the fact that the Weyerhaeuser Timber Company offered to pay only one-half of the value of the Klamath Indian forest land in Oregon.[23]

Crucial to the issue was the preservation of the Menominee forest and lumber mill as a source of livelihood to the employed tribal members, and as a source of income for all enrolled Menominees. Public Law 399, as amended on July 24, 1956, required a plan "for the protection" of the forest on a sustained yield basis, and for the protection of the water, soil, fish, and wild life." The general opinion on the reservation, reflected by the Menominee Indian Study Committee, indicated that the tribe wanted to "continue as a closed Menominee organization after the termination date, that . . . they could 'continue to hold hands as the Menominee Tribe of Indians' and hold . . . common property as before."[24] The Menominee Indian Study Committee's Business Advisory Board urged that conveyance of property was totally impractical, and the sale of the whole property would result in utter disaster for the Menominee people. The most logical, easily accomplished method for the tribe was the creation of a business corporation under Chapter 180 of the Wisconsin statutes. Such a corporation would receive title from the Secretary of Interior to the tribal forest and mill. It in turn would issue shares of voting stock to each enrolled Menominee. This recommendation and its corollaries provided the basic plan by which Menominee Enterprises, Incorporated, was created.

George Kenote said, "Menominee Enterprises was born out of necessity," since without a plan, the Secretary of Interior was empowered by Public Law 399 to surrender Menominee property to a trustee of his choice. Two years of serious planning by all groups produced the articles of incorporation and bylaws of the corporation. The final plan was reviewed by the Menominee General Council on January 9, 10, and 17, 1959. The plan was adopted 91 to 16 by secret ballot on January 17, 1959.[25]

The Menominee plan, submitted to the Secretary of Interior and put into practice at the time of termination, April 30, 1961, was designed "to promote the most beneficial use of Menominee property." Chapter 259 of the Wisconsin statutes created Menominee County, Wisconsin's seventy-second county. At the time of its creation among Wisconsin's counties, Menominee County ranked sixty-fourth in area, and last or seventy-second in total population, family income, high school graduates, total housing units classified as sound, and land in farms. Menominee County ranked first for nonwhite residents and unemployment, and second for the per cent of the population, ages five to thirty-four, enrolled in school.[26]

The new county, consisting of a single political town, provided normal county services, except that public education and the judicial process were administered by Shawano County. A town board, elected from precincts, also served as the county board. Chapter 258 of the Wisconsin statutes provided the method of taxation of forest land required by federal law for a sustained-yield forest. This method was based upon the principle that a forest required by law to operate on sustained yield had a fair market value equivalent to 40 per cent of a fair market value of a forest owned and operated without such restrictions.[27]

Under the economic plan that created Menominee Enterprises, Incorporated (MEI), in 1961 to hold and administer the tribal resources of land and forest, and the lumber mill, each Menominee received a 4 per cent negotiable bond with a face value of $3,000 scheduled to mature in the year 2000 A.D. In addition each was given a certificate of beneficial interest representing one hundred shares of common stock in the Enterprises which were to remain nonnegotiable until the end of 1973. The shares of stock were held and voted by a seven-member voting trust, three of whom were Menominee Indians, that selected the board of directors of the Enterprises.[28] An assistance trust was organized at the time of incorporation and awarded by the Advisory Council to the First Wisconsin Trust Company of Milwaukee. The assistance trust received guardian power to act as trustee on behalf of Menominee minors and persons under legal disability. This action placed the interests of 1,400 Menominees under the custody of the First Wisconsin Trust Company. It prevented guardianships from being scattered and provided a uniform control. Under the contract First Wisconsin had only one trustee on the ballot in the annual election, but they voted a disproportionate share of the votes at each election. These were usually cast in a block vote, thereby enabling the Wisconsin Trust to control the election results. When in March, 1972, Wisconsin permitted eighteen year olds to take charge of their own property, the First Wisconsin Trust Company released the stocks and bonds of such young Menominees. The company's voting bloc through maturation of its wards was reduced from 41.6 per cent of the total vote to about 18 per cent in 1973.

The Menominee Termination Plan was implemented April 30, 1961. The transition seemed to go smoothly. Yet, if one had followed the planning, negotiating, and decision making, there were danger signals that went unheeded by the Menominee Coordinating and Negotiating Committee, the chairman of the Advisory Council, and the Menominee delegates who pleaded

201

their cause in Madison and Washington. Too little attention was given to the loss of treaty hunting and fishing rights and to the rejection by government of further recognition of a Menominee as an Indian, thereby denying him medical care, aid in education, protection of tribal law, and protection of the tribal land. State and federal legislation stripped the Menominees of every treaty right ever guaranteed them.

From the outset Menominees protested the termination idea. Antoine Waupochick at the 1954 joint hearings asked for time, saying:

> Time is essential; withdrawal must be orderly, or we will face liquidation, for there are many in our tribe who do not know the white man's way of living. Those people will not know what to do when a tax collector comes around, and I am fearful that this problem will be met by such persons only by selling such property as they can sell. Eventually this may result in a situation which will leave our reservation checkerboarded. The Menominee people are painfully aware of this possibility by looking around at the Stockbridge, Chippewa, the Potawatomi, and other tribes in our areas, all of whom had reservations but lost them after they were allotted and given fee patents.[29]

Menominees protested termination in hearings in Madison before the state legislative committees. Representatives from Oconto County, including State Senator Reuben LaFave, joined the Indian protestors, chiefly because Oconto County objected to the loss of the three Menominee townships. At a committee meeting in June, 1959, Menominee Indians charged that the tribal leaders on the various termination committees were "dictators" who had lost the trust of the reservation people.[30] The small attendance at General Council meetings seems to indicate that the Menominee people, not understanding what was happening and fearful of the future, chose to stay away, probably in the hope that termination would not come.

"We Will Make It." This slogan on billboards, at the entrances to Menominee County, only hinted at the desperate struggle for survival that marked the first ten years of the new county's existence. From the April 30, 1961, termination deadline, exis-

202

tence for Menominee County and its small Indian population had been an uphill struggle. The problems faced by Menominee Enterprises, Incorporated, were enormous. The new corporation inherited a fifty-year-old mill, greatly in need of renovation, at a time when the lumber market was depressed. It fell heir to all the land within the county without a plan for recognizing individual rights to homesites. The MEI had to contend with 94 per cent of the tax burden that earmarked some $380,000 for local government, roads, education, welfare, utilities, and health care for the citizens of the county. Doubt, dissatisfaction, and complaints accompanied each decision made by the MEI board of directors during the first decade of operations.

Within two months of termination the board ordered that the land in use for homes or farms be purchased at a fixed value by the residents. In February, 1962, bills were sent to all home owners within the county. Most owners had no recourse but to offer their enterprise bonds to the corporation in payment for the land that had always been their own. By 1964 more than six hundred bonds had been used by the Menominee Indians to buy their own homesites.[31]

Termination resulted in the loss of federal contracts for the mill and the closing of the BIA public school. The reservation hospital at Keshena closed its door because of lack of funds to bring it up to state standards, and the Indians had to travel to Shawano, ten miles away, if they wanted medical care. During this time the dread word tuberculosis was again common among the Menominees. Wisconsin public health doctors checked on the tubercular scare. In 1965 they reported six hundred positive reactions among the two thousand Menominees tested. At this time the infant mortality rate for the county was three times that of the rest of the state, and over 90 per cent of the school children were in need of dental care.

The Indians were further discouraged when confronted by the Shawano police and court system. Used to a speedy hearing or dismissal in Indian court, the Menominees complained about being "lost" in jail for eighteen days awaiting a hearing, and of

203

having their children confined in the Shawano jail because of curfew violation.[32] The new state game and fish laws forced Menominees, who needed food, to hunt deer at night with dogs and car headlights, and to net and spear fish also at night. Conservation officers spotted violators from the air and radio-relayed locations to waiting police patrols. The poor Indian "captured" in such a raid sat out his fine in the Shawano jail, since there was little money among the Menominee Indians with which to pay a game violation fine.

Menominee County's estimated annual per capita income of eight hundred and eighty-one dollars ranked lowest in Wisconsin. Since the county lacked diversified industry, the Menominees had the state's highest unemployment rate. In 1968 an average of 24.4 per cent of the county's work force was unemployed. In an effort to remedy the situation, training programs were instituted, including three phases of the Manpower Development and Training Act.[33]

The Menominee Indian education program was made a part of Joint School District No. 8. Nine hundred and ninety-four elementary school children attended the four county schools. Both Keshena and Neopit maintained a public and a parochial grade school, but high school students had to travel to either Gresham or Shawano. Federal funds aided the district schools that served Menominee County students, and such funds also provided adult education classes and Headstart and Upward Bound programs within the county.

Welfare costs, which cost the county $49,723 in 1963, had doubled by 1968. The welfare program received money from federal, state, and town-county governments. Large families, illegitimacy, and high unemployment comprised the major causes of the high welfare demands in Menominee County.

Termination thus reduced the proud, independent, self-supporting Menominee nation to a poor, disorganized group of citizens dependent upon federal-state support for survival. The entire program was most costly to the federal government, whose termination program was passed originally to save money.

The tribe, which had previously used only $144,000 a year of federal funds, by December, 1960, had been allotted $2,357,-000. This money had been authorized to reimburse the Indians for termination study and planning expenses, upgrading the school program, building roads, sponsoring adult education programs, and health-welfare needs.[34] Despite the money, the Menominee situation in no way matched the condition found in any other county in Wisconsin. Two federal bills in 1961 and 1966 of over one million dollars each were passed to sustain county programs, and in 1964 the State of Wisconsin began contributing welfare aid. In addition the state granted one million dollars to individual Menominees to enable them to keep their shares in Menominee Enterprises, Incorporated.[35] Termination robbed the Menominees of their self-respect by reducing them to a state of near pauperism. In 1964, seven hundred and eighty-nine desperate Menominees signed a petition begging for the repeal of termination.

In an effort to save the county and the business corporation, the management firm of Ernst and Ernst was engaged in 1967 under a grant from the Economic Development Administration of the Department of Commerce to make a study of the industrial and recreational potential of the county. The study revealed that the logging and sawmill operations of Menominee Enterprises, Incorporated, managed each year since termination to increase its sales and reduce its losses. It was not until 1965, however, that the company began to realize a small profit. Nevertheless, the company was unable to meet all of the socio-economic responsibilities demanded of it by the county. The survey team advised the Menominees to renovate and update the mill and to expand production by adding the manufacture of veneer, dimension stock, and edge-glued coreboard, low density particle board, and charcoal.[36] Menominee Enterprises estimated the cost of such an expansion program at three and one-half million dollars. The big problem posed by the industrial expansion plan was that of money. The most promising avenues of development capital for the Menominee program remained as be-

205

fore, that of increased forestry cutting and the utilization of the recreational value from the scenic lakes and Wolf River.[37] By far the easiest plan to implement was that of developing the recreational potential of Menominee County.

As early as 1929 a recreational plan had been projected by the Indians to develop Menominee water resources, park and resort facilities. Chief Ernest Oshkosh at that time proposed the creation of an area Boy Scout camp and the establishment of Menominee trout hatcheries on the reservation. In 1947 the Menominee Advisory Council advocated a resort complex, featuring an Indian owned and operated two-hundred guest hotel with golf course, riding stables, and fishing guide services.[38] Foremost among the plans for recreational development in 1967 was the idea of a state or national park, since this had been considered among the alternatives for the disposition of the reservation at the time of termination. In fact in 1962, Menominee Enterprises, Incorporated, had announced a "Menominee Forest Lakes Vacationland Homes" plan in which six hundred homesites were to be developed and leased along the river and southeastern lakes.[39] It was in conjunction with this plan that the Indians purchased their homesites, but the idea drew little public response.

The desire to broaden the county's tax base and the uncertainty of what would happen when the federally granted funds expired led Menominee Enterprises to undertake construction of a multiseasonal tourist complex and to initiate the West Lake Project in 1967. The old 1947 plan was revived in part, as MEI leadership made plans for golf, horseback-riding, and snowmobiling courses with a large visitors destination center. The latter was to include an Indian cultural center, nature awareness center with auditorium, tourist information center, a picnic and camping center, and a boat storage center. One million dollars in financial assistance was allocated for the project by the Upper Great Lakes Regional Planning Commission in June, 1968. The money was quickly spent and only the tourist information center, shopping center, nature awareness center, and picnic-camping

206

development were completed.[40] This project has had little Menominee support because it was devised by the MEI leadership without consultation with the Menominee people.

The West Lake Project, an extension of previous uncompleted lake plans, called for the creation of a large lake to be made by dredging submarginal forest, swamp, and lake land near Keshena and the offering of forest-edge vacation sites at premium prices. MEI directors consulted with various engineering firms and recreational developers, including Neilan Engineers of Somerset, Pennsylvania, and the U.S. Land Company of Columbus, Ohio. Late in 1967, the MEI board of directors discussed their project with N. E. Isaacson and Associates, lake developers from Reedsburg, Wisconsin. Mr. Isaacson convinced the board that a lake development project needed not only engineering and construction, but also sales and financing. N. E. Isaacson, on July 9, 1968, entered into a joint "Lakes of the Menominees" venture with Menominee Enterprises, Incorporated. The agreement provided for the continued development of West Lake, hereafter to be called Legend Lake and the future creation of an East, or Spirit Lake, project.[41]

Almost immediately, Menominees began protesting the Legend Lake project. The costly advertising program, gimmicks that included a small Mississippi River showboat on the lake, and free steak dinners for prospective buyers were considered a wasteful expenditure of money. The opponents of the project insisted that the Legend Lake plan was never put to a vote. They maintained that on September 23, 1967, endorsement had been given to the creation of an economic development zone. That vote had not reflected approval for the sale of Menominee Indian land to the general public.[42]

N. E. Isaacson guaranteed the enterprise a sale of $500,000 the first year, some $1,500,000 the second year, and $2,000,000 in each of the third and fourth years. The firm gave the Menominees an initial payment of $750,000 for the land, after which the joint partners were to share on a fifty-fifty basis. In the event that the anticipated sales goals were not reached, the split was

207

to be on a sixty-forty basis with the Menominees receiving the larger share. The project called for the development of 2,600 lots in the 5,170-acre site. Under the proposal the area was divided into thirds and reserved into water area, subdivision sites, and a wilderness area to be left in its natural state. The price range for the lots in the Lakes of the Menominees project was "from $2,500 to over $15,000, with the average lot going for about $5,500." There were boat access areas spotted around the lake, which ranges in depth to seventy feet. By July 11, 1971, more than half, or 1,568 lots had been sold.[43]

Menominee Enterprises, Incorporated, received $1,850,000 through 1971 from the Legend Lake development project. The money was used to renovate and update the mill, pay mill taxes, pay bond interest, sponsor a forest inventory, and pay the initial costs of a new federal lawsuit.

DRUMS, Determination of Rights and Unity for Menominee Shareholders, a grassroots movement, emerged from meetings of dissident Menominees in Chicago, Milwaukee, and Menominee County. Local chapters of Menominees, unhappy with the Enterprises leadership, were organized. The Chicago-Milwaukee groups, protesting corporation lumber mill losses, discrimination against Menominee children in Shawano schools, and the "giving away" of Menominee land by the Legend Lake developers, sought advice and won the support of attorney Joseph Preloznik, director of the OEO-funded Wisconsin Judicare legal service agency.

DRUMS next moved into Menominee County where Genevieve Otradovec and her family and the family of Joseph Deer quickly organized a chapter and led an organized protest against Legend Lake. First demonstrations at the Legend Lake Company Lodge, protesting the sale of lots, occurred on July 4 and 5, 1970, and continued through November of that year. This pattern was repeated throughout the spring, summer, and fall in 1971 and 1972. Some of the demonstrations were peaceful, while others were quite militant, provoking arrests, and in at least one instance local police resorted to the use of crowd-control gas to prevent a DRUMS takeover of the Legend Lake Development Center's Lodge.[44] Indian author, Vine Deloria, Jr., speaker at a United American Indian rally in Milwaukee in March, 1971, pledged $3,000 to aid the DRUMS movement to prevent "a single handful of dirt" from leaving Indian hands and to seek a reversal in the termination policy.[45] Buffy Sainte-Marie and the Robert F. Kennedy Youth Project in Washington, D.C., also sent contributions to DRUMS.

Wisconsin Judicare, backed by DRUMS, brought a series of lawsuits against Menominee Enterprises, Lakes of the Menominees, and MEI directors and trustees. While court action was pending, DRUMS attempted to secure shareholders' proxy votes to enable the organization to vote the Voting Trust out of existence in the first ten-year election scheduled for December, 1970. Abolishment of the Voting Trust required a 51 per cent majority, or 1,600 Menominee votes. DRUMS secured an injunction forestalling the election from December to April, 1971, in order to better organize their campaign.[46] Patrick O'Donahue of the *Green Bay Press Gazette* staff in an interview poll conducted in the fall of 1970, reported that 60 per cent of the Menominees believed in the Enterprises, but at least 40 per cent favored a change in the Enterprises structure. Feelings were mixed on Legend Lake with most admitting that the tax base had to be increased. Surprisingly, despite the claim of DRUMS, 56 per cent of those interviewed approved of the First Wisconsin Trust Company's control of the children's stock.[47]

During the winter of 1970–71, DRUMS sent every Menominee a proxy and a letter explaining the issues and the need for eliminating the Voting Trust. In a specific March election for the first two of four additional trustees sanctioned by the Voting Trust, two DRUMS members, Georgianna Webster Ignace and Ada Deer, were elected. The important vote came on April 3, 1971. DRUMS received 119,320 of the voted shares to 118,-516 for the MEI. DRUMS lacked the necessary 51 per cent to dissolve the Voting Trust. The charge made by the DRUMS organization was that the First Wisconsin Trust "gang voted" its 48,000 votes to continue the trust.[48] The election increased the bitterness between the two groups. Amid the charges and countercharges a considerable number of Menominees still remained outside of the friction generated by both groups.

Everything in the county after 1969 hinged on DRUMS activity and the ill-fated Legend Lake project. The Neopit mill renovation was undertaken with the aid of Legend Lake funds after a devastating fire in June, 1970. The half-million-dollar project included new boilers and the installation of the most modern antipollution devices in the industry. The devices recycle the waste smoke after separating the fly ash from the smoke. The fly ash is collected and disposed of so that it does not enter the atmosphere. The improvement program also led to the replacement of the water debarker with a new, pollution-free mechanical debarker. The whole project made the Menominee mill at Neopit one of the most modern plants in the Midwest, and one in which the Menominee people took great pride.

The political rift went beyond Menominee County in charges fired by DRUMS leadership against the Shawano public schools. A two-hundred-member group, calling themselves Menominee County Parents and Students Committee for Better Education, charged the Shawano School District with discrimination against Menominee youth. Multiple suspensions, lack of communication between students and administrators, and the "quashing" of an Indian club at Shawano High School were cited as the group's major complaints.[49] On May 20, 1972, demanding an educational bill of rights for the high school students of Menominee County, suit was filed in United States District Court against Joint School District No. 8. In response to the suit the Shawano school board worked with the court and the Indian community to formulate a workable plan to combat anti-Menominee sentiment in the schools. During the 1972–74 school years, students "in trouble" in the Shawano and Gresham high schools remained in Keshena, where a special program was inaugurated. The classes, worked out by the Menominee County Community

Schools group, were held in the Visitor Destination Center at Keshena. More than fifty students attended these sessions.

The Menominee County Education Committee sought detachment from the Shawano School District and the creation of a new school district for the Menominees. Public hearings were held in January, 1974, both in Shawano and Keshena. On January 15, Board President Donald Juers informed the Agency School Committee that the Shawano Board of Education endorsed the plan for detachment. Citing a high rate of absenteeism and lack of motivation among Menominee children in the Shawano schools, Juers voiced the board's decision "that the people of Menominee County do have a right of self-determination in this matter and the success or failure of their efforts should be their own reward and responsibility."[50]

Following this action, the Agency School Committee voted five to three on January 26, 1974, in favor of detachment and gave approval for a referendum vote on the issue among the Menominees. This action triggered new debates on the issue. The major stumbling blocks to detachment were the problems of financing, especially in view of the uncertainty of Johnson-O'Malley funds from the federal government, and the need to find qualified school teachers with an understanding of Indian children. Bolstering the cause of need for their own education system through the twelfth grade was the persuasive argument that public school education in District No. 8 forced assimilation on Indian students to the detriment of the traditional Menominee Indian culture.

The referendum vote of April 3, 1974, resulted in the defeat of the detachment proposal by a vote of 328 to 294. The charge was made that the fifty-two non-Indian votes cast by Legend Lake property owners made the difference. Mrs. Christine Webster of the education committee called for legislative action to create a Menominee school district "over the heads of Legend Lake voters."[51] The education of Menominee youth remains as a vital problem for the Menominee people. The need for doctors, lawyers, nurses, and school teachers has not been met. Menominee culture can be preserved only if the Menominee young people begin to fill some of these vital positions for their people.

While the detachment issue developed, restoration interest increased. The defeat of DRUMS in the Voting Trust decision in April, 1971, strengthened the group's determination to obstruct the completion of the Legend Lake project and to seek a reversal of termination legislation. Protests at Legend Lake were renewed throughout 1972 amidst arrests and television reports. Demonstrators picketed Isaacson offices and projects throughout the state, and staged a highly publicized protest at the First Wisconsin Trust Company office in Milwaukee. In August, 1971, with DRUMS casting proxy votes, an MEI proposal, asking for the sale of Wolf River property, was overwhelmingly defeated. DRUMS was on the move! The group sponsored a dramatic two-hundred-and-twenty-two-mile March for Justice from Keshena to Madison in an effort "to pierce the iron-curtain of state-wide misinformation and ignorance surrounding tribal affairs."[52] The march began on October 2, 1971. In Madison a demonstration of some six hundred supporters cheered as Governor Patrick Lucey met the Menominee marchers on the capitol steps. The governor promised to help the Menominees work out their problems and to visit the county as soon as possible. This peaceful demonstration, more than any other action, gave emphasis to the Menominees' protests to termination, the sale of their homeland to outsiders, their sorry financial plight, and their desire to return to the protections offered by the federal treaties that had been discarded so hastily in 1954.

A crucial test for the DRUMS organization came in the November, 1971, trustees' election. Four DRUMS candidates, Ada Deer, Georgianna Webster Ignace, John Gauthier, and Carol Dodge, comprised a slate calling for the reversal of termination, an end to Legend Lake sales, the eventual end of the Voting Trust, and the democratizing of MEI. DRUMS realized a stunning victory as the four candidates were swept into office.

212

It was evident that after a decade of termination experience, the Menominee people were disenchanted with the old leadership, the Enterprises, and their financial problems. They were heartsick to see cottages owned by white outsiders along their lake shores. The new motel, gas stations, supermarket, and taverns meant little to the Menominees in the face of the latest loss of the land they cherished. Most unfortunate of all was the rejection by the Menominees of the men who worked so hard to make the county and the Enterprises a success. George Kenote, the man who left his Washington, D.C. job to help his people develop Menominee County, deplored what had happened. He stated:

> . . . reddish tactic — sloganeering — hate-targeting — underground press — big lie — racism — polarization — manipulation of media — these have engulfed a simple people and ruined them. The Menominee Indians have paid a terrible price. Judicare funded the funeral — called it social reform.
>
> Menominee Enterprises and Menominee County are looking at bankruptcy in cash — and worse, bankruptcy in leadership. The Drum beats a terrible dirge.[53]

213

Restoration

*Restoration is not a magic wand, that will immedi-
ately solve all the problems of the Menominees.
But it will make possible the solution to those
problems.*

Governor Patrick J. Lucey

President Richard Nixon's repudiation of the termination policy
during the summer of 1970 inspired the Menominees, led by
DRUMS, to seek the reversal of Menominee termination.[1] This
cause received a boost when Governor Patrick Lucey, keeping
the promise made to the March of Justice petitioners, visited
Menominee County in October, 1971. The governor told the
Menominees at that time that the Wisconsin Department of
Health and Social Services would no longer require forfeiture
of Menominee Enterprises bonds when an Indian applied for
welfare. Governor Lucey also discussed the possibilities of re-
versing termination, and he urged unity among tribal members
and some firm decisions on what would be the most desirable
policy for the tribe.[2]

DRUMS, MEI, and county officials began discussions in November, 1971, concerning the restoration of the reservation.
These meetings marked the first time that the various factions
joined together in serious discussion, and from the outset the

meetings were distinguished by remarkable agreement among the representatives.[3] Wisconsin's United States congressional delegates met with the Menominees in January, 1972, and Senator Edward Kennedy requested that attorneys from the Native American Rights Fund in Boulder, Colorado, assist the tribe in writing the request for restoration into a congressional bill.

Meeting in January, 1972, to fill four vacancies on the MEI board of directors, the Voting Trust elected a slate of four DRUMS candidates. This election clearly put DRUMS in control throughout the county. All Menominee corporate and governmental organizations were invited to join a joint legislative committee, chaired by Sylvia O. Wilber, to help prepare and introduce the necessary legislation. A Menominee delegation to achieve restoration went to Washington with the Menominee restoration bill in March, 1972. There, with the help of Mrs. LaDonna Harris, Phileo Nash, and James Goodell of the Robert Kennedy Youth Project, a National Committee to Save the Menominee People and Forest was organized.

Wisconsin's Senators William Proxmire and Gaylord Nelson on April 20, 1972, introduced Senate Bill No. 3514, calling for Menominee restoration. The bill, itself, stated the purpose:

> A bill to repeal the act terminating Federal supervision over the property and members of the Menominee Indian Tribe of Wisconsin; to reinstate the Menominee Indian Tribe of Wisconsin as a federally recognized, sovereign Indian tribe; and to restore to the Menominee Tribe of Wisconsin those Federal services furnished to American Indians because of their status as American Indians.[4]

Senator Proxmire in introducing the bill carefully outlined the history of Menominee County and the great financial burden created by the 1961 change in Indian status for the Menominee people. According to the senator's testimony, the cost of restoration of the reservation was set at $2,053,000. That figure was $1,421,000 less than the state and federal governments spent in Menominee County in 1971.

215

The Lakes of the Menominees project at Legend Lake called for the creation of three united lakes supplied with water from the original lake beds and diverted surplus water from Linzy Creek. Construction of the first two lakes "caused a reversal of the ground water table, which then caused the water levels . . . to rise by seepage."[5] Menominee outrage became very strident in September, 1970, when the Department of Natural Resources (DNR) authorized completion of the final phase, the third lake, of the Legend Lake project. DRUMS brought suit against the MEI and the Isaacson firm. In June, 1971, the DNR placed a restraining order on the project and conducted hearings on the environmental problems of seepage and the new septic tanks at the homesites. In September, Circuit Judge Lewis Charles in Ashland, Wisconsin, declared that the project had an adverse effect on the environment. However, since the developers swore that they were working in close cooperation with the DNR in the project, Judge Charles lifted the restraining order. The United States District Court in Milwaukee during the spring of 1971 also upheld the validity of the guardianship trust of the First Wisconsin Trust Company.

Following these decisions, DRUMS and the DRUMS dominated MEI increased pressure on the N. E. Isaacson firm and prospective buyers of Legend Lake property. By July, 1972, after intensive meetings, the N. E. Isaacson firm surrendered to Menominee pressure. A dissolution agreement in the case of the Lakes of the Menominees partnership went into effect July 8, 1972. By terms of the agreement the six hundred and ninety-nine unsold Legend Lake lots were divided between the MEI and N. E. Isaacson. Three hundred and twelve lots were consigned to Isaacson and Associates with permission to continue sales. The firm agreed to pay the MEI $250,000 and surrender the Legend Lake Lodge and the land around it to the Legend Lake Property Owners' Association. With four hundred lots in the project, the MEI became the largest single owner in the Property Owners' Association. Both parties agreed that present property owners were to be unaffected by the dissolu-

216

tion of the partnership. Current lawsuits against the DNR over the third lake project and the MEI over the original land sales also were not affected by the agreement.[6] Three weeks after the dissolution of the partnership, Judge William J. Duffy in Circuit Court, Green Bay, ruled that the original Legend Lake sales had taken place without the necessary two-thirds approval by the Menominee Indians. Judge Duffy ordered further land sales stopped on July 8, 1972.[7]

On May 2, 1973, Senators William Proxmire and Gaylord Nelson in the Senate and Congressman Harold V. Froelich in the House again introduced a Menominee restoration bill.[8] The bill was sent to the Indian subcommittees of the Committees of Interior and Insular Affairs for study. Senator James Abourezk, chairman of the Senate subcommittee, promised hearings on the bill during the summer of 1973.[9] The Wounded Knee confrontation threatened to delay action on all Indian affairs, but the congressional subcommittees kept the senator's promise to the Menominees. On May 25 and 26, 1973, the House subcommittee, headed by Congressman Lloyd Meeds of Washington, held a preliminary hearing on the Menominee restoration bill at Keshena, Wisconsin. This was the first official congressional committee hearing to be held in the land of the Menominees. The hearing enabled the Menominee Indians to urge immediacy in restoration and to express objections to amendments to their original bill.

The Indians' principal objection to the congressional bill was to a provision calling for a two-year delay before Menominee land would be returned to federal trust status and thereby become tax exempt. The Menominees expressed the belief that such a delay would completely bankrupt the Enterprises and bring financial ruin to the tribe. The Indians also protested the State of Wisconsin's retaining control of non-Indian hunting and fishing rights in Menominee lakes and rivers, and the amendment that would permit land sales within the reservation. State Senators Reuben LaFave and Herbert Grover from the Menominee Indian Study Committee of the state legislature asked

217

that the congressional bill be amended to permit the state to determine the form of government that Menominee County should assume when the land returned to reservation status.[10] Ada Deer spoke for the Menominee Voting Trust. She outlined the three major long-range effects of termination on the Menominee people, terming each "a disaster in itself." The effects cited were the transformation of Menominee County into a "pocket of poverty" that required massive infusions of federal and state aid for survival; the forced sale of tribal assets through the Legend Lake project; and, the destruction of democracy for the Menominees through the mechanics of the termination plan.[11] Sylvia Wilber, MEI chairwoman, urged immediate restoration. She declared,

> Restoration of the Menominee Tribe is the only salvation for Menominee Enterprises and the Menominee people. With Menominee lands safely back in trust, the almost $500,000 yearly paid in property tax can be used to update our mill. Our children and their children can be assured of retaining our most important asset, our ancestral lands.[12]

Following the Keshena meetings, the hearings were continued in Washington, D.C., during the week of June 25–29, 1973. In his introduction before the full subcommittee on June 28, Chairman Lloyd Meeds asserted:

> Restoration will not only go a long way to solving the immediate problem, but will also rectify a past wrong. The lands, the resources, the culture and the entity of the Menominee Indian Tribe remain substantially intact, though severely threatened. Restoration is feasible and practical, and common decency and justice require it.[13]

Governor Patrick J. Lucey of Wisconsin addressed the June 28 session. He said that the state study had convinced him to support the Menominee request for restoration. He added,

> Restoration is not a magic word that will immediately solve all the problems of the Menominees. But it will make possible the solution to those problems. It will relieve the pressure to sell Menominee lands to non-Menominees. It will remove the crippling property tax burden on the financially weak MEI, and return jointly-owned

218

Menominee land to a federal trust. It will bring an infusion of new federal funds for schools, health care, roads and other important public services. It will assure the Menominees a real choice over their own destiny, rather than the illusory choice by an economic situation which offers them few real alternatives.[14]

The Wisconsin State Supreme Court, meanwhile, reversed the decision of Circuit Judge William J. Duffy concerning Legend Lake land sales. In a ruling issued during the June hearings on Menominee restoration in Washington, the court ordered that the N. E. Isaacson firm could reopen the sale of its remaining three hundred and seventy-six lots to the public. This ruling came as a severe blow to the DRUMS organization and to the Menominee Indian people. Mrs. Wilber charged that the decision once again proved that "the law is written to protect the interests of non-Indians, shows little concern for the rights of Indian people."[15]

While most Menominees endorsed the concept of the restoration of trust status, echoes of a new protest reached Menominee County in the summer of 1973. American Indian Movement leaders, Russell Means and Dennis Banks, objected to DRUMS' consent to permitting the Legend Lake lots sold by the Isaacson-Enterprises partnership to remain under white ownership. During the week of June 14, 1973, AIM announced that Menominee County should become the scene of the second Wounded Knee.[16] Such action would have been disastrous to the cause of restoration and Menominee harmony. The tribe had already paid too high a price for termination. Menominee leadership was determined that nothing should interfere with a speedy hearing and return of Menominee land to trust status before all would be lost.

Senate hearings on restoration began in September, 1973, before the Subcommittee on Indian Affairs, chaired by Senator James Abourezk of South Dakota. The case of Menominee termination was again reviewed, and spokesmen representing every vested interest in national, state, and Menominee affairs in the matter were heard. Significant in the hearing was the concern voiced by George Kenote that the pending restoration legislation, like termination before it, had not been fully explained to the Menominee people. He also questioned the future of privately owned property, vested stock, business rights within Menominee County, and the need to safeguard the Menominee forests on a continuing sustained-yield basis should restoration become a reality. At the hearing the Menominees presented letters of support from Indian tribes throughout the United States. Charles Trimble, executive director of the National Congress of American Indians, expressed the united Indian view, when he described the dedication of the 30th National Congress to the concept of "Restoration Now," not only for the Menominee tribe, but for the return to Indianness by all American Indian people.[17]

House bill 10717, originally sponsored by Congressman Harold V. Froelich and recommended by the House Subcommittee on Indian Affairs, passed the United States House of Representatives on October 16, 1973, by a vote of 404 to 3. On December 5, the Senate Interior Committee recommended a slightly amended bill. This measure was considered and passed the Senate on December 7. The House concurred with the Senate amendments, and the bill went to the President. Describing the event as "an important turning point in the history of the American Indian people," President Nixon privately signed the Menominee Restoration Act into law on December 22, 1973.[18] Thus, the policy of wrong, the policy of forcibly terminating Indian tribal status was clearly reversed.

Public Law 93–197, the Menominee Restoration Act, made provision for the return of the Menominee Indians to full tribal status and the return of tribal assets to trust status. Prominent in the new legislation was the call for the opening of the tribal roll, closed since 1954, and the writing of a new constitution. The problems contingent upon the return of the Menominees to full tribal status were delegated to an elected nine-member Menominee Restoration Committee for solution, and a one-year time limit was imposed by Congress for implementation

220

of a restoration plan. Central problems to be resolved included the transfer of Menominee Enterprises, Incorporated, assets to federal protection, the tax-base and property rights of non-Menominees on the reservation, future local government, and the completion of a tribal roll.[19]

The historic significance of Public Law 93–197 and Menominee restoration was eclipsed by the wasted thirty-four-day occupation of the abandoned Alexian Brothers' Novitiate at Gresham, Wisconsin. The takeover on January 1, 1975, was instigated by young members of the Menominee Warrior Society, who had lost a bid for seats on the Menominee Common Stock and Voting Trust in the December election. This group also opposed the transfer of Menominee land and assets to federal trust status.[20]

On April 23, 1975, the Menominee reservation in an unprecedented action was restored. The ceremony in Washington, D.C., was presided over by Secretary of Interior Rogers C. B. Morton.[21] The Menominee Restoration Committee was given the responsibility of administering Menominee affairs until the transfer plans and new constitution were put into effect.

The tribal roll, closed since June 17, 1954, was reopened on May 16, 1975. Qualifications for enrollment were one-quarter Menominee Indian blood and a blood relationship with someone on the 1954 roll or any other official Menominee tribal roll. All Menominees enrolled in the initial enrollment period before midnight, August 13, 1975, qualified to participate in restoration elections and in the vote on the new constitution. During that time period 2,342 applicants were approved by the enrollment committee, four hundred and seventeen were denied acceptance, and a small number of these appealed their petition for membership.[22]

Restoration repealed Public Law 280 for the Menominees and assured the tribe that legal jurisdiction would be returned to them as soon as they were ready to accept the responsibility. On November 17, 1975, the federal government authorized the Menominees to establish a tribal police force, adopt a tribal law and order code, and undertake correctional functions. The State of Wisconsin on March 1, 1976, retroceded their jurisdictional powers over the Menominees, and the tribe was authorized to establish a court of Indian offenses.[23] Control of hunting and fishing rights was restored to the Menominees by the Wisconsin Supreme Court on May 6, 1975. In the case of *Van Camp* v. *MEI* the court ruled against Legend Lake property owners and other non-Menominees hunting and fishing on Menominee lands and in Menominee waters.[24]

The motto of the restoration committee throughout the transfer period was "Federal Protection, not Domination." The federal paternalism that many feared as a result of restoration has not materialized. The Menominees willingly accepted the responsibility that had been theirs since 1961 and turned it to their advantage. The constitution voted and accepted by the tribe in November, 1976, made provision for the future election of a nine-member council to govern and administer all reservation programs. Meanwhile, a restoration committee undertook to direct the council elections and give advice in tribal management. In the matter of restoration the Bureau of Indian Affairs permitted the Menominees to take full advantage of the principle of self-determination. Vital to the success of the whole endeavor and the future security of the Menominees was the receipt of an Economic Development Administration grant of six million dollars with which to renovate the Menominee lumber mill. New equipment was purchased and enlargement was immediately undertaken. By 1978 new, modern Menominee milling operations were in full production.

The reversal of termination won by the united effort of the Menominee Indian tribe stands as a hallmark in United States Indian legislation. Rogers Morton hailed the Restoration Act as a "milestone in Indian efforts to achieve social and economic equality." The secretary also admitted that the termination policy was a mistake and restoration had corrected the error.[25] The real credit for what has happened belongs to the Menominee Indians. Like their ancestors before them, the Menominee people did not yield to outside pressures, but worked together to preserve their land and their business. Throughout Menominee history there have been repeated threats to the very survival of the tribe. It is a credit to the heart and spirit of the Menominee people that each such threat has been diverted to the tribe's eventual advantage. The "We Can Make It" signs that marked the entries into Menominee County can be replaced by signs that read: "We Have Made It!"

Now that the Menominee reservation has been restored, perhaps the sacred drum of the Menominees will again be heard by the people, and the Menominee Indians, having experienced the bitterness and disappointments of leadership struggles and economic desperation, can return to a happy and productive life in the scenic splendor of their lakes and forests.

Notes

CHAPTER I

1. Walter J. Hoffman, *The Menomini Indians*, United States Bureau of American Ethnology (hereafter cited as BAE), *Fourteenth Annual Report*, 39-43. A version of the origin myth appears in Alanson Skinner, *Material Culture of the Menomini*, 46-47.

2. Robert Hruska, "The Riverside Site: A Late Archaic Manifestation in Michigan," *Wis. Arch.*, n.s., Vol. XLVIII, No. 3 (September, 1957), 145-257.

3. S. A. Barrett and Alanson Skinner, "Certain Mounds and Village Sites of Shawano and Oconto Counties, Wisconsin," *Bulletin* of the Public Museum of Milwaukee, Vol. X, No. 5 (March 4, 1932), 401-522; Chandler W. Rowe, *The Effigy Mound Culture of Wisconsin*, No. 3, Milwaukee Public Museum Publications in Anthropology (1970).

4. Skinner, *Material Culture of the Menomini*, 379-81.

5. Huron H. Smith, "Ethnobotany of the Menomini Indians," *Bulletin* of the Public Museum of Milwaukee, Vol. IV, No. 1 (1923), 14-20; Phebe Jewell Nichols, "Weavers of Grass: Indian Women of the Woodlands," *Wis. Mag. of History*, Vol. XXXVI, No. 2 (Winter, 1952-53), 130-33.

6. Many legends exist about this interesting Algonquian hero. Hoffman, *The Menomini Indians*, 66-209, provides one of the most complete collections of Menominee myths. He cites the White Rabbit

origin of Mä'näbus. Alanson Skinner, *Medicine Ceremony of the Menomini, Iowa, and Wahpeton Dakota, with Notes on the Ceremony Among the Ponca, Bungi, Ojibwa, and Potawatomi*, Museum of the Am. Indian (1920), 15-189, identifies Mä'näbus as being Light or Great Dawn. Leonard Bloomfield, *Menomini Texts*, Vol. XII, Am. Ethno. Soc. (1932), tells the tales and has the accompanying Menominee texts.

7. Reuben Gold Thwaites, ed., *Jesuit Relations and Allied Documents*, LIV (1669-71), 201.

8. Skinner, *Material Culture of the Menomini*, 332-34.

9. Albert Ernest Jenks, "Wild Rice Gatherers of the Upper Lakes: A Study in American Primitive Economics," BAE *Nineteenth Annual Report*, Pt. 2, 1897-98, 1013-1137; H. Clyde Wilson, "A New Interpretation of the Wild Rice District of Wisconsin," *Am. Anthro.*, Vol. LVIII, No. 6 (December, 1956), challenges Jenks's widespread use of rice by so many tribes, but the Menominee position remains secure.

10. Thwaites, *Jesuit Relations*, LIX (1673-77), 93-95.

11. Bacqueville de la Potherie, *Histoire de l'Amérique Septentrionale* (1722), published in *Wis. Hist. Coll.*, Vol. XVI, "The French Regime in Wisconsin," Pt. 1, 8–9.

12. Felix Keesing, *The Menomini Indians of Wisconsin: A Study of Three Centuries of Cultural Contact and Change*, Memoirs of the Am. Phil. Soc., X (1939), 29-30, challenges the antiquity of birch bark among the Menominees. The abundance of birch trees in the original habitat negates Keesing's analysis.

13. Pierre Margry, *Découvertes et établissements des Français dans l'ouest et dans le sud de l'Amérique*, Pt. 1, "Voyages des Français sur les grands lacs et découverte de l'Ohio et du Mississippi, 1614-84," 118-19.

14. *Ibid.*, 20.

15. Thwaites, *Jesuit Relations*, XLV (1659-60), 219.

16. Frank Hamilton Cushing, "Primitive Copper Working: An Experimental Study," *Am. Anthro.*, VII (January, 1894), 93-117.

17. Hruska, "The Riverside Site," 239-45.

18. Skinner, *Material Culture of the Menomini*, 282-83.

19. Hoffman, *The Menomini Indians*, 206. Bloomfield, *Menomini Texts*, has two versions of the legend, 252-65.

CHAPTER II

1. C. W. Butterfield, *History of the Discovery of the Northwest by Jean Nicolet in 1634 with a Sketch of His Life*, 57.

2. Pierre Radisson, "The Fourth Voyage," *Wis. Hist. Coll.*, XI, 78.

3. Emma Helen Blair, trans. and ed., *The Indian Tribes of the Upper Mississippi Valley and Region of the Great Lakes*, Vol. 1, Pt. 2, 310-13.

4. *Ibid.*, 312-13.

5. Margry, *Découvertes et établissements des Français*, I, 96-99. Also printed in *Wis. Hist. Coll.*, XI, 26, and *Documents Relative to the Colonial History of the State of New York*, IX, 803. Hereafter cited as *New York Colonial Documents*.

6. John Gilmary Shea, *Discovery and Exploration of the Mississippi Valley with Original Narratives of Marquette, Allouez, Membré, Hennepin and Anatase Douay*, xxii.

7. Joseph S. La Boule, "Claude Jean Allouez: The Apostle of the Ottawas," *Parkman Club Publications*, No. 17; John Gilmary Shea, *History of the Catholic Missions among the Indian Tribes of the United States, 1529-1854*, 348-73; and, Sister M. Rosaria Manthey, O.S.F., "Missionary Activity Among the Menominee, 1846-84." M.A. thesis, 1955.

8. Thwaites, *Jesuit Relations*, LIV, 205.

9. *Ibid.*, 219 and 227.

10. *Ibid.*, 231 and 235.

11. Shea, *History of Catholic Missions*, 348-73; Thwaites, *Jesuit Relations*, LXII, 203-205.

12. Thwaites, *Jesuit Relations*, LVI, 133.

13. *Ibid.*, LVII, 287.

14. *Ibid.*, Letter from Father André, LVIII, 273-75.

15. *Ibid.*, "Marquette's First Voyage and Journal," LIX, 93-97.

16. *Ibid.*, LVII, 273-303.

17. Margry, *Découvertes et établissements des Français*, II, 310.

18. Duluth to de la Barre, Michilimackinac, April 12, 1684, *Wis. Hist. Coll.*, XVI, 14-24.

19. *New York Colonial Documents*, III, 436-37.

20. M. de Denonville to M. de Seignelay, Ville Marie, Aug. 25, 1687, *ibid.*, IX, 336-44; Rev. P. F. X. Charlevoix, S. J., *History and General Description of New France*, trans. by John Gilmary Shea, III, 279-89.

21. Margry, *Découvertes et établissements des Français*, "Prise de Possession par Nicolas Perrot," V, 33-34.

22. *New York Colonial Documents*, IX, 619-26.

23. M. de Pontchartrain to Count Frontenac, April 28, 1697, *ibid.*, 805-808.

24. Ratification of the peace with the Indians, August 1761, *ibid.*, 722-25; and, Charlevoix, *History of New France*, V, 141-54.

25. Gov. de Vaudreuil to the Council of Marine, Oct. 14, 1716, *Wis. Hist. Coll.*, XVI, 341–44.

26. Margry, *Découvertes et établissements des Français*, V, 121.

27. Gov. de Vaudreuil to the Minister, Oct. 11, 1723, *Wis. Hist. Coll.*, XVI, 437.

28. Charlevoix visits Wisconsin, *ibid.*, 411.

29. Du Tisné to de Vaudreuil, Jan. 14, 1725, *ibid.*, 450-51.

30. Memoir of the King to Gov. de Beauharnois, May 14, 1728, *New York Colonial Documents*, IX, 1002–1006.

31. Rev. Emanuel Crespel, "DeLignery's Expedition against the Foxes," *Wis. Hist. Coll.*, XVII, 47-53.

32. Messrs. de Beauharnois and d'Argemait to the French Minister of War, Sept. 1, 1728, *ibid.*, V, 92-95.

33. Marin to de Beauharnois, May 11, 1730, *ibid.*, XVII, 88-100.

34. *Ibid.*

35. Gilles Hacquart, Intendant of New France to the French Minister of War, January 15, 1731, *ibid.*, XVII, 129-30.

36. Louis Henri Deschamps, Sieur de Boishebert to Beauharnois, Feb. 28, 1732, *ibid.*, 148-52.

37. Letters of de Beauharnois to the French Minister, 1733–35, *Wis. Hist. Coll.*, XVII, 130–219.

38. Census of the Indian Tribes, Oct. 12, 1736, *New York Colonial Documents*, IX, 1052-58; *Wis. Hist. Coll.*, XVII, 274-75.

39. De Beauharnois to the French Minister, Oct. 16, 1737, *Wis. Hist. Coll.*, XVII, 274–75.

40. Speeches to Marquis de Beauharnois, July 18, 24, and 25, 1742, *ibid.*, 396-402.

41. *Ibid.*, 451-55.

42. "Partnership to Exploit LaBaye," *Wis. Hist. Coll.*, XVIII, 9-10.

43. Operation of the French in New England and New York, 1745, 1746, *New York Colonial Documents*, X, 34.

44. M. de Beaucourt and Michel to de Beauharnois, Aug. 20, 1746, *ibid.*, X, 122.

45. La Jonquiere to the French Minister, Sept. 16, 1751, *Wis. Hist. Coll.*, XVIII, 76-80.

46. Richard McCarty to Marquis de Vaudreuil, Sept. 2, 1752, Menominee Indians, Archives of the Great Lakes–Ohio Valley Ethnohistory Research Project, Indiana University. Original MS. in Loudon Collection, Pease and Jeninson, French Series, III, pp. 654+, Huntington Library.

47. Report from Fort Duquesne, 1756, M. Dumas, Commandant, *Wis. Hist. Coll.*, XVIII, 163; Joseph Tasse, "Memoir of Charles Langlade, *ibid.*, VII, 130–33.

48. Louis Antoine de Bougainville, *The American Journal of; Adventure in the Wilderness*, trans. and ed. by Edward P. Hamilton, 6 and 8.

49. *Ibid.*, 8-9.

50. Report by Adjutant Malartic, *New York Colonial Documents*, X, 840.

51. Montcalm's Journal, from Chevalier de Lévi, MSS, *Wis. Hist. Coll.*, XVIII, 204.

52. Bougainville, *Adventure in the Wilderness*, 145.

53. *Ibid.*

54. Journal of the Expedition against Fort William Henry, July 12 to Aug. 16, 1757, from the Département de la Guerre, *New York Colonial Documents*, X, 598-616.

55. Thwaites, *Jesuit Relations*, VI, 297.

CHAPTER III

1. Lt. James Gorrell's Journal, *Wis. Hist. Coll.*, I, 25-26.

2. *Ibid.*, 33 and 38; Lt. Hutchin's Journal, April 14, 1762, to Sept. 24, 1762, in the Papers of Col. Henry Bouquet, in Menominee, 1750-77, Great Lakes-Ohio Valley Ethnohistory Archives, Indiana University.

3. Louis B. Porlier, "Capture of Mackinaw, 1763: A Menominee Tradition," *Wis. Hist. Coll.*, VIII, 228-30; Howard H. Peckham, *Pontiac and the Indian Uprising*, 109-10.

4. Alexander Henry, *Travels and Adventures in Canada and Indian Territory between 1760 and 1776*, 77-91; Raymond McCoy, *The Massacre of Old Fort Mackinac (Michilimackinac)*, 108-65; Francis Parkman, *The Conspiracy of Pontiac*, 269-70.

5. Thomas Gage to Sir William Johnson, Montreal, Aug. 12, 1763, *The Papers of Sir William Johnson*, X, 787-88.

6. A meeting with the Menominees, Niagara, July 17, 1764, *ibid.*, IV, 487-89.

7. Capt. William Howard to Sir William Johnson, Michilimackinac, June 24, 1765, *ibid.*, XIV, 808-809.

8. Jonathan Carver, *Three Years' Travels Through the Interior Parts of North America for More than Five Thousand Miles*, 9-11.

9. Joseph Tasse, ed., "Memoir of Charles Langlade," *Wis. Hist. Coll.*, VII, 123-87; A. Grignon, "Seventy-two Years Recollection of Wisconsin," *ibid.*, III, 224.

10. "The Narrative of Peter Pond," in *Five Fur Traders of the*

Northwest, ed. by Charles M. Gates, 33-34.

11. Maj. A. S. de Peyster to Capt. Langlade, Michilimackinac, April 18, 1777, *Wis. Hist. Coll.,* XVIII, 220-21.

12. Maj. de Peyster to Sir Guy Carleton, Michilimackinac, June 4, 1777, *ibid.,* VII, 405-407.

13. De Peyster to Langlade and Gautier, Oct. 26, 1778, *ibid.,* XVIII, 371-72.

14. De Peyster's speech to the western Indians, July 4, 1779, *ibid.,* 377-90.

15. Sinclair to Haldimand, Michilimackinac, Feb. 17, 1780, and May 29, 1780, *ibid.,* XI, 147-48 and 151-53.

16. John Long, *Voyages of an Indian Interpreter and Trader,* 15.

17. De Peyster to Haldimand, Michilimackinac, June, 1780, *Wis. Hist. Coll.,* XII, 51.

18. Grignon's "Recollections," *ibid.,* III, 256-59 and 265. Local writers persist in reporting a tradition that says "the first white man on the Menominee was a Negro," who at an unknown date was killed at Peshtigo, Wisconsin, at the site of "Nigger Hill."

19. McCoy, *Massacre of Old Fort Mackinac,* 54.

20. Donald Jackson, ed., *The Journals of Zebulon Montgomery Pike,* I, 102.

21. *Ibid.,* 107-108.

22. *Ibid.,* 21-22.

23. Charles Reaume to Capt. Dunham, Green Bay, June 4, 1807, N. A., RG 107, D 163 (3), Sec. of War, Letters Rec'd., Menominee, 1800-12, Great Lakes-Ohio Valley Ethnohistory Archives, Indiana University.

24. James W. Biddle, "Recollections of Green Bay in 1816-17," *Wis. Hist. Coll.,* I, 52.

25. Capt. J. B. Glegg to Col. Edward Baynes, York, Nov. 11, 1812, William Wood, ed., *Select British Documents of the Canadian War of 1812,* I, 419-22.

26. N. Boileau to Interpreter Joseph Roe, Dec. 8, 1812, *Mich. Pioneer and Hist. Coll.,* XV, 196-97.

27. Gov. Ninian Edwards to Sec. of War William Eustis, June 29, 1812, History of Illinois, 1778 to 1830, 330, in Menominee, 1800-12, Great Lakes-Ohio Valley Ethnohistory Archives, Indiana University.

28. M. Irvin, U. S. Factor, to William Eustis, Sec. of War, Detroit, Aug. 6, 1812, N. A., RG 107, I 266 (6), Letters Rec'd, in *ibid.*

29. Thomas Forsyth to Gen. Gibson at Vincennes, July 26, 1812, *ibid.*

30. Joseph Roe to Nicolas Boilvin, Prairie du Chien, March 12, 1813, *ibid.*

31. Grignon's "Recollections," *Wis. Hist. Coll.*, III, 269–70; McAfee, *History of the Late War in the Western Country,* 317–30.

32. Dickson to Lt. John Lawe, Dec. 25, 1813, Feb. 4, 6, and 27, 1814, *Wis. Hist. Coll.*, X, 105, 112, and XI, 282, 289, 292, 299, and 300.

33. Dickson to Lt. Lawe, Feb. 14, 1814, *ibid.*, XI, 293–94.

34. Brymner, "Capture of Fort McKay," *ibid.*, 256–63.

35. Lt. Col. George Croghan to the Sec. of War, J. Armstrong, Aug. 9, 1814, *Niles Weekly Reg.*, Sept. 10, 1814, p. 5; McAfee, *History of the Late War in the Western Country,* 426–37.

CHAPTER IV

1. William Clark, N. Edwards, A. Chouteau to William Crawford, Oct. 18, 1815, *Am. State Papers, Indian Affairs,* II, 10.

2. William H. Puthuff to Lewis Cass, Aug. 31, 1815, Records of the Mich. Supt. of Indian Affairs, Letters Rec'd and Sent, 1814-18, N. A., Microcopy 1: Roll 2, West. Hist. Coll., University of Oklahoma. Hereafter cited as Records of the Mich. Supt.

3. John O'Fallon to Gen. Duncan McArthur, Aug. 18, 1816, *ibid.*

4. Col. John Bowyer to Cass, Oct. 1, 1816, *ibid.*

5. Cass to the Indian Office, Sept. 3, 1814, *ibid.*

6. James Mason to Cass, Supt. of Indian Trade Papers, Letters Sent, Vol. C, N. A., M 16: Roll 3, 292–93.

7. Bowyer to Cass, July 22, 1817, Records of the Mich. Supt., N. A., M 1: Roll 3, Pt. 2, 147–49.

8. Irwin to Bowyer, July 24, 1817, *ibid.*, 165–67.

9. Cass to Maj. Puthuff, *ibid.*, M 1: Roll 4.

10. Treaty with the Menominee Indians at St. Louis, March 30, 1817, original handwritten treaty #86 in Ratified Indian Treaties, 1722-1869, N. A., M 668: No. 4, Frames 0311-15. Ratified Dec. 26, 1817, Frames 0316-17.

11. Bowyer to Cass, July 22, 1817, *Wis. Hist. Coll.*, XIX, 466–67.

12. Jedidiah Morse, *Rept. of the Sec. of War of the U.S. on Indian Affairs,* Appendix, 117.

13. Cass to David Ogden, June 21 and Oct., 1818, Records of the Mich. Supt., N. A., M 1: Roll 4, Pt. 3, 237.

14. Treaty Journal, Aug. 11, 1827, Menominee, 1823-30, Great Lakes-Ohio Valley Ethnohistory Archives, Indiana University.

15. S. C. Stambaugh to Pres. Andrew Jackson, Sept. 8, 1830, Green Bay Agency Papers, 1824–32, N. A., M 234; Roll 315, Frames 302–305.

16. Treaty Journal, Ratified Treaties, 1827-32, RG 75, Records of the BIA, N. A., M T494: Roll 2, Frames 1-12, in the West. Hist. Coll., University of Oklahoma.

17. Henry B. Brevoort and James Doty to Pres. John Q. Adams, June 16, 1824, Records of the Mich. Supt., N. A., M 234: Roll 419, Frames 75-76.

18. Treaty at Prairie du Chien, Treaty No. 139, Ratified Indian Treaties, N. A., M 668: Roll 5, Frames 403-88, in West. Hist. Coll., University of Oklahoma.

19. Thomas L. McKenney to Lane Barbour, Sec. of War, Office of Indian Affairs, Green Bay Agency, 1824-27, N. A., M 234: Roll 315, Frame 530.

20. Cass to Pres. John Q. Adams, Jan., 1828, *ibid.*, M 234: Roll 420, Frame 532.

21. Treaty of Butte des Morts, Treaty No. 148, Ratified Indian Treaties, N. A., M 668; Roll 6, Frames 61-74; Doc. Relating to the Negotiations of Indian Treaties, 1801-69, Ratified Treaties, 1827-32, RG 75, Records of the BIA, M T494: Roll 2, Frames 1-48.

22. Keesing, *The Menomini Indians,* 103.

23. Paul Kane, *Wanderings of an Artist among the Indians of North America,* 23.

24. Grignon, "Recollections," *Wis. Hist. Coll.,* III, 285.

25. Nichols, *Oshkosh, the Brave,* 21.

26. Kane, *Wanderings of an Artist,* 22-23.

27. "Visit to the Menominees," *The Friend: A Religious and Literary Journal,* eleventh month 24, 1840, Vol. XXXIX, No. 4, p. 73.

28. H. Atkinson to Gaines, Sept. 28, 1827, Rept. of the Comm. of Indian Affairs, 1827, Doc. No. 2, Item No. 6, 155-56 and 142-43.

29. Winnebago War, 1827, Smith's, Dixon's, and Johnston's Cos., Mich. Vol., Index, RG 94, N. A. Names copied as they appear on the individual service records:

Addick Once (Little Reindeer)
Ah-meek (The Beaver)
Ashekaw-bo-wee (One Who Changes Place Standing)
Aw-she-awta-shee (Receding Cloud)
Ayshe-ke-nett (The Remaining)
Aysh-kun (The Horn)
Cah-noh (Carron)
Cheche-gon-a'way (Man with a Straight Tail)
Che-kaw-me-ke-shin (One that Flies Low)
Eno-gu
Eyam-e-taw (The Raw Deer-skin)

Eyam-e-taw (son of Eyam-e-taw)
Kah-kahche-kayu
Ka-kon-won-equay (Long Hair)
Kaw-ge-ga be-tun (Man Always in the Same Place)
Kaw-keech-kee
Kaw-ke-gay-she
Kay-on-a-mick
Keche-na-gon (Great Sand)
Ke-che-pe-ko-wan
Ke-che-ton-o-gnet (Great Cloud)
Ke-ne-ki-yet (Vulture that __?_)
Kene-u-o-gee-maw (Vulture Chief)
Ken-e-woh' o-tay-neco-te (The One Brought by the
    Vulture)
Ke-she-ah-coo-tay (The Cloud that Sings)
Ke-sh-sheek
Ke-we-shay (The Vulture)
Ko-man-e-kin (Great Wave)
Ko-man-e-kin (Son of Shaw-won-ungg)
Kon-non-o-quet (The Cloud Cut)
Kos-kos-ky
Ma-goo-saw
Ma-ish-ke-wit (Son of Mo-wa-sha)
Ma-me-ah-to-maw (The Man Who Calls for Help)
Ma-me-nonce (The One Who Sails)
Ma-on-Say (War Chief)
Mayah-che-waw-bo mee (One Who Sees All)
May-aw-ko-may (Straight Nose)
May-ish-ke-wit (Son of Wah-Cheshe)
Me-ah-ge-shick (One Standing in the Sky)
Menom-no-gnet (Beautiful Cloud)
Me-she-took (The Collector)
Mi-ah-go-o
Milch-oge-maw (The Great Chief)
Mis-quan-wack (Red Cedar)
Mon-e-do-maig (Fish Devil)
Muck-waw (The Bear)
Much-way (The Wolf)
Na-bwoh-cos-pay (Foolish Woman)
Naw-naw che-ke' sheen
Nay-gooth
Ne-geek (The Otter)

Ne-gon-o-quom (Thunder Going Forward)
Ne-maw che-u (Left Handed)
Oge-amy-shay (Little Chief, Son of Cotton)
Oge-maw-mo-ke′u (Chief Rising from the Earth)
Oge-maw-shaw (Little Chief, Son of Mas-caw)
Oge-maw-shay (Little Chief)
O Meech (Juice of the Pipe)
O me-guon (The Warrior)
O me-g-won (The Feather, Son of Oshaw-wo-nim)
Onaw-congg (The Stars)
Onaw-ge-say
Onaw-kay-u (Raw Hide)
Ope-she-mean (Small Acorn)
Osa-ue-ha′pit (The One that is in His Nest)
Oshaw-won-e-gaw bow-ee (Man Standing in the South)
Oshaw-won-no guet (Yellow Cloud)
Oshe-nee-nee (Well Made Man)
Owon-ish-kame (Foggy Man)
Pa-maw-bo-mee (One Who Visits All)
Pa-maw-sa-gay (Shadow of the Moon)
Peco-che-nee-nee (Man of the Woods)
Pe-de-dah (One Who Comes Making a Noise)
Pe-mo-net-tah
Pe-na-quon (Falling Feathers)
Pe-naw-kaw (One Taking Something From Above)
Pe-peek (Pigeon Hawk)
Pe-peek-we-saule (Little Pigeon Hawk)
Pe-pone-na-na′u (Winter Bird)
Pe-she-pe-kaw
Pe-tah-ton-no-quet a-peet (One Between Two Clouds)
Po-we-kon-nay (One Who Changes His Feathers)
Sa-ne-bon (The Ribbon, Son of Won-nesh-cum)
Saw-gaw-no-quet (End of the Clouds)
Say-ge-toag (One that Frightens)
Say-kaw-bo-may
Sha-kon-aw-go (Future)
Shal-wow-tock
Shaw-che-skaw
Shaw-win-o-ko-nay-bee
She-bah-naw-go (The Papage)
Sho-bon-yay (Chevalier)
Sho-min (The Raisin)
Sin-e-bon (The Ribbon, Son of Mas-ke-wit)

234

*Skash-O (1st Chief, The Fingernail, O-skash)
Tah-wos-ah'bon (Daybreak)
Teme-naw-o'way
Te-pay-cut-toh (The Belt)
Tuck-waw-gon-nay (Autumn Duck)
Wa-tos-say (The Warrior)
Waub-ah-coo-sa'u (White Tree)·
Waub-au-nim (Potawatomie, The White Dog)
Waub-au-nim
Waub-e-ne-mee (White Thunder)
Waub-un-uck (White Star)
Waw-boose (The Rabbit)
Waw-bo-saw'ke (White Crawfish)
Waw-keech
Waw-kon (Winnebago, Rattle Snake)
Waw-poose (The Hare)
Way-baw-tuck
Way-e-no-ash
Way-she-one (Pointed Face)
Way-she-te-nee (Handsome Shoulder)
We-ak-we-nay-o-o (Whirlwind)
We-aw-wit-ne-oo (One That is Named)
We-ko-nosh-o-gee-maw (Chief of Long Continuance)
We-no-shah-gaw
We-shoo-gaw
Woh-kaw-che'won (Crooked Steam)
Louis Griffon 1st Lt.
Lewis Rause 1st Lt.

30. Victor O'Daniel, *The Right Rev. Edward D. Fenwick, O. F.,* 354-55; Manthey, "Missionary Activity among the Menominee, 1846-1884," 12-13.

31. "Documents Relating to the Catholic Church in Green Bay," *Wis. Hist. Coll.,* XIV, 176-84.

32. U.S. Circuit Court Record, *Green Bay Hist. Bull.* (n.d.), Vol. III, No. 2, 1-10; Tenney, "A Case of Lex Talionis," Tenney Papers, Wis. Hist. Soc. The Tenney account makes Oke-wah a Pawnee Indian.

33. S. C. Stambaugh to Sec. of War, Sept. 8, 1830, Green Bay Agency, 1824-32, N. A., M 234: Roll 315, Frames 302-19.

34. Capt. William Powell's "Statement," in Additions and Corrections, *Wis. Hist. Coll.,* X, 497-98.

35. John V. Smith, "Eleazar Williams and the Lost Prince," *ibid.,* VI, 308 and 333.

36. Stambaugh Treaty, Treaty No. 161, Ratified Indian Treaties,

Jan. 14, 1826-Sept. 21, 1832, N. A., M 668: Roll 6, Frames 286-350.

37. Jos. M. Street to Clark, July 31, Aug. 1 and 9, Oct. 24, Nov. 15, 1831, Clark Papers, VI, Menominee, 1831-32, Great Lakes-Ohio Valley Ethnohistory Archives, Indiana University; Elbert Herring, *Rept. of the Comm. of Indian Affairs,* Nov. 19, 1831, Doc. No. 2, 173-74 and 192-94.

38. T. P. Burnett to Clark, June 29, 1831, Clark Papers, VI, 422-24.

39. J. M. Street to Clark, March 2 and May 12, 1831, *ibid.,* 230-32, 250-53, 348-50, and August 1, 1831, 466.

40. Street to Clark, Nov. 15, 1831, *ibid.*

41. Journal of the Council by E. G. Mitchell, *Rept. of the Comm. of Indian Affairs,* 1831, 202-204.

42. Clark to E. Herring, April 6, 1832, Clark Papers, VI; Capt. Henry Smith, "Indian Campaign of 1832," *Wis. Hist. Coll.,* X, 182–83.

43. Felix St. Vrain to Clark, April 18, 1832, N. A., RG 107, Menominee, 1831–32, Great Lakes–Ohio Valley Ethnohistory Archives, Indiana University.

44. Black Hawk's War Roll, Henry S. Baird Papers, 1832-35, Wis. State Hist. Soc.; Stambaugh Battalion Index, Black Hawk War, RG 94, N. A.

45. Publius V. Lawson, *Story of Oshkosh, His Tribe and Fellow Chiefs.*

46. George Boyd to Gov. Porter, Aug. 12, 1832, Boyd Papers, *Wis. Hist. Coll.,* XII, 287-88.

47. Treaty of 1832, Preamble, Ratified Indian Treaties, 1722-1869, Jan. 24, 1826-Sept. 21, 1832, N. A., M 668: Roll 7, Treaty No. 179, Frames 141–60.

48. George Catlin, *Letters and Notes on the Manners, Customs, and Conditions of the North American Indians,* II, Letter No. 52, 147-48.

49. George Featherstonhaugh, *Canoe Voyage up the Minnay-Sotor,* II, 175-80.

50. Speeches of Oshkosh and Silver, Oct. 13, 1835, sent by George Boyd to Comm. Herring, Oct. 18, 1835, Green Bay Agency, Letters Rec'd by the Office of Indian Affairs, M 234: Roll 316, Frames 290-92.

51. Sec. of War to Gov. Dodge, July 7, 1836, Carter, *Territorial Papers, Wis. Terr.,* XXVII, 611-13; and, Gov. Dodge to the Acting Sec. of War, Aug. 12, 1836, 638–39.

52. Louise Phelps Kellogg, "The Menominee Treaty at the Cedars, 1836," *Wis. Academy of Sciences, Arts, and Letters,* XXVI, 127-35.

53. Documents Relating to the Negotiations of Indian Treaties, Treaty No. 209, N. A., M T494: Roll 3, Frame 443.

54. Treaty of the Cedars, Ratified Indian Treaties, Treaty No. 209, Sept. 3, 1836, N. A., M 668: Roll 8, Frames 191-234.

CHAPTER V

1. *Rept. of the Comm. of Indian Affairs,* 1839, Doc. No. 2, No. 45, 485.

2. Charges filed by Morgan L. Martin against George Boyd, Letters Rec'd by the Office of Indian Affairs, Green Bay Agency, 1840-43, N. A., M 234: Roll 318, Frames 262-65 and 308-309.

3. Boyd to Henry Dodge, May 21, 1839, Wis. Supt., 1836 10, N. A., M 234: Roll 948 (letters arranged chronologically in the M 234: Roll 900 series); correspondence from Boyd to Commissioner Crawford, Letters Rec'd by the Office of Indian Affairs, Green Bay Agency, N. A., M 234: Roll 318, Frames 58-60 and 77-84, and Roll 319, Frames 168-70.

4. Schoolcraft to Crawford, Dec. 24, 1840, *ibid.,* N. A., M 234: Roll 318, Frame 209.

5. Capt. Merrill to Gov. Dodge, Jan. 8, 1841, *ibid.,* N. A., M 234: Roll 948.

6. Oscar G. Schilke and Raphael E. Solomon, *America's Foreign Coins,* 188.

7. Dodge to Crawford, Feb. 12, 1841, Wis. Supt., 1841-48, N. A., M 234: Roll 949.

8. Talk with Oshkosh and Menominee Chiefs, Dodge to Crawford, Feb. 25, 1841, Letters Rec'd by the Office of Indian Affairs, Green Bay Agency, 1840-43, N. A., M 234: Roll 318, Frames 473-82.

9. War Dept.'s Summation of the Boyd Charges, March 2, 1841, *ibid.,* Frames 505-20.

10. Tribal Roll; George W. Lawe, Oct. 20, 1842, *ibid.,* Frames 750-69.

11. Petition of the Wis. Legislature, July 6, 1843, *ibid.,* Frames 855-56, and Dec., 1845, Green Bay Agency, 1844-47, M 234: Roll 319, Frame 235.

12. Arthur G. Ellis to Dodge, Annual Report, 1845, *ibid.,* M 234: Roll 319, Frame 347.

13. A. Ellis to Dodge, *Rept. of the Comm. of Indian Affairs,* 1846, Doc. No. 4, 255; Petition of Menominee Chiefs, Green Bay Agency, Dec. 3, 1845, N. A., M 234: Roll 319, Frames 526-30.

14. *Ibid.,* Feb. 19, 1847, Frames 781-85.

15. *Ibid.,* Nov. 14, 1846, Wis. Supt., 1841–48, N. A., M 234: Roll 949.

16. W. Medill to Dodge, March 30, 1848, Letters Rec'd by the Office of Indian Affairs, Green Bay Agency, 1844-47, N. A., M 234: Roll 320, Frame 172.

17. Treaty of 1848, Treaty No. 253, Oct. 18, 1848, William Medill, commissioner, Ratified Indian Treaties, N. A., M 668: Roll 10, Frames 1-14.

18. Indian Office Special Files, No. 226, Report of Thomas Wistar, Jr., to the Sec. of Interior Thomas Ewing, Sept. 13, 1849. Photostatic copy at the Wis. State Hist. Soc.

19. "Visit to the Menominees," objections offered by La Motte, *The Friend,* eleventh month 10, 1849, Vol. XXIII, No. 8, 56.

20. *Ibid.,* eleventh month 24, 1849, Vo. XXIII, No. 10, 73.

21. *Ibid.,* eleventh month 10, 1849, No. 8, 57. *The Friend* description of Oshkosh appears in Chapter IV, 104.

22. *Ibid.,* twelfth month 22, 1849, No. 14, 106.

23. *Ibid.,* third month 10, 1850, No. 26, 201.

24. *Ibid.,* third month 23, 1850, No. 27, 209-11, and third month 30, 1850, 217-18.

25. Ebenezar Childs to William Bruce, Aug. 1, 1849, Letters Rec'd by the Office of Indian Affairs, Green Bay Agency, 1848-50, N. A., M 234: Roll 320, Frames 246-48. There is an account of the Wistar-Menominee episode in James F. Dorrance, Jr., "The Menominee Indians, 1848-58: The Making of the Menominee Reservation."

26. Bruce to Orlando Brown, Aug. 6, 1849, Letters Rec'd by the Office of Indian Affairs, Green Bay Agency, 1848-50, N. A., M 234: Roll 320, Frames 253-66.

27. *Ibid.,* Sept. 24, 1849, Frames 344-45.

28. E. S. Miner, "Coroner's Report," Jan. 30, 1850, *ibid.,* Frames 574-78.

29. Unidentified newspaper article, "Trouble with the Winnebagoes — All Returning to Wisconsin," n.d., *ibid.,* Frame 588.

30. Report of William Bruce on the Exploration of the Crow Wing, Aug. 19, 1850, *ibid.,* Frames 757-69.

31. Ebenezar Childs on the Exploration of the Crow Wing, Aug. 4, 1850, *ibid.,* Frames 773-77, William Powell's report, Frames 771-72, and the Journal of Talbot Prickett, Frames 800-806.

32. William Bruce to Bishop Henni, July 18, 1850, *ibid.,* 1851-52, M 234: Roll 321, Frame 119, Affidavits concerning Bonduel's removal, Frames 120-87, and Father Bonduel to Bruce, July 28, 1849, Frame 115.

33. C. Grignon to the Office of Indian Affairs, Sept. 18, 1850, *ibid.*, 1848-50, N. A., M 234: Roll 320, Frames 915-16.

34. Menominee Council, Sept. 7, 1855, *ibid.*, M 234: Roll 322, Frames 678-91.

35. Menominee Petition to the President, Sept. 4, 1850, *ibid.*, M 234: Roll 320, Frames 929-30 and 975-81; and *Proceedings of the Wis. Hist. Soc.*, 1912, 175.

36. James Duane Doty to Millard Fillmore, n.d., Letters Rec'd by the Office of Indian Affairs, Green Bay Agency, 1851-52, N. A., M 234: Roll 321, Frames 78-80.

37. Orlando Brown to Doty, Jan. 22, 1850, *ibid.*, Frame 87.

38. Petitions to Pres. Fillmore, May 10, 1851, *ibid.*, Frames 268-71 and 272-74; two petitions, April 15, 1851, Frames 340-46.

39. Elias Murray to Luke Lea, Oct. 2, 1851, *ibid.*, Frames 405-406.

40. Court Commissioner for the Circuit Court for the County of Winnebago, March 27, 1852, *ibid.*, Frame 529; and William Converse Haygood, "Red Child, White Child: The Strange Disappearance of Caspar Partridge," *Wis. Mag. of History,* Vol. LVIII, No. 4 (Summer, 1975), 259-312.

41. Partridge Case, Testimony and Events, Letters Rec'd by the Office of Indian Affairs, Green Bay Agency, 1851-52, N. A., M 234: Roll 321, Frames 492-558.

42. Petition with four hundred signees, April 1, 1852, *ibid.*, Frames 629-30, others, Frames 631-36.

43. Menominee Chiefs to the President, Nov. 3, 1852, *ibid.*, Frames 595-96.

44. Menominee Chiefs to Elias Murray, Dec. 6, 1852, *ibid.*, 1853-55, N. A., M 234: Roll 322, Frame 186.

45. Resolution of the Wis. Leg., *ibid.*, Frame 171.

46. F. Huebschmann to George H. Manypenny, Dec. 31, 1853, *ibid.*, Frames 364-65.

47. Treaty with the Menominees, 1854, Treaty No. 269, Ratified Indian Treaties, N. A., M 668: Roll 10, Frames 353-68.

48. Keesing, *The Menomini Indians,* 150-52.

49. Menominee Council, Sept. 7, 1855, Letters Rec'd by the Office of Indian Affairs, Green Bay Agency, 1853-55, N. A., M 234: Roll 322, Frames 678-91.

50. *Ibid.*, Frames 687-91.

51. F. Huebschmann to George Manypenny, Nov. 24, 1855, *ibid.*, Frames 709-48.

52. Treaty of 1856, Treaty No. 302, Ratified Indian Treaties, N. A., M 668: Roll 12, Frames 59-72.

53. Menominee Chiefs to F. Huebschmann, June 27, 1854, Letters Rec'd by the Office of Indian Affairs, 1853-55, N. A., M 234: Roll 322, Frames 421-22.

54. F. Huebschmann to George Manypenny, Oct. 27, 1854, *ibid.*, Frames 434-36.

55. A. D. Bonesteel to Charles E. Mix, Commissioner of Indian Affairs, Sept. 11, 1858, *ibid.*, M 234: Roll 323, Frames 599-600.

CHAPTER VI

1. Council of the Menominee Tribal Chiefs, Letters Rec'd by the Office of Indian Affairs, Green Bay Agency, 1856-60, N. A., M 234: Roll 323, Frames 615-17.

2. Augustus Bonesteel to Charles Mix, Aug. 2, 1860, *ibid.*, Frames 1063-75.

3. A. Bonesteel to J. W. Denver, Dec. 1, 1858, *ibid.*, Frame 635.

4. A. Bonesteel to Commissioner Greenwood, Oct. 25, 1860, *Rept. of the Comm. of Indian Affairs,* 1860, Green Bay Agency, 35-36, and Bonesteel to Greenwood, March 23, 1860, Letters Rec'd, Green Bay Agency, 1856-60, N. A., M 234: Roll 323, Frames 1035 and 1577.

5. Agency Report on Employees, 1862, Letters Rec'd by the Office of Indian Affairs, Green Bay Agency, 1861-64, N. A., M 234: Roll 324, Frames 512-13.

6. Moses M. Davis to W. P. Dole, Sept. 27, 1862, *Rept. of the Comm. of Indian Affairs,* 1862, Green Bay Agency, 328-39; M. M. Quaife, "The Panic of 1862 in Wisconsin," *Wis. Mag. of History,* IV, 166-95.

7. Menominee Chiefs to Moses Davis, Aug. 12, 1863, and Davis to W. Dole, Aug. 15, 1863, Letters Rec'd by the Office of Indian Affairs, Green Bay Agency, 1861-64, N. A., M 234: Roll 324, Frames 546-49, and *The War of the Rebellion,* Ser. 1, Vol. XXII, Pt. 2, 372-73.

8. *Ibid.*, and *Rept. of the Comm. of Indian Affairs,* 1865, 438.

9. The Service Record of each Civil War soldier in this chapter was read at the National Archives, Washington, D.C., Adjutant General's Office, Military Service Record, Civil War, Record Group 94.

10. Frederick L. Dyer, *A Compendium of the War of the Rebellion,* III, *Regimental Histories,* Wisconsin 17th Regiment.

11. Robert R. Jones, "Menominee Notes," MSS, BU., Wis. State Hist. Society.

12. Private Joseph Kah-ke-ma-hot, Co. F., 38th Wis. Infantry Regi-

ment, Adjutant General's Office, Military Service Record, Civil War, N. A., RG 94.

13. Peter T. Arstad, ed., "A Civil War Medical Examiner: The Report of Dr. Horace O. Crane," *Wis. Mag. of History,* Vol. XLVIII, No. 3 (Spring, 1965), 230.

14. *List of Pensioners on the Roll, January 1, 1883, Western States,* IV, 507.

15. Contract between R. A. Jones and Menominee Chiefs, Aug. 22, 1854, Letters Rec'd by the Office of Indian Affairs, Green Bay Agency, 1861-64, N. A., M 234: Roll 324, Frames 140-48, 169-70, and J. V. Suydam to F. Huebschmann, Feb. 18, 1854, *ibid.,* M 234: Roll 322, Frame 375.

16. M. M. Davis to D. N. Cooley, Sept. 25, 1865, *Rept. of the Comm. of Indian Affairs,* 1865, 439.

17. Menominee Petition to N. G. Taylor, July 15, 1868, *ibid.,* M 234: Roll 326, Frames 358-61, 724-25, and 730-37.

18. Richard P. Delaney, "The Menominee Forest to 1908," Menominee Indian Papers, Federal Record Center, Kansas City, Accession No. 62A400, Agency Box 33. Hereafter cited as FRC Kansas City.

19. Keshena Speech, "The Menominees," *Oshkosh City Times,* Feb. 23, 1870. Handwritten copy in the George Hyde Papers, Wis. State Hist. Society, MSS Ax.

20. Jones, "Menominee Notes," MSS, BU., Wis. State Hist. Society.

21. Morgan L. Martin to N. G. Taylor, Sept. 25, 1868, *Rept. of the Comm. of Indian Affairs,* 1868, 293.

22. Petition of the Menominee Indian Chiefs to Pres. Johnson, Keshena, Sept. 1, 1869, Letters Rec'd by the Office of Indian Affairs, Green Bay Agency, 1868-69, N. A., M 234: Roll 326, Frames 313-14.

23. Morgan L. Martin to E. S. Parker, Aug. 1, 1869, *Rept. of the Comm. of Indian Affairs,* 1869, 438.

24. Testimonial Statement of Charles Bagley and Daniel Crawford, June 7, 1870, Letters Rec'd by the Office of Indian Affairs, 1870-71, N. A., M 234: Roll 327, Frames 197-203.

25. Menominee Chiefs to Lt. J. A. Manley, Feb. 15, 1870, *ibid.,* Frames 591-92.

26. J. D. Cox to Commissioner Ely S. Parker, Aug. 19, 1870, *ibid.,* Frames 367–68.

27. C. Delano to the Commissioner of Indian Affairs, *ibid.,* Frames 952-53.

28. Thomas N. Chase to E. P. Smith, Sept. 30, 1873, *Rept. of the Comm. of Indian Affairs,* 1873, 178.

29. B. H. Bristow to C. Delano, Oct. 16, 1871, *ibid.,* Frames 898-99.

30. J. Murdock of the Keshena Improvement Co. to Thomas Chase, Oct. 18, 1873, Letters Rec'd by the Office of Indian Affairs, Green Bay Agency, 1873, N. A., M 234: Roll 329, Frames 30-31 and 42-43.

31. T. Chase to H. R. Clum, Nov. 10, 1873, *ibid.*, Frame 122.

32. T. Chase to E. P. Smith, April 10, 1874, *ibid.*, M 234: Roll 330, Frames 168, 212, and 123-28.

33. Menominee Petitions, April 5, 1874, *ibid.*, Frame 464, and Sept. 1, 1874, Frame 280.

34. Joseph C. Bridgeman, Aug. 20, 1877, *Rept. of the Comm. of Indian Affairs,* 1877, 203.

35. Manthey, "Missionary Activity Among the Menominee," 57. The original letter to the Catholic Chiefs, Feb. 6, 1872, was lost in the fire that destroyed the Archives of St. Michael's Mission, St. Michael Friary, 1955, Keshena, Wis.

36. George and Louise Spindler, *Dreamers without Power; The Menomini Indians,* 91-141.

37. D. P. Andrews, Aug. 13, 1883, *Rept. of the Comm. of Indian Affairs,* 1883, 157.

38. *Rept. of the Comm. of Indian Affairs,* 1890, 236.

39. T. Jennings to the Commissioner of Indian Affairs, Aug. 25, 1886, *ibid.,* 1888, 249.

40. E. Stephens to the Commissioner of Indian Affairs, *ibid.,* 1881, 177.

41. D. P. Andrews, Aug. 13, 1883, *ibid.,* 1883, 157.

42. Delaney, "The Menominee Forest," 4, FRC Kansas City.

43. *Ibid.,* 5.

44. T. J. Morgan to the Secretary of Interior, *Rept. of the Comm. of Indian Affairs,* 1889, 89.

45. E. Stephens to the Commissioner of Indian Affairs, *ibid.,* 1881, 177.

46. *United States Statutes-at-Large,* XXV (1889), 673.

47. *Ibid.,* XXVI, Public Law 153 (1890), 146, and "Menominee Logging," *Rept. of the Comm. of Indian Affairs,* 1891, 88-90.

48. Delaney, "The Menominee Forest," 5, and J. R. Kinney Report, June 30, 1934, FRC Kansas City.

CHAPTER VII

1. *Roster of Wisconsin Troops in the Spanish-American War,* Soldiers Rehabilitation Board, n.d.

2. U.S. Congress, "Sale of Certain Timber on the Menominee Reservation," House Doc., 287, 59 Cong., 1 sess., *Cong. Rec.*, XLVI, 1905; Nels O. Nicholson and Lloyd O. Grapp, "Preliminary Forest Management Plan for the Menominee Indian Reservation" (1930), Accession No. 62A400, Agency Box 12, FRC Kansas City.

3. *Ibid.*, and "The Menominee Forests to 1908" (typed MSS), Accession No. 62A400, Agency Box 33, FRC Kansas City.

4. U.S. Congress, House, "Cutting Timber on the Menominee Indian Reservation," March 16, 1907, *Cong. Rec.*, XLVIII, 3410-14; Public Law 74, Chap. iii, 60 Cong., 1 sess., *Statutes at Large*, Vol. XXXV, No. 51 (1908).

5. *Ibid.*

6. Robert M. La Follette, "Cutting Timber on Indian Reservations in Wisconsin," address to 60 Cong., 1 sess., Senate Report 110, Jan. 23, 1908.

7. "The Government in the Lumber Business," Dec. 9, 1908, 5-7, Accession No. 61A566, FRC Chicago.

8. Barrow, Wade, Guthrie and Co., "Report on Tribal Trust Fund," June 30, 1934 (typed MSS), Accession No. 66A837, FRC Chicago.

9. Report by Peter LaMotte on the Organization of the Government at Neopit, April 4, 1911 (typed MSS), Accession No. 61A566, FRC Chicago.

10. Supt. A. S. Nicholson to W. L. Fisher, June 6, 1911, Forestry Reports and Correspondence, 1906-14, Green Bay Agency, Accession No. 61A566, FRC Chicago.

11. E. E. Carter to William W. Morris, Nov. 18, 1909, *ibid.*

12. "The Government in the Lumber Business," Dec. 9, 1908, Accession No. 61A566, FRC Chicago.

13. Ogden Brooks, "Forest Fire at Neopit," *Shawano County Advocate*, Aug. 2, 1910, in Records of the U.S. Court of Claims, Selected Records of General Jurisdiction, Case File 44304, *Menominee Tribe of Indians* v. *The United States*, FRC Suitland, Maryland. Hereafter cited as WNRC.

14. Supt. A. S. Nicholson, "Annual Narrative Report," 1911 and 1915, Keshena, RG 75, N. A.

15. John Francis, Jr., to the Commissioner of Indian Affairs, Keshena Agency Papers, Accession No. 22295-1913-044, RG 75, N. A.

16. "National Memorial to North American Indian," *New York Times*, Feb. 22, 1913.

17. "Visiting Chiefs Go on Sightseeing Trip," *ibid.*, Feb. 24, 1913.

18. "The Inaugural Parade," *ibid.*, March 5, 1913.

19. Unidentified Indian to Judge Edward E. Ayer, Jan. 10, 1914,

Forestry Reports and Correspondence, 1906-14, Accession No. 61A566, FRC Chicago.

20. *Ibid.*; Menominee Indian Council Proceeding Minutes sent to the Commissioner of Indian Affairs, Jan. 15, 1915, Keshena, Accession No. 16691-1915-054, RG 75, N. A.

21. Supt. Edgar A. Allen, "Annual Narrative Report, 1920," *ibid.*

22. Supt. A. S. Nicholson, "Annual Narrative Report, 1917," *ibid.*

23. Raymond Weber, "Report of White Pine Blister Rust Control on the Menominee Reservation" (1947), Accession No. 69A672, Agency Box 8, Kansas City.

24. Raymond Caswell, "Blister Rust Control Report of the Menominee Indian Reservation, 1933," Annual Reports on Blister Rust Control, 1933–60, Accession No. 69A672, Agency Box 11, FRC Kansas City.

25. Supt. E. A. Allen To Rev. Philip Gordon, Jan. 14, 1924, Corr. to the Supt., G-L, 1921-24, Accession No. 61A565, FRC Chicago.

26. Samuel Blair, Dept. of Interior, to Charles H. Burke, June 10, 1925, Accession No. 42723-1925-054, RG 75, N. A.

27. Supt. William R. Beyer, "Annual Narrative Report, 1933," Keshena, RG 75, N. A.

28. Lewis Meriam, and others, *The Problem of Indian Administration,* Institute for Government Research, 1928.

29. Phebe Jewell Nichols, "Report on the Condition of the Menominees, 1928," in Menominee Tribal Minutes, Nov., 1928, Pt. 1, 87–98, Accession No. 57174–1928–054, Keshena, RG 75, N. A.

30. "Chief Says Tribe Is to Reorganize," *Leader-Advocate,* Shawano, Wis., Oct. 3, 1929, and "Offers Indians Land for Parks," *Milwaukee Journal,* Sept. 26, 1929.

31. *New York Times,* March 17, 1929.

32. Isaak Walton League, Antigo, Wis., to the Commissioner of Indian Affairs, Feb. 16, 1929; James T. Drought, Milwaukee Evergreen Club, to John C. Schafer, Jan. 3, 1929; John H. Burke to Supt. William Beyer, Nov. 23, 1928, Accession No. 8607-22-054, Keshena, RG 75, N. A.

33. Mary McGairs, Field Report, Jan. 17, 1931, Accession No. 13977-1931-054, *ibid.*

34. J. Henry Scattergood, "Memorandum after Visit to Menominee Indian Lumber Operations," Aug. 5–7, 1929, Central Corr. Files, 1907-39, Menominee, Accession No. 5900-1928-339, RG 75, N. A.

35. "Proud Menominee Indians Refuse Federal Road Aid," *New York Times,* July 31, 1933; "Self-Reliant Menominees," *The Literary Digest,* Aug. 26, 1933, p. 33.

36. Hughes Report, July 20, 1932, Menominee Reservation, Accession No. 62A400, Agency Box 10, FRC Kansas City; "Menominee Indian Mills Management," *Milwaukee Journal,* April 2, 1933.

37. Lee Muck, "Report upon the Statement of Hughes, Schurman, and Dwight to the Advisory Board of the Menominee Indians," Jan. 15, 1933, 63 pp., Accession No. 62A400, Agency Box 10, FRC Kansas City.

38. "Per Capita Payment to the Menominee Indians," *Statutes-at-Large,* XLVIII (1934), 964; Lee Winner and Walter J. Ridlington, "A Plan for Continuous Forest Control on the Menominee Indian Reservation," June, 1954 (typed MSS), Accession No. 69A672, Agency Box 11, FRC Kansas City.

39 "Menominee Tribal Claims," *Statutes-at-Large,* XLIX (1934), 1085; U.S. Congress, House Report No. 1412 on Public Law 413, 74 Cong., 1 sess., July 1, 1935.

40. "Rules and Regulations Governing the Transactions of Business and Election of Officers of the Menominee Indian Tribe," and "Constitution of the Menominee Indian Tribe," Central Classified Files, Accession No. 9646-A-1936-054, Keshena, RG 75, N. A.

41. Robert Marshall, "Indian Self-Government in Relation to the Management of the Menominee Indian Mills" (1935), U.S. Dept. of Forestry (typed MSS), Central Classified Files, Accession No. 00-1935-100, *ibid.*

42. Minutes of the Menominee General Council, Dec., 1934, Accession No. 13740-1934-054, *ibid.;* Act of June 15, 1934, *Statutes-at-Large,* XLVIII (1934), p. 965.

43. Dan J. Sully to James Frechette, Appleton, Wis., March 22, 1941, Accession No. 21684-1938-154, RG 75, N. A.

44. Minutes of the Menominee General Council, Dec., 1942, Pt. 13, Accession No. 9646-E-1936-054, *ibid.;* "Narrative Supplement to Annual Forestry Report," Menominee Indian Reservation (1943), Accession No. 69A672, FRC Kansas City.

45. "Indian Women Work for Victory," *Indians in the War,* 49; "Blister Rust Control Report of the Menominee Reservation" (1960), Annual Reports 1933-60, *ibid.*

46. Winner and Ridlington, "Plan for Continuous Forest Control" (1954), Accession No. 69A672, *ibid.*

47. *Indians in the War,* 8-41.

48. Swampland Case No. 44294, *U.S. Court of Claims Reports,* 95:232, decided Dec. 1, 1941, and June 5, 1944, *U.S. Court of Claims Reports,* 101:863.

49. *Ibid.*; "State Can Have $1,500,000 if 2 Sign Papers," *Capital Times,* Madison, Wis., April 26, 1945.

50. Minutes of the Menominee Advisory Council, Aug. 12 and Sept. 9, 1947, Menominee Agency, Accession No. 66A837, FRC Chicago.

51. Fred H. Daiker to James Arentson, Sept. 5, 1947, in Minutes of the Menominee Advisory Council, Feb. 24, 1948, *ibid.*

52. Minutes of Special Meeting of the Menominee Advisory Council, Keshena, Oct. 3, 1950, *ibid.*

53. Minutes of the Menominee Advisory Council, July 13, 1951, *ibid.*

54. Minutes of the Menominee Advisory Council, June 7, April 25, and Aug. 9, 1949, *ibid.*; Auditor Reports on the Menominee Garment Factory, Accession No. 569538, Agency Box 2, FRC Kansas City.

55. *United States Court of Claims Reports,* Case No. 44296, 102: 555; 44298, 101:10; 44300; 44303, 107:22; 44304; 44305; and 44306, 121:492. "Comments Concerning Recovery Suits," 9–10, Accession No. 62A400, Agency Box 10, FRC Kansas City; Records of General Jurisdiction, Case File No. 44304, Accession No. NCWN 71-1157, WNRC.

56. *Ibid.*, 121-492; Extracts from Menominee General Council, June 16, 1951, Accession No. 62A400, Agency Box 10, FRC Kansas City.

CHAPTER VIII

1. Minutes of the Menominee Advisory Council, Keshena, April 3, 1952, Accession No. 66A837, FRC Chicago.

2. U.S. Congress, "Per Capita Payment for Menominee Indian Tribe," Extension of Remarks by the Hon. Melvin R. Laird, Feb. 9, 1953, 83 Cong., 1 sess., *Cong. Rec.*, Appendix A534.

3. U.S. Congress, House 42828, May 19, 1953, 83 Cong., 1 sess., *Cong. Rec.*, Vol. XCIX, No. 4, 5124.

4. U.S. Congress, Committees on Interior and Insular Affairs, Statement of the Hon. Melvin R. Laird, March 10, 1954, "Termination of Federal Supervision over Certain Tribes of Indians," Joint Hearings before a subcommittee of the Committees of Interior and Insular Affairs, Pt. 6, *Menominee Indians of Wisconsin,* 83 Cong., 2 sess., 1954, *Cong. Rec.*, 579-772. Hereafter cited as *Termination of Federal Supervision, Joint Hearings.*

5. "Menominees' Full Freedom Assured at General Council," *Shawano Evening Leader,* June 22, 1953, 1; *Freedom with Reservation:*

246

The Menominee Struggle to Save Their Land and People, 7-12; Gary Ordfield, "Ideology and the Indian: A Study of Termination Policy," Chap. 1.

6. Statement of Monroe Weso, March 12, 1954, and Exhibit No. 2, Resolution of June 20, 1953, *Termination of Federal Supervision, Joint Hearings*, 736-38; George W. Kenote, *A Personal Memorandum for Menominee Youth, 1972: A Glance at Catastrophe, Judicare Style*, 5-6.

7. U.S. Congress, Senate, "Termination of Federal Supervision over Property and Members of the Menominee Indian Tribe of Wisconsin," Amended House Report 2828, July 24, 1953, 83 Cong., 1 sess., *Cong. Rec.*, XCIX, Pt. 7, 9742-46.

8. Public Law 399, *Statutes-at-Large*, Vol. LXVIII, p. 250.

9. Menominee Enrollment Act, *ibid.*, p. 965.

10. Menominee General Council Minutes, Dec. 11, 1954, Accession No. 66A827, FRC Chicago, p. 28.

11. Final Roll, Menominee Tribe of Indians of Wisconsin, *Federal Register*, XXII, Dec. 12, 1957, 9951-72.

12. Personal records and affidavits by name in Menominee Central Correspondence Files, Green Bay, Accession No. 14332-08-053, RG 75, N. A.

13. Garland P. Wood, "Basic Data Regarding Reservation Resources," 7 pp. (typed MSS), Burton R. Fisher Collection, Wis. State Hist. Society.

14. Articles on Laird v. Neuberger, *Green Bay Press Gazette*, April 8, May 8 and 13, 1958: Public Law 85–77, *Statutes-at-Large*, Vol. LXXI, p. 257.

15. "Termination Report for the Menominee Indian Tribe," Draft of Sen. Richard L. Neuberger, Aug. 19, 1957, Minutes of the Menominee Advisory Council, Dec., 1957, Accession No. 66A837, FRC Chicago.

16. "Memorandum of the Legislative Council of Wisconsin as to Menominee Indian Reservation and Proposed Legislation," Report of the Menominee Indian Study Committee, April 30, 1959, MSS in the Burton R. Fisher Collection, Wis. State Hist. Society.

17. "Menominees Favor Their Own County," *Green Bay Press Gazette*, Sept. 16, 1958; "Menominee Indian Tribe, Questions and Answers on Proposed Legislation," prepared by attorneys for the tribe, May 25, 1959, 5-7, Burton R. Fisher Collection, Wis. State Hist. Society.

18. Kenote, *Personal Memorandum for Menominee Youth, 1972*, 12.

19. Irene Dixon Mack, Minutes of the Menominee General Council Meeting, Jan. 17, 1959, Accession No. 66A837, FRC Chicago.

20. *Ibid.*

21. Constance W. Deer, Article for the People's Forum, sent to the *Green Bay Press Gazette*, March 23, 1959, in the Menominee Indian Papers, MSS BU, Wis. State Hist. Society; Mrs. Deer to J. R. Donoghue, March 24, 1958, *ibid.*

22. "Alternatives for Ownership and Management of Menominee Resources," for the Indian Study Committee, June, 1958, Burton R. Fisher Collection, Wis. State Hist. Society.

23. "Report of the Coordinating and Negotiating Committee," *Menominee News,* Keshena, Wis., Feb. 24, 1958, 2, in the Burton Fisher Collection, Wis. State Hist. Society.

24. *Ibid.*, 3; "Amendment to Menominee Termination," *Statutes-at-Large,* Vol. LXVIII, p. 250.

25. Minutes of the Menominee General Council, Jan. 17, 1959, Accession No. 66A837, FRC Chicago; "Menominee Indian Tribal Property: Plan for Future Control," *Federal Register,* Vol. XXVI, No. 82, April 29, 1961, 3727-55.

26. Wayne H. Weidemaun and Glenn V. Fuguitt, *Menominee: Wisconsin's 72nd County,* 3.

27. "Menominee Indian Tribal Property," *Federal Register,* Vol. XXVI, No. 82, April 29, 1961, 3728.

28. U.S. Congress, "Amending the Menominee Termination Plan," House Report 1824, House Misc. Reports on Public Bills, IV, 86 Cong., 2 sess., 7-8; *Freedom with Reservation,* Chap. 2.

29. U.S. Congress, *Termination of Federal Supervision, Joint Hearings,* 741.

30. John Wyngaard, "Indian Minority Fights Termination," *Green Bay Press Gazette,* June 11, 1959, 18.

31. "Land of the Menominees, Menominee County, 1961-69," Appendix E, *Report of the Wisconsin Legislative Committee, 1969,* VIII, 53-55.

32. James Ridgeway, "The Lost Indians," *New Republic,* Vol. 153, No. 23, Dec. 4, 1965, 17–20.

33. *Report of the Wisconsin Legislative Council, 1969,* VIII, 25-26.

34. *Freedom with Reservation,* 12-14.

35. *Ibid.*, 14-15; *Report of the Wisconsin Legislative Council, 1969,* VIII, 28-29.

36. Ernst and Ernst, "Opportunities for Economic Development, Menominee County, Wisconsin," March, 1967, 46-7, Burton R. Fisher

Collection, Wis. State Hist. Society.

37. Duncan Alfred Harkin, "Issues in Economic Development: The Menominee County, Wisconsin Case," 77–82 and 175–78. Unpublished Ph.D. dissertation, Department of Agricultural Economics, University of Wisconsin, 1966.

38. Minutes of the Menominee Indian Advisory Council, "Proposal for the Resort Development of the Menominee Indian Reservation," Accession No. 66A837, FRC Chicago.

39. "Indians Will Lease Cabin Sites," *Milwaukee Sentinel*, March 24, 1962; "Menominees Offer Reservation Lots," *Green Bay Press Gazette*, June 12, 1962.

40. "Progress Report and Information, Visitors Destination Center," Economic Development Administration Project, No. 06-01-00653, Jan. 23, 1969, Burton R. Fisher Collection, Wis. State Hist. Society.

41. Kenote, *Personal Memorandum for Menominee Youth, 1972,* 33–37; Patrick O'Donahue, "Lake of the Menominees: Legend Lake Development Is Joint Effort to Reduce Indian Taxes," *Green Bay Press Gazette*, July 11, 1971, Sec. A 6.

42. *Freedom with Reservation,* 29–31.

43. O'Donahue, "Lake of the Menominees," *Green Bay Press Gazette,* July 11, 1971.

44. Kenote, *Personal Memorandum for Menominee Youth, 1972,* 38; O'Donahue, "Indian Group Marches to Regain Control," *Green Bay Press Gazette,* July 12, 1970.

45. O'Donahue, "Deloria Urges Menominees to Fight Termination," *Green Bay Press Gazette*, March 19, 1971.

46. "Menominee Meeting Limited by Injunction," *ibid.,* Dec. 13, 1970.

47. O'Donahue, "Indians Divided in Dispute between DRUMS, Enterprises," *ibid.,* Sept. 20, 1970.

48. "Menominees to Cast Crucial Votes," *ibid.,* April 2, 1971; Nancy O. Lurie, "The Menominee Indians," *Indian Historian,* Vol. IV, No. 4 (Winter, 1971), 42.

49. "Shawano Curriculum Criticized by Indians," *Green Bay Press Gazette,* April 22, 1969; "School Racial Rifts Charged at Keshena," *ibid.,* March 3, 1971.

50. "Board of Education Will Back Detachment," *Shawano Evening Leader,* Jan. 15, 1974.

51. "Menominees Reject Own School District," *Green Bay Press Gazette,* April 5, 1974.

52. *Freedom with Reservation,* 87-90; "Indians Launch Madison

Trek," *The Herald-Leader* (Menominee, Mich.), Oct. 3, 1971.

53. Kenote, *Personal Memorandum for Menominee Youth, 1972,* 2-3.

CHAPTER IX

1. U.S. Congress, Richard M. Nixon, "The American Indian — Message from the President of the United States," House Doc. 91-363, July 8, 1970, 91 Cong., 2 sess., *Cong. Rec.,* Vol. CXVI, No. 114, 6438.

2. "The Special Case of the Menominees," *Green Bay Press Gazette,* July 15, 1970; *Freedom with Reservation,* 89–90; "Lucey Tours Land of Menominees," *Eagle Star* (Marinette, Wis.), Oct. 25, 1971.

3. *Freedom with Reservation,* 93-95; "Indians Favor Return to Reservation Status," *Eagle Star,* Jan. 24, 1972; Robert Woltmar, "Menominee DRUMS," *Akwesasne Notes* (Roosevelttown, N. Y.), Vol. III, No. 2, March, 1971.

4. U.S. Cong., Senate bill 3514 and Statements, April 20, 1972, 92 Cong., 2 sess., *Cong. Rec.,* Vol. CXVIII, No. 62, 6450-56.

5. *Freedom with Reservation,* 30-31.

6. Edward H. Blackwell, "Developer, Indians to End Partnership," *Milwaukee Journal,* July 8, 1972.

7. "Judge Orders Land Sale Halt," *Herald-Leader* (Menominee, Mich.), July 25, 1972.

8. U.S. Cong., "Menominee Restoration Bill," Senate 1687, House 7421, 93 Cong., 1 sess., *Cong. Rec.,* Vol. CXIX, Pt. II, 8159–66, and Extension of Remarks, E2765.

9. Senator James Abourezk, chairman of the Senate Subcommittee on Indian Affairs, to P. K. Ourada, April 16, 1973, personal correspondence.

10. U.S. Cong., "Menominee Restoration Act," Hearings before the Subcommittee on Indian Affairs on House Report 7421, 93 Cong., 1 sess., 1973, Serial No. 90–20, 398 pp.

11. *Ibid.,* 33.

12. Statement of Mrs. Sylvia Wilber before the Subcommittee, May 25, 1973, *ibid.,* 41.

13. Statement of the Honorable Lloyd Meeds, June 28, 1973, *ibid.,* 249.

14. Statement of the Honorable Patrick J. Lucey, June 28, 1973, *ibid.,* 276.

15. Patrick O'Donahue, "Menominee Official Raps State Court Land Ruling," *Green Bay Press Gazette,* July 8, 1973.

16. TV 11 Newscast, WLUK, Green Bay, Wis., June 14, 1973.

17. U.S. Cong., *Menominee Restoration Act,* Hearings before the Subcommittee on Indian Affairs on Senate 1687, 93 Cong., 1 sess., *Cong. Rec.,* Sept. 17 and 26, 1973, special individual printing, 377 pp.

18. U.S. Cong., 93 Cong., 1 sess., *Cong. Rec.,* Oct. 16, 1973, House 9096–9105; *Weekly Compilation of Presidential Documents,* Vol. IX, No. 52.

19. *Public Law 93–197,* 93 Cong., House Report 10717, Dec. 22, 1973, 4 pp.

20. *Aq-ua-Chamine,* The Menominee Restoration Committee Newsletter, Vol. II, No. 1, Jan. 19, 1975. The *New York Times* for Jan. and Feb., 1975, carries the account of the occupation.

21. "Government Gives Reservation Back to the Menominees," *New York Times,* April 24, 1975.

22. *Aq-ua-Chamine,* Vol. II, No. 5, May 20, 1975, and Vol. II, No. 12, Nov. 20, 1975.

23. *Federal Register,* Nov. 24, 1975, 54450, and March 9, 1976, 10114.

24. *Aq-ua-chamine,* Vol. II, No. 6, May 31, 1975.

25. *New York Times,* April 24, 1975.

Bibliography

Manuscript Materials

ARCHIVES OF THE GREAT LAKES–OHIO VALLEY ETHNO-
HISTORY PROJECT. GLENN A. BLACK MUSEUM
OF ARCHAEOLOGY, INDIANA UNIVERSITY

Colonel Henry Bouquet Papers, 1750–77.
William T. Clark Papers. Original papers in the State Historical Society of Kansas.
Menominee Indians, 1634–1833. Collected Papers. 12 vols.

FEDERAL RECORD CENTER, CHICAGO, ILLINOIS

Barrow, Wade, Guthrie and Company. "Report on Tribal Bonds," June 30, 1934. Menominee Indian Papers. Accession No. 66A837.
———. "Report on the Tribal Trust Fund," June 30, 1934. Menominee Indian Papers. Accession No. 66A837.
Correspondence of the Superintendent, 1921–24. Menominee Indian Papers. Accession No. 61A565.
Forestry Reports and Correspondence. Green Bay Agency. Accession No. 61A566.
"The Government in the Lumber Business." Written for Senator Robert La Follette by the U.S. Forest Service at Neopit, December 9, 1908. Accession No. 61A566.
LaMotte, Peter. "Organization of the Government at Neopit," April 4, 1911. Accession No. 61A566.
"The Menominee Scholarship for Higher Education, Plan of Operation." Menominee Agency, January 14, 1947. Accession No. 66A837.
253

Minutes of the Menominee Advisory Council. Accession No. 66A837.

"Proposal for the Resort Development of the Menominee Indian Reservation." Menominee Indian Advisory Council, 1947. Accession No. 66A837.

FEDERAL RECORD CENTER, KANSAS CITY, MISSOURI

"Advance Release." Department of Interior, Office of Indian Affairs, July 5, 1945. Accession No. 62A400.

Auditor Reports on the Menominee Garment Factory. Accession No. 569538.

Caswell, Raymond. "Blister Rust Control Report of the Menominee Indian Reservation, 1933." Annual Reports on Blister Rust Control, 1933–60. Accession No. 69A672.

"Comments Concerning Recovery Suits." Accession No. 62A400.

Delaney, Richard P. "Clear Cut Case" (1945). Accession No. 55A6.

———. "The Menominee Forest to 1908." Accession No. 62A400.

Hughes Report, July 30, 1932. Menominee Reservation. Accession No. 62A400.

Muck, Lee. "Report upon the Statement of Hughes, Schurman, and Dwight to the Advisory Board of the Menominee Indians," January 15, 1933. 63 pp. Accession No. 62A400.

"Narrative Supplement to the Annual Forestry Report." Menominee Indian Reservation (1943). Accession No. 69A672.

Nicholson, Nels O., and Lloyd O. Grapp. "Preliminary Forest Management Plan for the Menominee Indian Reservation," 1930. Accession No. 62A400.

Weber, Raymond. "Report of White Pine Blister Rust Control on the Menominee Reservation," 1947. Accession No. 69A672.

Winner, Lee, and Walter J. Ridlington. "A Plan for Continuous Forest Control on the Menominee Indian Reservation," June, 1954. Accession No. 69A672.

FEDERAL RECORD CENTER, SUITLAND, MARYLAND

Brooks, Ogden. "Forest Fire at Neopit." *Shawano County Advocate*, August 3, 1910. Records of the U.S. Court of Claims, Selected Records of General Jurisdiction, Case File 44304. *Menominee Indian Tribe* v. *The United States.*

Records of General Jurisdiction. Case File 44304. *Menominee Indian Tribe* v. *The United States.* Accession No. NCWN 71–1157.

NATIONAL ARCHIVES (N.A.)

Black Hawk's War. Stambaugh Battalion Index. Record Group 94.

Central Classified Files. Menominee. Record Group 75. Accession No. 35051–1932–155.

Central Correspondence Files, 1907–39. Menominee. Record Group 75. Accession No. 5900–1928–339.

"Constitution of the Menominee Tribe of Indians." Central Classified Files. Record Group 75. Accession No. 9646–A–1936–054, Keshena.

Keshena Agency Papers. Record Group 75. Accession No. 22295–1913–044.

Letters Received by the Secretary of War. Record Group 107.

Marshall, Robert. "Indian Self-Government in Relation to the Management of the Menominee Indian Mills," 1935. Central Classified Files. Record Group 75. Accession No. 00–1935–100, Keshena.

Menominee Tribal Minutes. Record Group 75, Accession No. 57174–1928–054, Keshena.

Military Service Records. Civil War. Adjutant General's Office. Record Group 94.

"Superintendents' Annual Narrative Reports, 1911–1933." Keshena, Record Group 75.

Winnebago War, 1827. Michigan Volunteers, Index. Record Group 94.

STATE HISTORICAL SOCIETY OF WISCONSIN

Henry S. Baird Papers, 1832–35. Black Hawk's War Roll.

Deer, Constance W. Article to the *Green Bay Press Gazette,* March 23, 1959. Menominee Indian Papers, MSS BU.

Burton R. Fisher Collection. University of Wisconsin Menominee Termination Advisory Board Papers.

Jones, Robert R. "Menominee Notes." 6 pp. Menominee Indian Papers, MSS BU.

Keshena Speech. "The Menominee." George Hyde Papers, MSS Ax. Also published in the *Oshkosh City Times,* February 23, 1870.

Morgan Martin Papers, 1645–1829. Microcopy 36. Original MSS in the Neville Museum, Green Bay, Wisconsin.

Menominee Indian Papers, MSS BU.

"Summary Statement of Withdrawal Status," March 12, 1956.

Tenney, Horace T. "A Case of Lex Talionis." Tenney Papers. MSS Wis., BE. Box 1.

WESTERN HISTORY COLLECTIONS
UNIVERSITY OF OKLAHOMA

Documents Related to the Negotiations of Indian Treaties, 1801–69. Ratified Treaties. Record Group 75, Records of the Bureau of Indian Affairs. National Archives, Microcopy T494.

Letters Received by the Office of Indian Affairs, 1824–81. Green Bay Agency, 1824–81. National Archives, Microcopy 234.

Ratified Indian Treaties, 1722–1869. National Archives, Microcopy 668.

Records of the Michigan Superintendency of Indian Affairs. Letters Received and Sent by the Superintendent, 1814–18. National Archives, Microcopy 1.

Records of the Wisconsin Superintendency of Indian Affairs. Letters Received and Sent by the Superintendent, 1841–48. National Archives, Microcopy M234.

Government Documents

REPORTS

American State Papers: Documents Legislative and Executive of the Congress of the United States, December 4, 1815–March 3, 1827. Class II, Indian Affairs, Vol. II. Washington, D.C., Gales and Seaton, 1834.

Annual Reports of the Menominee Indian Agents, and the Commissioner of Indian Affairs, 1827–80. Washington, D.C., Government Printing Office.

Carter, Clarence Edwin, ed. and comp. *Territorial Papers of the United States. Territory of Michigan,* Vol. XI. *Wisconsin Territory,* Vol. XXVII. Washington, D.C., Government Printing Office.

McAfee, Robert B. *The History of the Late War in the Western Country.* Lexington, Worsley and Smith, 1816.

23 Cong., 1 sess., Sen. Doc. 512. "Correspondence on the Emigration of Indians." II, 1835.

FEDERAL REGISTER

Final Roll, Menominee Tribe of Indians of Wisconsin. Vol. XXII, December 12, 1957.

"Menominee Indian Tribal Property: Plan for Future Control." Vol. XXVI, No. 82, April 29, 1961.

Report of the Secretary of Interior. Office of Indian Affairs. Washington, D.C., Government Printing Office, 1935.

STATUTES-AT-LARGE

Act of June 15, 1934. XLVIII (1934).

"Amendment to Menominee Termination." LXVIII (1956).

256

Menominee Enrollment Act. XLVIII (1934).

"Menominee Tribal Claims." LXIX (1934).

"Per Capita Payment to the Menominee Indians." XLVIII (1934).

Public Law 74, Chap. 3, 60 Cong., 1 sess. XXXV, No. 51 (1908).

Public Law 85–77. LXXI (1958).

Public Law 153. XXV (1889) and XXVI (1890).

Public Law 399. LXVIII (1954).

UNITED STATES CONGRESS: *Congressional Record*

59 Cong., 1 sess., House Doc. 287, "Sale of Certain Timber on the Menominee Reservation." XLVI, 1907.

60 Cong., 1 sess., House Debate, "Cutting Timber on the Menominee Indian Reservation." Senate 4040. XLVIII, Part 4, March 16, 1907.

60 Cong., 1 sess., Senate Report 110, Address to the 60th Congress by Robert M. La Follette. "Cutting Timber on Indian Reservations in Wisconsin," 1908.

71 Cong., 3 sess., House 17052. LXXIV, Part 4, 1931.

74 Cong., 1 sess., House Report 1412 on Public Law 413, July 1, 1935, LXXIX, Part 10.

83 Cong., 1 sess., "Per Capita Payment for Menominee Indian Tribe." Extension of Remarks of the Hon. Melvin R. Laird, February 9, 1953, Appendix.

83 Cong., 1 sess., House 2828. Vol. XCIX, No. 4, May 19, 1953.

83 Cong., 1 sess., "Menominee Termination." XCIX, Pts. 7 and 8, 1953.

83 Cong., 2 sess., Committees of Interior and Insular Affairs. *Termination of Federal Supervision over Certain Tribes of Indians, Joint Hearings before a Subcommittee of the Committees of Interior and Insular Affairs*, Pt. 6, *Menominee Indians of Wisconsin*, 1954.

86 Cong., 2 sess., House Report 1824, "Amending the Menominee Termination Plan." House Misc. Reports on Public Bills, IV, 1957.

91 Cong., 2 sess., House Doc. 91–363, Richard M. Nixon. "The American Indian—Message from the President of the United States." Vol. CXVI, Part 17, 1970.

92 Cong., 2 sess., Senate 3514 and Statements. Vol. CXVIII, No. 62, 1972.

93 Cong., 1 sess., Senate 1687, House 7421, "Menominee Restoration Bill." CXX, Part 11, 1973.

93 Cong., 1 sess., Hearings before the Subcommittee on Indian Affairs of the Committee on Interior and Insular Affairs, House of Representatives on House Report 7421, May 25–26 and June 28, 1973, 398 pp.

93 Cong., 1 sess., Hearings before the Subcommittee on Indian Affairs of the Committee on Interior and Insular Affairs, United States Senate on Senate 1687, Sept. 17 and 26, 1973, 378 pp.

United States Court of Claims Reports

Menominee Tribe of Indians v. *The United States.* Case Nos. 44296, 102:555; 44298, 101:10; 44300; 44303, 107:22; 44304; 44305; and 44306, 121:492.
Swampland Case, No. 44294, 101.

Wisconsin Legislative Committee: Menominee Indian Study Committee

Report of the Wisconsin Legislative Committee, 1965 and *1969.* Menominee Indian Study Committee. Vols. III (1966) and VIII (1970). Compliments of State Senator Reuben LaFave.
Report of the Wisconsin Legislative Council. Menominee Indian Study Committee. *History of Federal Legislation.* Madison, 1965.

Unpublished Manuscripts

Dorrance, James F., Jr. "The Menominee Indians, 1848–58: The Making of the Menominee Reservation." M.S. thesis, University of Wisconsin, 1955.
Harkin, Duncan Alfred. "Issues in Economic Development: The Menominee County, Wisconsin Case." Ph.D. dissertation, Department of Agricultural Economics, University of Wisconsin, 1966.
Manthey, Sister M. Rosaria, O.S.F. "Missionary Activity among the Menominee, 1846–84." M.A. thesis, Catholic University of America, 1955.
Orfield, Gary. "Ideology and the Indian: A Study of the Termination Policy." M.A. thesis, University of Chicago, 1965.
Riesberry, Janet. "History of the Menominee Nation, 1816–56." M.A. thesis, University of Wisconsin, 1939.

PERSONAL CORRESPONDENCE

Abourezk, Senator James, to P. K. Ourada, April 16, 1972.
Dodge, Atlee, to P. K. Ourada, February, 1973.

Published Primary Material

Auburey, Thomas. *Travels through the Interior Parts of North America.* London, 1789. Reprinted as *With Burgoyne from Quebec.*

Ed. by Sydney Jackman. Toronto, Macmillan, 1963.

Biddle, James W. "Recollections of Green Bay in 1816–17." *Wisconsin Historical Collections,* I (1903).

Black Hawk. *Autobiography.* Ed. by Donald Jackson. Urbana, University of Illinois Press, 1964.

Blair, Emma Helen, trans. and ed. *The Indian Tribes of the Upper Mississippi Valley and Region of the Great Lakes as Described by Nicolas Perrot, French Commandant in the Northwest; Bacqueville de la Potherie, French Royal Commissioner in Canada; Morrell Martson, American Army Officer; and Thomas Forsyth, United States Agent at Fort Armstrong.* 2 vols. Cleveland, Arthur H. Clark Company, 1911.

Bougainville, Louis Antoine de. *The American Journal of; Adventure in the Wilderness.* Trans. and ed. by Edward P. Hamilton. Norman, University of Oklahoma Press, 1964.

Boyd, George. "Papers of Indian Agent Boyd." *Wisconsin Historical Collections,* XII (1892).

"Canada, correspondence générale," from the Archives de Ministère de Colonies, Paris. *Wisconsin Historical Collections,* XVI and XVIII; also printed in the *Michigan Pioneer and Historical Collections,* XXIV (1905).

Charlevoix, Pierre François Xavier de. *History and General Description of New France.* Trans. by John Gilmary Shea. 6 vols. Chicago, Loyola University Press, 1965. Originally published in 1744.

Childs, Ebenezar. "Recollections of Wisconsin Since 1820." *Wisconsin Historical Collections,* IV (1906).

"A Civil War Medical Examiner: The Report of Dr. Horace O. Crane." *Wisconsin Magazine of History,* Vol. XLVIII, No. 3 (Spring, 1965).

Document Transcriptions of the War of 1812 in the Northwest. Transcribed by Richard C. Knopf. Columbus, Ohio Historical Society, 1958.

Documents Relative to the Colonial History of the State of New York. Procured by John Homeyn Brodhead. 11 vols. Albany, Weed Parsons and Company, 1853.

Dyer, Frederick L. *A Compendium of the War of the Rebellion: Regimental Histories.* Vol. III, *Wisconsin Regiments.* New York, Thomas Yoseloff, 1959.

Featherstonhaugh, George. *Canoe Voyage up the Minnay-Sotor.* 2 vols. London, 1847.

Gorrell, Lt. James. "Journal." *Wisconsin Historical Collections,* I (1903); also printed in *The Papers of Sir William Johnson.*

Grignon, Augustin. "Recollections." *Wisconsin Historical Collections,* III (1857).

————. "Seventy-two Years Recollection of Wisconsin." *Wisconsin Historical Collections*, VII (1876).

Hamilton, Milton W., ed. *The Papers of Sir William Johnson.* 14 vols. Albany, The University of the State of New York, 1921–65.

Henry, Alexander. *Travels and Adventures in Canada and Indian Territory between 1760 and 1776.* New York, I. Ripley, 1809.

Jackson, Donald, ed. *The Journals of Zebulon Montgomery Pike.* 2 vols. Norman, University of Oklahoma Press, 1961.

Kane, Paul. *The Wanderings of an Artist among the Indians of North America from Canada to Vancouver's Island and Oregon through the Hudsons Bay Company's Territory and Back Again.* Toronto, The Radisson Society, 1925. Originally published in 1859.

La Potherie, Bacqueville de. *Histoire de l'Amérique Septentrionale.* Paris, 1722. Published in the *Wisconsin Historical Collections*, XVI (1902).

List of Pensioners on the Roll, January 1, 1883. Vol. IV, *Western States.* Washington, D.C.: Government Printing Office, 1883.

Long, John. *Voyages of an Indian Interpreter and Trader.* Chicago, R. R. Donnelley, 1922.

"M'Call's Journal of a Visit to Wisconsin in 1830," and accompanying documents. *Wisconsin Historical Collections*, XII (1892).

McKenney, Col. Thomas L. "The Winnebago War of 1827." *Wisconsin Historical Collections*, V (1907).

Margry, Pierre. *Découvertes et établissements des Français dans l'ouest et dans le sud de l'Amérique.* Première partie, "Voyages des Français sur les grands lacs et découverte de l'Ohio et du Mississippi, 1614–84." Paris, Imprimerie D. Jouaust, 1876. An English translation is in the Burton Collection, Detroit Public Library. A microfilm copy of the translation was borrowed to verify the author's interpretation.

Marquette, Jacques S. *Voyages of Marquette.* March of America Facsimile Series, No. 28. Ann Arbor, University Microfilms, Inc., 1966.

Menominee Petition to President Millard Fillmore, September 4, 1850. *Proceedings of the Wisconsin Historical Society*, 1912.

Morse, Jedidiah. *Report to the Secretary of War of the United States on Indian Affairs, Comprising a Narrative of a Tour.* New Haven, Howe and Spalding, 1822.

"The Narrative of Peter Pond." Reproduced in *Five Fur Traders of the Northwest.* Ed. by Charles M. Gates. St. Paul, Minnesota Historical Society, 1965.

Powell, Capt. William. "Statement." *Wisconsin Historical Collections*, X (1888).

Radisson, Pierre. "The Fourth Voyage." *Wisconsin Historical Collections,* XI (1888).

Roster of Wisconsin Troops in the Spanish-American War. Madison: Brigadier General Ralph M. Immel, president, Soldiers Rehabilitation Board, n.d. First printed in the *Sentinel Almanac and Book of Facts, 1899.*

Steck, Francis Borgia. *The Jolliet-Marquette Expedition, 1673.* Quincy, Illinois, Franciscan Fathers, 1928.

Thwaites, Reuben Gold, ed. *Jesuit Relations and Allied Documents: Travels and Explorations of the Jesuit Missionaries in New France 1610-1791.* 59 vols. Cleveland, Barrows Brothers, 1896-1901.

"Visit to the Menominees," *The Friend: A Religious and Literary Journal,* Vol. XXXIX, No. 4 (1849), and "Cope's Diary," Quaker Collection, Haverford College Library, Haverford, Pennsylvania. Xeroxed copies courteously sent by the Library. Alfred Cope Articles, "A Mission to the Menominees," *Wisconsin Magazine of History,* Vol. XLIX, No. 4 (1966-67).

Wood, William, ed. *Select British Documents of the Canadian War of 1812.* 3 vols. Toronto, Champlain Society, 1920; Facsimile edition, New York, Greenwood Press, 1968; *Michigan Pioneer and Historical Collections,* XV (1889).

Secondary Books

Adams, Arthur T., ed. *The Explorations of Pierre Esprit Radisson.* Loren Kallsen, modernizer. Minneapolis, Ross and Haines, 1961.

Bloomfield, Leonard. *Menomini Texts,* XII. Publications of the American Ethnological Society. New York, G. E. Strickert and Company, 1928.

Brinton, D. G. *American Hero Myths.* Philadelphia, H. C. Watts and Company, 1882.

———. *The Myth of the New World.* Philadelphia, David McKay, 1905.

Brophy, William A., Sophie D. Aberle, and members of the Truman Commission on Indian Rights. *The Indian: America's Unfinished Business.* Norman, University of Oklahoma Press, 1966.

Butterfield, C. W. *History of the Discovery of the Northwest by Jean Nicolet in 1634 with a Sketch of His Life.* Cincinnati, Robert Clarke and Company, 1881.

Colden, Cadwallader. *The History of the Five Indian Nations Depending on the Province of New York.* New York, T. H. Morrell, 1866.

Cuneo, John R. *Robert Rogers of the Rangers.* New York, Oxford University Press, 1959.

Davidson, John Nelson. *Muh-he-ka-ne-ok: A History of the Stock-bridge Nation.* Milwaukee, S. Chapman, 1893.

Densmore, Frances. *Menomini Music.* Bulletin 102. Smithsonian Institution, Bureau of American Ethnology. Washington, D.C., Government Printing Office, 1932.

Freedom with Reservation: The Menominee Struggle to Save Their Land and People. National Committee to Save the Menominee People and Forests. Coordinating editor Deborah Shames. Madison, Impressions, Inc., 1972.

Gilsdorf, Gordon. *Wisconsin Catholic Heritage.* N.p., Madison, 1949.

Green, Howard. *The Reverend Richard Fish Cadle: A Missionary of the Protestant Episcopal Church in the Territories of Michigan and Wisconsin in the Early Nineteenth Century.* N.p., Waukesha, Wisconsin, 1936.

Hagan, William T. *The Sac and Fox Indians.* Norman, University of Oklahoma Press, 1958.

Hamilton, Edward P. *Braddock's Defeat.* Norman, University of Oklahoma Press, 1959.

Hoffman, Walter J. *The Menomini Indians.* United States Bureau of American Ethnology, *Fourteenth Annual Report, 1892–93.* Washington, D.C., Government Printing Office, 1896.

Indians in the War. Chicago, U.S. Department of Interior, 1945.

Ingalls, E. S. *Historical Album, Menominee County, Michigan, 1863–1963.* Centennial edition. Culbert Swann Production Company, 1963.

Keesing, Felix. *The Menomini Indians of Wisconsin: A Study of Three Centuries of Cultural Contact and Change.* Memoirs of the American Philosophical Society, X. Philadelphia, The American Philosophical Society, 1939.

Kellogg, Louise. *The British Régime in Wisconsin and the Northwest.* Madison, Wisconsin State Historical Society, 1935.

———. *The French Régime in Wisconsin and the Northwest.* New York, Cooper Square Publishers, 1968. First published in 1925.

Kenote, George W. *A Personal Memorandum for Menominee Youth, 1972: A Glance at Catastrophe, Judicare Style.* Private printing, 1972. Courtesy of Mr. George W. Kenote.

Kingsford, William. *The History of Canada.* 9 vols. Toronto, Roswell and Hutchinson, 1888.

La Boule, Joseph S. "Claude Jean Allouez: The Apostle of the Ottawas," *Parkman Club Publications,* No. 17. Milwaukee, Edward Keogh, printer, 1897.

Lavender, David. *The Fist in the Wilderness.* Garden City, Doubleday, 1964.

262

Lawson, Publius V. *Story of Oshkosh, His Tribe and Fellow Chiefs.* N.d., n.p. Price 25¢, in the Phillips Collection, University of Oklahoma Library.

McCoy, Raymond. *The Massacre of Old Fort Mackinac (Michilimackinac).* Bay City, Michigan, Raymond McCoy, 1946.

Meriam, Lewis, and the Commission. *The Problem of Indian Administration.* Baltimore, Johns Hopkins Press, 1928.

Nichols, Phebe Jewell. *Oshkosh, the Brave: Chief of the Menominees and His Family.* Centennial edition. Menominee Indian Reservation, 1954.

O'Daniel, Victor. *The Right Reverend Edward D. Fenwick, O. F.* New York, Frederick Pustet Company, 1920.

Parkman, Francis. *The Conspiracy of Pontiac.* New York, Collier Books, 1962. Originally published in 1851.

————. *Count Frontenac and New France under Louis XIV; of France and England in America,* Pt. V. Boston, Little, Brown and Company, 1923.

————. *Montcalm and Wolfe, France and England in America.* 2 vols. Boston, Little, Brown and Company, 1903.

Peckham, Howard H. *Pontiac and the Indian Uprising.* Princeton, Princeton University Press, 1947.

Phillips, Paul Chrisler. *The Fur Trade.* 2 vols. Norman, University of Oklahoma Press, 1961.

Ritzenthaler, Robert E., and Pat Ritzenthaler. *The Woodland Indians of Western Great Lakes.* American Museum of Science Books, New York, Natural History Press, 1970.

Rowe, Chandler W. *The Effigy Mound Culture of Wisconsin.* Milwaukee Public Museum Publications in Anthropology, No. 3, Milwaukee, Greenwood Press, 1970.

Sawyer, Alvah L. *History of the Northern Peninsula of Michigan, Its people, Its Mining, Lumber, and Agricultural Industries.* 3 vols. Chicago, Lewis Publishing Company, 1911.

Shea, John Gilmary. *Discovery and Exploration of the Mississippi Valley with Original Narratives of Marquette, Allouez, Membré, Hennepin and Anatase Dovay.* New York, Redfield, 1853.

————. *History of the Catholic Missions among the Indian Tribes of the United States, 1529–1854.* New York, J. P. Kennedy, Excelsior Catholic Publishing House, 1882.

Skinner, Alanson. *Material Culture of the Menomini.* Indian Notes and Monograph Series. Edited by William H. Hodge. New York, Museum of the American Indian, Heye Foundation, 1921.

Smith, Elizabeth Alice. *James Duane Doty: Frontier Promoter.* Madison, State Historical Society of Wisconsin, 1954.

Smith, Huron H. *Ethnobotany of Menomini Indians. Bulletin* of the Public Museum of the City of Milwaukee, Vol. IV, No. 1. Milwaukee, Advocate Publishing Company, 1923.

Spindler, George and Louise. *Dreamers without Power: The Menomini Indians.* New York, Holt, Rinehart and Winston, 1971.

Stevens, Frank E. *The Black Hawk War.* Chicago, Frank E. Stevens, 1903.

Terrell, John Upton. *Furs by Astor.* New York, Morrow, 1963.

Weidemaun, Wayne H., and Glenn V. Fuguitt. *Menominee: Wisconsin's 72d County.* Department of Rural Sociology, University of Wisconsin, Population Note No. 3 (April, 1963).

Wells, R. W. *Wisconsin in the Civil War.* Milwaukee, *Milwaukee Journal,* 1962. Originally published as a thirty-nine installment series in the *Milwaukee Journal.*

Periodicals

Ames, Daniel W., and Burton R. Fisher. "The Menominee Termination Crisis," *Human Organization,* Vol. XVIII, No. 3 (Fall, 1959).

Barrett, S. A., and Alanson Skinner. "Certain Mounds and Village Sites of Shawano and Oconto Counties, *Bulletin* of the Public Museum of Milwaukee, Vol. X, No. 5 (March 4, 1932).

Brunson, Alfred. "Memoir of Honorable Thomas Pendleton Burnett," Appendix No. 8, *Wisconsin Historical Collections,* II (1903). Reprint.

Brymner, Douglas. "Capture of Fort McKay, Prairie du Chien, in 1814," *Wisconsin Historical Collections,* XI (1888).

Crespel, Rev. Emanuel. "DeLignery's Expedition Against the Foxes, 1728," London translation of 1797, *Wisconsin Historical Collections,* XVII (1906).

Cruikshank, Ernest Alexander. "Robert Dickson, The Indian Trader," *Wisconsin Historical Collections,* XII (1892).

Cushing, Frank Hamilton. "Primitive Copper Working: An Experimental Study," *American Anthropologist,* VII (January, 1894).

Dousman, Rosalie Laborde. *Wisconsin Historical Collections,* XIX. Biographical sketch.

Ellis, Albert G. "Some Accounts of the New York Indians into Wisconsin," *Wisconsin Historical Collections,* II (1903).

Hart, Paxton. "The Making of Menominee County," *Wisconsin Magazine of History,* Vol. XLIII, No. 3 (Spring, 1960).

Haygood, William Converse. "Red Child, White Child: The Strange Disappearance of Caspar Partridge," *Wisconsin Magazine of History,* Vol. LVIII, No. 4 (Summer, 1975).

Horsman, Reginald. "Wisconsin and the War of 1812," *Wisconsin Magazine of History,* Vol. XLVI, No. 1 (Autumn, 1962).

Hruska, Robert. "The Riverside Site: A Late Archaic Manifestation in Michigan," *Wisconsin Archaeologist,* n.s., Vol. XLVIII, No. 3 (September, 1957).

Jenks, Albert Ernest. "Wild Rice Gatherers of the Upper Lakes: A Study in American Primitive Economics," *Nineteenth Annual Report of the Bureau of American Ethnology,* Pt. 2, 1897–98. Washington, D.C., Government Printing Office, 1900.

Juoan, Henri. "Jean Nicolet, Interpreter and Voyageur in Canada, 1618–42," trans. by Grace Clark, *Wisconsin Historical Collections,* XI (1888).

Kellogg, Louise Phelps. "The Menominee Treaty at the Cedars, 1836," *Wisconsin Academy of Sciences, Arts, and Letters,* Vol. XXVI. Madison, 1931.

———. "The Story of Wisconsin, 1634–1848," *Wisconsin Magazine of History,* II (1918–19).

———. "Wisconsin Indians During the American Revolution," *Wisconsin Academy of Sciences, Arts, and Letters,* Vol. XXIV. Madison, 1929.

Luric, Nancy Oestreich. "The Menominee Indians," *Indian Historian,* Vol. IV, No. 4 (Winter, 1971).

Nichols, Phebe Jewell. "In the Moon of Sugar-making," *Wisconsin Magazine of History,* Vol. XXXII, No. 3 (March, 1949).

———. "Weavers of Grass: Indian Women of the Woodlands," *Wisconsin Magazine of History,* Vol. XXXVI, No. 2 (Winter, 1952–53).

Pease, Theodore Calvin. "Revolution at Crisis in the West," *Journal of the Illinois Historical Society,* Vol. XXIII, No. 4 (January, 1931).

Porlier, Louis B. "Capture of Mackinaw, 1763: A Menominee Tradition," *Wisconsin Historical Collections,* VIII (1879).

Quaife, M. M. "A Forgotten Hero of Rock Island," *Journal of the Illinois Historical Society,* Vol. XXIII, No. 4 (January, 1931).

Ridgeway, James. "The Lost Indians," *New Republic,* Vol. 153, No. 23, December 4, 1965.

Scanlan, P. L. "Nicolas Boilvin, Indian Agent," *Wisconsin Magazine of History,* Vol. XXVII, No. 2 (December, 1943).

"The Self-Reliant Menominees," *The Literary Digest,* August 26, 1933.

Snelling, William J. "LaButte des Morts—The Hillock of the Dead," *Wisconsin Historical Collections,* V (1867–69).

Tasse, Joseph. "Memoir of Charles de Langlade," trans. by Mrs. Sarah Fairchild Dean, *Wisconsin Historical Collections,* VII (1876).

U.S. Circuit Court Record, *Green Bay Historical Bulletin,* Vol. III, n.d.

Wilson, H. Clyde. "A New Interpretation of the Wild Rice District of Wisconsin," *American Anthropologist,* Vol. LVIII, No. 6 (December, 1956).

Newspapers

Akwesasne Notes. "Guardianship Upheld," Vol. III, No. 2, March, 1971.

————. Waltmar, Robert. "Menominee DRUMS," Vol. III, No. 2, March, 1971.

Aq-ua-Chamine (Menominee Talking). The Menominee Restoration Committee Newsletter, Vol. II, 1975.

The Capital Times (Madison, Wisconsin). "Covering the Campus," September 28, 1956.

————. "State Can Have $1,500,000 if 2 Sign Papers," April 26, 1945.

Eagle Star (Marinette, Wisconsin). Select articles.

Green Bay Advocate (Green Bay, Wisconsin). Mixed-blood Payment List, October 5, 1848, and July 5, 1849.

Green Bay Press Gazette (Green Bay, Wisconsin). The *Press Gazette* permitted free access to their large clipping files on the Menominee Indians. The articles of Patrick O'Donahue, Eileen Hammer, and the general news stories were particularly valuable.

Herald-Leader (Menominee, Michigan). "Indians Launch Madison Trek," October 3, 1971.

Leader-Advocate (Shawano, Wisconsin). "Chief Says Tribe Is to Reorganize," October 3, 1929.

Menominee News (Keshena, Wisconsin). Termination information. Copies in the Burton R. Fisher Collection, Wisconsin State Historical Society.

Milwaukee Journal. Blackwell, Edward H., "Developer, Indians to End Partnership," July 8, 1972.

————. Lurie, Nancy Oestreich, "Ads Tell One Story, Indians Another," September 6, 1970.

————. "Menominee Indian Mill Management," April 2, 1933.

Milwaukee Sentinel. "Indians Will Lease Cabin Sites," March 24, 1962.

New York Times. "Forty Indians in Parade," March 4, 1913.

————. "The Inaugural Parade," March 5, 1913.

————. "National Memorial to North American Indians," February 22, 1913.

————. "Proud Menominee Indians Refuse Federal Road Aid," July 31, 1933.

————. "Visiting Chiefs Go on Sightseeing Trip," February 24, 1913.

Niles Weekly Register. Vol. III, No. 4, September 26, 1812, and September 10, 1814.

Oshkosh Times (Oshkosh, Wisconsin). Thwaites, Reuben G., "Oshkosh: The Last of the Menominee Sachems," April 22, 1876.

The Patriot (Prairie du Chien, Wisconsin). June 19, 1850.

Post-Crescent (Appleton, Wisconsin). Wyngaard, John, "Obstacles Face Bills to Free Menominees: Oconto Objects," April 21, 1959.

Shawano Evening Leader (Shawano, Wisconsin). "Back of the Hand," Pt. 3, October 6, 1954.

————. "New Anti-Pollution Devices for MEI Mill," May 11, 1971.

TV 11 Newscast, WLUK, Green Bay, Wisconsin, June 14, 1973.

Index

269